A PASSION FOR THE IMPOSSIBLE:
The Life of Lilias Trotter

A Passion for the IMPOSSIBLE

Miriam Huffman Rockness

The Life of Lilias Trotter

Harold Shaw Publishers
Wheaton, Illinois

North Wind
BOOKS

North Wind Books bring to the reader a series of biographies, imaginative literature, and popular theology designed to encourage people to follow God's call to purposeful and holy living. Men and women who enter into this joyous lifestyle do so only as they learn how to apply Christian doctrine to daily life. North Wind Books are dedicated to making spiritual direction more meaningful.

ISBN 0-87788-512-5

Edited by Lil Copan and Miriam Mindeman

Cover and inside design by David LaPlaca

Library of Congress Cataloging-in-Publication Data

Rockness, Miriam Huffman, 1944-
A passion for the impossible : the life of Lilias Trotter / by Miriam Rockness.
p. cm.
ISBN 0-87788-512-5
1. Trotter, I. Lilias (Isabella Lilias), 1853-1928. 2. Missionaries—Algeria—Biography. 3. Missionaries—England—Biography. 4. Artists—England—Biography. I. Title
BV3587.T76R63
266'.0092—dc21
[B]
98-26140
CIP

05 04 03 02 01 00 99

10 9 8 7 6 5 4 3 2

This book is dedicated to all the pilgrim-souls who,
like Lilias and her brave mission band,
have devoted their lives to bringing the light and life
and love of Jesus Christ to the Arab world.

Contents

Full many a gem of purest ray serene
The dark unfathom'd caves of ocean bear:
Full many a flower is born to blush unseen,
And waste its sweetness on the desert air.

—Thomas Gray, "Elegy Written in a Country Church-yard"

FOREWORD

Over the past twenty years I have devoted much time to studying the lives of Christians. Reading biographies and autobiographies of nineteenth- and twentieth-century saints has shaped my spirituality, encouraged me in my walk with God, and caused me to ponder anew the role of books in the process of spiritual formation. One striking lesson learned from spending time with pilgrims from bygone eras is that next to disciplined daily time in prayer and the Scriptures, the reading of devotional literature and biographies ranks extremely high among formative influences. Indeed, many Christians who have made significant contributions to the church testify to the profound impact of books—especially biographies—on their spiritual development.

The life story of Lilias Trotter is destined to become part of that long line of influential biographies. It is my hope and prayer that many people—especially teachers of all age groups, pastors, missionaries, and young Christians who are listening for God's call—will read this important book.

Miriam Rockness's portrait of Trotter makes an important contribution to our knowledge of missions in general and Miss Trotter in particular. Although it is not the first biography of this woman, this is a thoroughly researched book based on hitherto untapped primary sources. Written for a modern audience, *A Passion for the Impossible: The Life of Lilias Trotter* admiringly reveals the life of a wealthy British woman who gives up a comfortable life as an artist and socialite to become a missionary to the Muslims of Algeria. In the pages of this carefully crafted story we learn how one woman who became radically obedient to the Lord Jesus Christ became a missionary pioneer. Trotter was at least a century ahead of her time in developing ways to reach Muslims with the gospel. She realized that the Algerians would not receive the gospel through traditional evangelism tools of proclamation and persuasion. Instead, she employed a combination of literature and art, undergirded by a lifestyle of love and encouragement.

Rockness has given us an important book. It will help prepare us to witness to the complex world of the new millennium.

LYLE W. DORSETT
Wheaton College
Wheaton, Illinois

PREFACE

John Ruskin, in his 1883 Oxford lecture, "The Art of England," tells of meeting a young woman, Lilias Trotter, who challenged his prejudices about artists: "For a long time I used to say, in all my elementary books, that except in a graceful and minor way, women could not draw or paint. I'm beginning lately to bow myself to the much more delightful conviction that no one else can."[1] Exhibiting a half dozen framed pages from her Norwegian sketchbook for his students to copy, Ruskin advised, "You will in examining them, beyond all telling, feel that they are exactly what we should all like to be able to do, and in the plainest and frankest manner shew us how to do it—more modestly speaking, how, if heaven help us, it can be done."[2]

Eight decades later, Sir Kenneth Clark, in the introduction to his book *Ruskin Today,* mentions Ruskin's "ecstasy" over the drawings of Lilias Trotter, noting that she is no longer remembered—thereby inferring that she was not of artistic consequence. Today, a century after Ruskin's historic lecture, the exhibition paintings along with thirty-four other leaves from Lilias's sketchbook are buried in the Print Room of the Ashmolean Museum in Oxford, filed in the Long Cabinet of the Ruskin Art Collection—a hidden testament to potential recognized, promise unrealized.

Who was this talent of whom Ruskin spoke so highly? Lilias Trotter was born in 1853 into a wealthy Victorian family residing in London's fashionable West End. She was reared with all the privileges and prerogatives of her class, including education, travel, and culture. Like many young women of independent means in her era, she was actively involved in volunteer service organizations such as the fledgling Young Women's Christian Association (YWCA). She enjoyed a close personal friendship with Ruskin, who believed that under his tutelage she could become one of the nation's finest artists. Why, then, did someone with her prospects and talent disappear completely from the artistic scene? Did she simply not meet up to her potential?

To begin to answer this, we must look at vignettes drawn in succeeding years of Lilias's life: In her twenties, she is in London, far exceeding the boundaries of convention in her volunteer work. Unlike most women of her class who dabble in such service to avoid the potential boredom of a life of leisure, Lilias is carving out a career at once innovative and daring. She develops radical programs for the Welbeck Street Institute—opening the first public restaurant in London for women and transforming a discarded nightclub into a hostel for women of the street, providing them shelter and training for wholesome employment.

At age thirty-four in 1888, Lilias arrives in the city of Algiers to live among the Arab people of Algeria. Independent of any organization, knowing not one person nor a sentence of Arabic, and without a clue how or where to begin, she and two friends launch a pioneer work drawing only on their own resources.

Lily, a decade later, is in Algiers, walking through the narrow streets of the Arab section of the old town. Children crowd round this tall, slender woman, begging her attention as she works her way to her home, 2 Rue Du Croissant, at the end of the crowded street. An Arab woman calls out from an upper story, "Lili, come see my children. They are sick!" Lilias dresses the abscessed foot of one child and holds the other feverish child in her arms. As she leaves, another Arab woman says, "No one ever—ever loved us like this!"[3]

In 1902, at the age of forty-nine, Lilias is in an oasis in the Sahara desert. She is seated among white-robed figures in a book-lined room spread with camel-skins as a guest in the *zaouria,* a fraternity house of a Sufi brotherhood (fellowship of Islamic mystics). It is exceedingly rare for a woman to receive such an invitation. She drinks coffee and talks about mysteries of "The Way"—the long road to union with God undertaken by these mystic seekers—endeavoring to establish common ground with them regarding the human soul-hunger for God.

A quarter century later, Lilias is living in El Biar, a suburb of Algiers, at the headquarters of the Algiers Mission Band. Inspired by her vision, the group comprised of thirty members joins together to bring the life and light and love of Christ to Algeria. Lilias is white-haired and bedridden, but in no way inactive. With watercolors and paintbrush, she captures images of North Africa—landscapes and houses, figures and flowers—culled from an almost forty-year love affair with Algeria for her sketchbook, *Between the Desert and the Sea.*

From these glimpses alone Lilias would be a person worth learning about. But set into the context of her privileged background and extraordinary prospects, her story is even more intriguing. The life of Lilias Trotter challenges the very meaning of success and talent, potential and fulfillment in any place or time. Her story, as revealed in the events of her life, her writings, and her art, offers a convincing alternative for any woman or man who longs to take on the impossible, to make a difference not only in time but in eternity.

My own introduction to Lilias Trotter was through her written legacy—out-of-print books and leaflets, many beautifully illustrated by her. These works were handed over to me, one by one, by Jane and Betty Barbour, two retired sisters who feared that the writings might be lost during the eventual disbursement of their personal library. Each new edition from the Barbours, arriving through the mail over a period of years, penetrated to my soul, each one exuding a rare blend of earthiness and holiness.

Over time, a passion grew in me to find everything written by or about Lilias Trotter and then to make these works known to others. I discovered that I was not alone in my appreciation. In response to my queries, Elisabeth Elliot wrote, "Delighted to hear from you and find you're another Lilias Trotter fan! . . . I quote her and tell people about her whenever I can."[4] English author Patricia St. John responded: "I was delighted to hear of someone else who loved Miss Trotter's books as I do. As a girl, I think that *Parables of the Cross* helped me spiritually more than any other book, barring the Bible. During my years in Morocco, *The Master of the Impossible* was a constant strengthener of my faith."[5]

It was, however, my meeting with Marjorie Mead and Lyle Dorsett of North Wind Books, and Wendell Evans of Arab World Ministries (AWM), that ultimately led me to Loughborough, the United Kingdom Headquarters of AWM and the home of the Trotter archives, to do research for a biography so that I could reintroduce Lilias Trotter and her now out-of-print works in the hopes that some of those works would be reprinted. When at last I settled in at Loughborough for a month-long immersion in the diaries, journals, and papers, it seemed like the end of a decade-long pilgrimage. In fact, however, it was the beginning of another pilgrimage. I had examined Patricia St. John's fine work, *Until the Day Breaks* (OM Publishing, 1990), which synthesizes and provides commentary on two helpful out-of-print biographical sources written by women who actually knew Miss Trotter. With the foundation of the biographical works plus the primary sources of the diaries and journals, I still longed to know even more about this remarkable woman, particularly about the formation and development of her inner life.

My search continued, propelled by unresolved questions: What early influences in the home and family affected the formation of Lilias's character? What factors influenced the development of her faith? How did she reconcile the stewardship of her gifts with her sacrifice of a vocation in art? What compelled her to leave a prospering ministry in England to serve in Algeria, and, later, what kept her in North Africa? Did she ever waver in her resolve or regret her decision? How did she maintain the vision and sustain the stamina to persevere against so many seemingly insurmountable obstacles? Who, at the deepest level, was Lilias Trotter?

I embarked on two separate journeys: a journey back in time to examine the early, formative years of her life—the England Era—and a journey inward to her soul through the diaries and journals of the final forty years of her life—the Algerian Era.

The journey backward proved to be a formidable challenge; she left so few tracks to guide someone tracing early influences. It required detective work, sleuthing out relatives and institutions that she served and that served her, a mission impossible without the full collaboration of AWM and, in particular, Alasdair McLaren. The search sent me pounding the pavement of the West End of London, map in hand, locating the homes and haunts of her childhood and youth. In time, with much trans-Atlantic communication to Trotter family members and friends, Ruskin scholars, and the archivist for YWCA of Great Britain, piece by piece, information was added to the jigsaw puzzle of her early years. There were surprises—a disappointing dead end in my effort to trace "45 Ruskin letters to Lilias Trotter . . . being prepared for publication"[6] referred to in a tantalizing footnote to Ruskin's *Brantwood Diaries;* and the discovery of the published collection of her mother's letters to five-year-old Lily—by far the most intimate glimpse into the dominant influences of her early years.

Meanwhile, the journey inward, the Algerian Era, was as forthcoming with information as the England years were reluctant because of the treasure of Lilias's early journal-letters (1888–1898), followed by thirty compact, leather-bound, page-a-day diaries (1899–1928), supplemented by travel journals—a study in both beauty and economy of space. Day by day, decade upon decade, through the seasons of her life, Lilias simply recorded the facts, filtered through her heavenly vision: God's working out his eternal purposes on a land, in a people. From these records, illuminated by exquisite watercolors and strong sketches—a museum in miniature—emerges a country, intimate and varied, and a people, "bright and living."[7]

Ultimately and most profoundly, however, a life emerges, indeed, evolves, from England's lovely Lily to Algiers's beloved "Lalla Lili": a soul in progress. Stamped on every page of her journals and diaries is a woman at once fully immersed in the practical realities of everyday living and engaged in assimilating those realities through an eternal perspective that recognized no boundaries of time or space.

It is from the tension of these two realities—temporal and eternal—that hard spiritual truths are hammered out which later appear in Lilias's devotional books, elegant and reasoned. Light-giving lessons are harvested through her common daily rounds, tested through crises, and sustained through a lifetime of change and growth. The lessons are as relevant to the mellowed Lilias of later years as to the fiery "Tiger Lily" of youth, and they are wholly applicable today to young and old alike, regardless of life circumstances.

This is the story of a soul drawn, whenever possible, from primary sources or eyewitness accounts, and from Lilias's original journal-letters, diaries, and travel journals rather than later edited versions. Throughout this book, any excerpt marked "Journal" or "Diary" or marked with a date alone is an excerpt from one of these sources of Lilias. To preserve a sense of Lilias's changing perspective or the changing times, as well as to maintain the immediacy and intimacy of the original material, Lilias's informal grammar and her choice of spellings is used (be it the English, French, or Arabic version of the word in question) when quoting directly from her works.

There are certain challenges in the attempt to reconstruct the life of a person seven decades after the fact: Her own records were not intended to be an "inner account" and her faults, whatever they might have been, tend to be obscured by time and by her extraordinary contributions. Yet the unadorned facts of her life speak her story—the silences during particularly dark times; the rush of words and watercolors through times of joy; and the subtle interactions and transactions of her daily life.

As to the question that pulsates throughout the journey into the life of Lilias Trotter, "How does one measure the sacrifice against the yield?" I offer the counsel given to Lily in a letter from her mother: "The way to arrive at truth in this, as in all other cases, is to hear what every one has to say, and to compare one account with another."[8]

Part One

The England Era

1853–1887

Garden Lily

Garden lilies grow in fertile, well-drained soil. They require shelter from cutting winds, shade for the roots and lower stems, and full or partial sun for the heads.

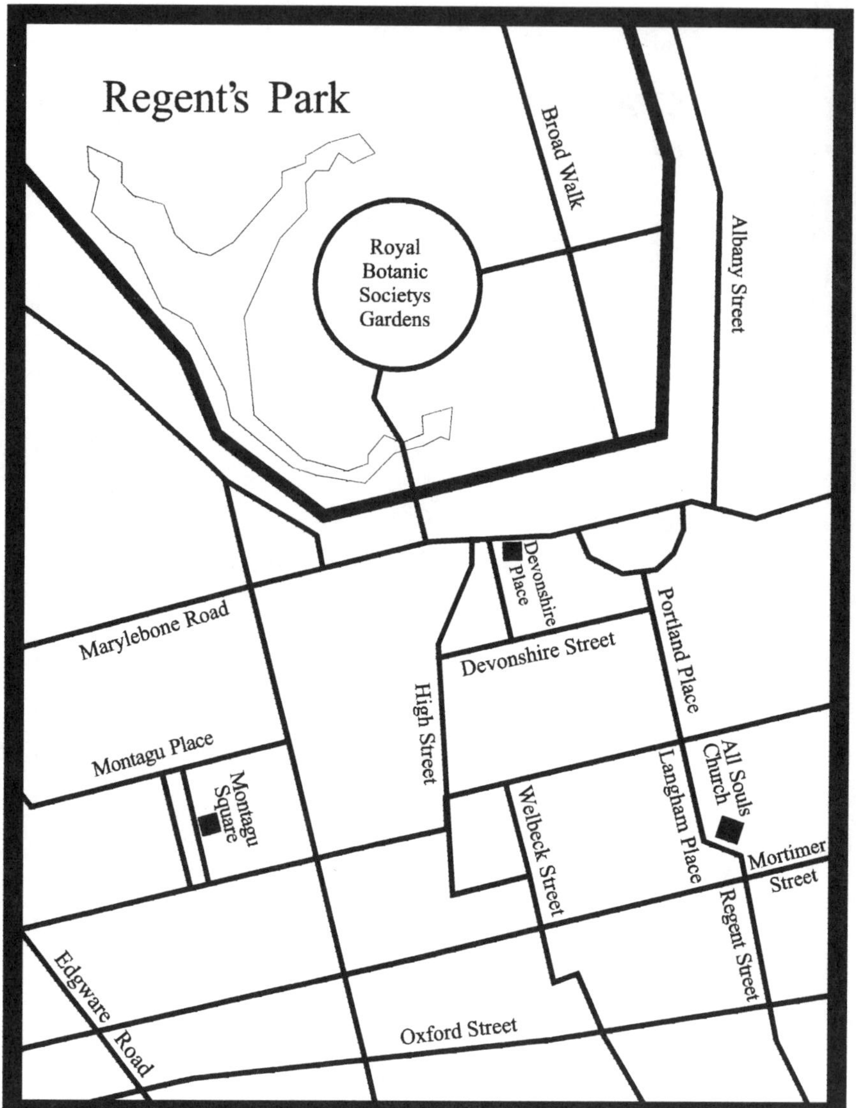

Map of Lilias's London

1
DEVONSHIRE PLACE*

1853

The Alexander Trotter family lived the happy, disciplined life of the Victorian upper classes; godly, serious, kind to the poor at a distance, sheltered from all that was offensive. So Lilias grew, beloved and loving, in the sheltered atmosphere of a stable home surrounded by beauty and culture.

—Patricia St. John, *Until The Day Breaks*[1]

---

*The reader is strongly encouraged to refer to the historical setting to part one, found in appendix A.

In London's fashionable West End between Baker Street and Portland Place and immediately south of Regent's Park, was "the best property in Marylebone,"[2] according to town planner John Nash. There, at Devonshire Place House on the corner of Devonshire Street and Upper Harley, Isabella Lilias Trotter was born on 14 July 1853 to Alexander and Isabella Trotter. Nearby, tall traditional terrace houses laid out along the sedate Georgian squares housed families similar to the Trotters, families who were inspired by Victorian ideals, grounded on biblical principles, and guided by Samuel Smile's self-help maxims.

One block from Regent's Park, the Trotter offspring supervised by governesses—like other children living in this prized location—played in the open fields of the Park or the adjoining gardens of Park Square while mothers enjoyed offerings from the Royal Botanical Society and garden shows. A short two blocks off Portland Place, Lilias's father like other breadwinners of the area—merchants and bankers and professional men—was connected by the royal mile of Regent Street to the royal borough and, just another two miles "down river," to the Bank of London, Royal Exchange, and Stock Exchange—in short, to the political and economic centers of the world.

By stagecoach these men had an easy return in the evening to home and family and the pleasures of West End society. In that environment, dinner parties were a preferred form of entertainment, and conversation was honed to an art. West End society not only discussed the books and letters fresh from the London presses, but it entertained the writers who penned them—Dickens, Trollope, the Brownings, James. Residents flocked as well to the exhibitions of the Royal Art Society and rubbed shoulders with the artists who painted them—Turner, Rossetti, Hunt—as well as the critics who promoted or panned them, most notably, the irrepressible John Ruskin.

Into this privileged world, Lily was welcomed by a brood of children from her father's first marriage to Jacqueline Otter, which had ended in Jaqueline's premature death four years before. Alexander Trotter supported his large and growing family from his prosperous career as a stockbroker for Capel, Norbury, and Trotter Co., located in the City. The stock brokerage firm, at the time, was one of the two most important firms on the Stock Exchange and in London. Recruited to join the firm at the age of twenty-three and joining the Stock Exchange the following year, young Alexander was a member of the Atheneum Club, the most intellectually elite of all London's clubs. His reputation as a man "with high qualities of intellect and acquirement"[3] was demonstrated early with his publication at the age of twenty-five of a lucid and thoroughly documented study of the financial positions of the states of the North American Union.

When, in 1851, thirty-five-year-old Isabella Strange married the thirty-seven-year-old widowed stockbroker, she was initiated immediately into the first-time roles of wife, homemaker, and mother to six children all under the age of fourteen. Lily's birth in 1853, followed respectively by Alexander and Margaret four and seven years later, brought the additional challenge of blending the children from the two marriages into one strong family unit, a feat accomplished "most harmoniously."[4]

Isabella clearly relished these roles. Devonshire Place House was a "choice London mansion,"[5] by her own description, beautifully situated just off Regent's Park. Spacious rooms comfortably accommodated the growing and changing family; conservatory and greenhouse allowed range for the nature-loving Isabella to cultivate and enjoy beloved plants and flowers. A staff of servants—personal and domestic—lightened her task, freeing her for the responsibilities of nurturing the lively family.

On the surface, the Trotter family could be seen as the picture of Victorian respectability; indeed, they were archetypical of the "cult of family" modeled auspiciously by Queen Victoria and Prince Albert. Their religious instruction was guided by the Church of England at St. Marylebone Parish Church located two blocks from their home. So enamored were Alexander and Isabella by the popular parish curate, Pelham, that they named their youngest child, Alexander Pelham, after him. The Trotter sons were educated at Harrow School, a public school in an outlying London suburb, continuing their studies at the University in Cambridge or at military college. The daughters were tutored by governesses at home polishing their skills in German and French, along with other refinements such as art and music. Sons and daughters alike enjoyed the enrichments of location and privilege: offerings from the Royal Botanical and Zoological Institutes at nearby Regent's Park, summers on the continent, and holidays in the country or by the seashore at Cromer.

Yet, like any other home, the real action took place beneath the surface. Lily was greeted at birth by four brothers—Coutts and William in their early teens, twelve-year-old Henry and ten-year-old Edward—and their two younger sisters, Jaqueline and Emily. Early on, Lily learned to stand her ground, agitated by the teasing typical of brothers. Her nickname, "Tiger Lily," was probably inspired by an incident, laughingly recalled years later, when Lily sprang to the defense of her kitten, rescuing the tormented with one hand and boxing the ear of the tormentor with the other.

Environment alone, however, does not account for Lily's spirit. Born of a mix of strong Scottish blood, she was given names, Isabella and Lilias, linked to both her maternal (Strange) and paternal (Trotter) lineage. Lilias's strong-willed, fiercely independent forebears exhibited many of the character traits which years later would mark their namesake. Likewise, the unique artistic gift and sensibility which would inform Lilias's life and work were clearly evident in her ancestral line.

Isabella Lumisden Strange, Lily's maternal great-grandmother, was considered to be a woman of "much originality and strength of character."[6] Granddaughter of the Bishop of Edinburgh, she was fervently pro-Scotland and a Jacobite: She embraced the cause of Prince Charles Edward Stuart, Young Pretender in his attempt to restore the Stuart monarchy by seizing the British throne from the Hanoverian George II. She was so adamant in her politics that Isabella made it a condition of her favor that her then suitor, Robert Strange, fight for Prince Charles Edward Stuart. Fight Robert did, right up to the fateful Battle of Culloden, identifying himself so completely with the cause that he engraved a plate for new bank-notes for the dynasty that was never to be. After the decisive defeat of 16 April 1746, soldiers came to search for him as he hid in the house of his ladylove. Resourceful Isabella deftly lifted her hoop skirt, under which the fugitive took refuge. She continued to work steadily at her needlework, caroling a Jacobean song, while the soldiers searched in vain. Robert's faithfulness was rewarded with Isabella's hand in marriage two years later. Not easily discouraged by the political defeat, the couple named their first son Charles Edward, long after it was fashionable to do so! The willingness to follow her personal convictions regardless of risk or cost was a trait that would likewise distinguish her great-granddaughter, Isabella Lilias Trotter.

If Robert Strange sacrificed safety in order to embrace Isabella's political causes, she sacrificed security for her talented husband's artistic ideals. Exiled for three years on the Continent due to his radical politics, Robert pursued his art, studying in Rouen, Paris, and with the Italian masters in Italy. After the amnesty extended to Jacobites, the young couple returned to London and enjoyed a ten-year respite, while Robert distinguished himself as an engraver "in the very first European rank"[7] and as an educator, importing collections of the best classical prints from Italy and issuing them at low cost to improve the public's taste—a proclivity which would be evidenced in Lilias's adult-long passion to print and propagate, at her own expense, edifying literature for the masses. The following twenty years, however, were marked by flux in favor and finances, as Robert battled the Prince of Wales and the Royal Academy of Art for his principles and causes. He and Isabella alternated living in Britain and on the Continent as his position rose and fell—they, like Lilias, caring less for security in art or politics than for their deeply-felt convictions. Finally, the tide of favor turned toward him in 1787, ending four decades of uncertainty, when his engraving of Benjamin West's painting of the royal family won him a knighthood.

Sir Robert Strange stood among the best in Europe as a pure historical line engraver and was considered foremost of his day in England. The description of his art in *The Dictionary of National Biography* is strongly suggestive of the sketchbook drawings of his great-granddaughter Lily, whose work, almost a century later, would catch the eye of yet another challenger of the Royal Academy, John Ruskin. The dictionary description points to "a certain distinction of style and a pervading harmony of treatment" in Strange's art, and adds, "His lines, pure, firm, and definite, but essentially flowing, lend themselves to the most delicate and rounded contours, from which all outline disappears."[8]

The third son of Robert and Isabella was Thomas Lumisden Strange, Lily's maternal grandfather, whose portrait hung in Devonshire Place House as a daily reminder of the man who, in contrast to his father, made his name and won his knighthood for diplomacy. Born and raised in London, with a four-year Italian interlude, Thomas chose the path of law, studying first at Westminster school and then Christ Church, Oxford. He was appointed Chief Justice of Nova Scotia, where his reputation for exceptional tact and diplomacy won him an appointment to Madras as Recorder and President of the Court and knighthood preceding his departure to this difficult post. There Thomas and his second wife, Louisa Burrough, an artist in her own right, produced their large family. After nineteen years of distinguished service, they returned to England, where a year later he was created Doctor of Civil Law at Oxford. His work, *Elements of Hindu Law,* published seven years later, remained for many years the great authority on this subject.

Thomas and Louisa's second daughter, Isabella—Lilias's mother—was one year old when the family returned to England, where they divided their time between the academic community of Oxford and their London home at Great George Street. She, like her grandmother Isabella before her and her daughter after her, was described as a person of originality—not surprising considering the environment in which she was raised. Political and religious leaders and thinkers of the day were frequent visitors at the Strange home—Drummonds, Dundases, Anstruthers, Arbuthnots, and Eyres, to name a few. One can only wonder, given the mix of people and places to which she was exposed over the years, just when and where Isabella first met Alexander Trotter, brother of her second cousin's husband, and the man who would someday be her husband and the love of her life.

On the paternal side, Lilias Stuart, Lily's grandmother, married her own Alexander Trotter in 1797. Through this union, the elder Lilias, daughter of John Stuart of Allanbank, would bequeath more than her given name to the younger Lilias: blood of the Stuart dynasty coursed through her veins, reinforcing with royal ties the Strange family's allegiance to the Young Pretender, Bonnie Prince Charlie. Tradition maintains that the Trotter name originated in 1314, when an ancestor—a knight—"trotted" home on horseback from the Battle of Bannockburn with news of victory in the long war for independence from England. Later Trotter descendants settled in the border county of Scotland on an estate at Kettlesheils in Berwickshire.

The year of the Stuart/Trotter union, 1797, forty-two-year-old Alexander, Paymaster of the Navy, acquired the estate of Dreghorn, located near Edinburgh in the ancient county of Midlothian. Over the next decade he added countless acres to his estate and five sons to his family. Active in national and municipal affairs, Alexander was influential in the development of the City of Edinburgh, being connected with drawing up "A Plan of Communication Between the New and Old Towns of Edinburgh," which united the romantic charm of the Old Town, built around a castle high on a hill, with the unmatched elegance of the New Town, with its crescents, squares, and wide streets.

Alexander's fourth son and namesake, Lilias's father, was born in 1814 at Dreghorn within the shadow of Edinburgh's Old Town. Young Alexander lived in the beautiful lowlands of Scotland until his early twenties, when he left his homeland to pursue a career in London, the financial capitol of the Empire. At the recommendation of his uncle, Sir Coutts Trotter, Alexander became a partner at the James Capel & Co. stock broking firm. The move to London during a time of unprecedented economic prosperity was fortuitous for himself and, in time, for his family. It was a decision which later would have an important effect in the development of Lilias's spiritual and leadership potential.

2

APRIL DAYS OF CHILDHOOD

1853—1866

You are right to be glad in His April days while He gives them. Every stage of heavenly growth in us is lovely to Him; He is the God of the daisies and the lambs and the merry child hearts!

—*Parables of the Cross*[1]

The 1850s was a profitable time for Lilias's family. The stock brokering firm of Capel, Norberry & Trotter continued to act as brokers for Coutts Bank, a Trotter connection of both family and business. The firm expanded Coutts banking interests, acting "as brokers to a number of foreign railway companies," including companies in the United States of America.[2]

Alexander Trotter, long interested in the financial transactions of the young States, was toying with the idea of a business trip to visit overseas clients and to travel the newly-constructed railroad lines. Isabella, fully occupied with the care of five-year-old Lily and her baby brother, teased her husband, saying, "the one stipulation in giving her consent to Papa's crossing the ocean was that she should accompany him,"[3] secure in the belief that neither he nor she would undertake the venture.

The next day, however, Alexander engaged four berths aboard an oceanliner for himself, his son William, his unsuspecting wife, and her personal maid, Thrower. And in October of 1858, the four set sail for the new world. The letters written to Lily during the four months of separation offer a lively and witty documentation of the "First Impressions of the New World on Two Travelers from the Old." They also provide for posterity the most intimate glimpse of Alexander and Isabella, and the dynamics of their marriage. Out of the 308 pages of letters (originally not intended for publication) emerge compelling portraits of the two most significant influences of Lily's life.

Isabella was described in her sister's memoirs, *Bygone Days,* as "affectionate, thoughtful and unselfish—a devoted wife and mother—a kind and loving sister to us all."[4] Indeed, the Isabella who shines through the letters to Lilias is warm-hearted with an expansive personality that reached out to friend and stranger alike. Her sympathetic nature made her a stout advocate for the disadvantaged, whether slave, native American dispossessed of land, or prisoner or orphan living in suffering—and it was that same natural concern for others that was evidenced in subsequent years by her daughter.

More than sympathy bound Isabella to people or causes. She brought an open mind to each new situation, making a conscious effort to balance impression with fact, emotion with objective consideration. Traveling through slave and free states during the fire of growing controversy preceding the Civil War, Isabella wrote in a surprisingly adult manner to her five-year-old daughter: "I shall give you the testimony of everyone as I gather it for you to put together that you may be able to form your deductions,"[5] a posture which, no doubt, encouraged in Lilias that same balanced objectivity. Her growing conviction as she conversed with slave and freeman alike compelled her in time to relate her own view of slavery as "lowering and degrading the moral tone, both of the white and black population," concluding, "I have seen nothing to lessen, and everything to confirm the strong impression I have always entertained respecting it. Besides what we have seen we have read as much as we could on the subject."[6]

Isabella read widely, keeping up with contemporary journals such as the *Edinburgh Review* and current writers of note. She was conversant on many topics, with her interests ranging from the domestic arts of gardening and decorating to matters urbane. She shared her husband's fascination with astronomy, geology, and botany, and, in her zeal for collecting, she was very much the Victorian woman, gathering pebbles for memorials, leaves to press and mount, seeds and cuttings for the greenhouse at Devonshire Place House.

Isabella's soul resonated to beauty, whether in architecture, interior design, a work of art, or the natural order. Letters she wrote from the New World capture her poetic perspective: a river "full of life and animation . . . a most tender green"; waterfalls by moonlight "lit up and shining like the brightest silver."[7] Her description of a sunset—"the most exquisite shades of colouring from clear blue, shading to a pale green, and then to a most glorious golden colour"—anticipates her daughter's descriptions, four decades later, accompanying watercolors of an Algerian sky.[8] Likewise, Isabella's appreciation for the subtle manifestations of beauty—the form of trees without leaves; seed-vessels in the long grown prairie grass—took expression in Lily's classic work, *Parables of the Christ-Life,* based on the seed-vessels of North Africa.

Isabella found strength and comfort in the familiar rites and rituals of the Church of England, yet religion, for her, went beyond the institution to a personal faith. At an early age she manifested strong religious principles that were met at times with considerable challenge in an environment where open-mindedness and tolerance were valued. Her own brother Thomas, a pious theist, ceased to be a Christian in Madras, while watching a supposed convert at the gallows proclaim his faith in Rama, not Christ. He set down his experience in the publication "How I ceased to be a Christian," and from then on left a legacy of "controversial writing" on a variety of religious subjects. The invariable tension surrounding such divergent points of view must have strengthened and defined Isabella's thinking while softening the sharp edges of orthodoxy, schooling her in a respect for differing viewpoints. Her own views, in turn, were respected, if not fully embraced. Her sister writes that she "gently and firmly held her way. Her influence in the family was felt and acknowledged"[9]—a position Lilias would one day maintain within her tolerant, yet at times uncomprehending, "greater family circle."

Isabella's evangelistic zeal was in no way stifled by opposition. She describes her encounter in the States with a young slave girl, "a real life Topsy," to whom she witnessed about Christ, urging "the duty of prayer upon her as strongly and simply" as possible. After discovering that the young girl could not read, she writes, "I shall try this morning to get her an alphabet, in order to encourage her to make another attempt to learn to read."[10] Here she prefigures an image of her daughter Lily, years later, with young girls gathered about her in an Arab courtyard as she intructs them, so that they too could have direct access to the words of the Bible.

Isabella's mother heart and wit permeate the letters written to "My dear little girl," going beyond endearments as she views each new experience from the eyes of her child. She records her observations, enclosing sketches and picture cards, and collects stones and "corn pop" to bring back to England, always relating the wonders of the unknown world to sites and situations familiar to Lily: the streets of Washington "two or three times the width of Portland Place"; the peaks of the White Mountains "higher than Ben Nevis." Attempting to describe the grandeur of Niagara Falls to Lily, she whimsically leaves a blank space for her "to fill up with [her] imagination, for no words can convey any idea of the scene."[11]

The sole souvenirs from Lily's childhood are a drawing and a sketchbook, inscribed in her mother's hand, "Lily—Sept. to Dec. 1858," a touching evidence of her sensitivity to the child left behind seen in the way she provided Lily the tools to record her experiences during their separation. This likewise suggests a mother's awareness and encouragement of her daughter's budding artistic talent. Significantly, the first drawings are dock scenes, captured in detail and perspective surprising in one so young, with people standing on a wooden platform waving to ships in the distance. The rest of the sketchbook is filled with images and imaginations of a Victorian childhood: tree house and castle; seacoast and bathing machine; somber-faced women with long skirts, nipped-in waists, and plume-decorated hats; men in waistcoats and stove pipe hats. A pipe-smoking gnome perches on the shoulder of a dubious host; kittens and cats scamper through pages decorated with alphabet books, toys, and other vestiges of childhood.

The final pages of the sketchbook show evidence of the advent of Christmas, bringing the safe return of Lily's parents, anticipated by her mother in her final letter: "In a few hours more, we shall, I trust, have the joy and gladness of seeing all your dear faces again, and be rejoicing together over our safe return from our interesting and delightful expedition to the NEW WORLD."[12]

Lily's father, Alexander Trotter, emerges from his wife's many letters as a man of high principles, strong character, and steady temperament. A large man, standing six feet three inches tall, he must have seemed the very tower of security to his children. His personality won the trust and affection of others, eliciting this tribute from Isabella's sister: "I can not name my dear brother-in-law without dwelling on his charming character of love, gentleness, generosity, unselfishness."[13]

Alexander took a keen interest in people and was fair-minded and tolerant sometimes to a fault in his determination to give people the benefit of the doubt. Isabella, writing to Lily about her papa's refusal to comment on a certain preacher's sermon observes, "I must draw my own conclusion from his silence. He will only admit that the pew was very comfortable and the cushion soft, and as he was kept awake all last night by mosquitoes, the inference to be drawn is not difficult."[14]

The letters show also that Alexander had a great respect for the dignity of all individuals, regardless of their station or rank in society, and he sought to understand divergent points of view. Throughout their American travels, in free state and slave, he invited dialogue with slaves, owners, and traders alike with much the same earnestness with which Lily would seek one day to understand the prostitutes at Victoria Station, the cloistered Arab women, and the mystic seekers of the Algerian Southlands. Alexander enjoyed engaging new acquaintances in conversation, drawing upon their expertise, be they professor, statesman, scientist, or local hotel chef famed for special omelets!

Lily's father had a curious mind and was constantly seeking out new experiences, then living them to the full, often to Isabella's alarm. Letters are laced with reports of "Papa's" derring-do: his precarious walks along the brittle rock edging precipices; his taking the wheel of the engine on the Baltimore & Ohio railway and driving the train himself; his riding out a hurricane in the Atlantic, standing on the ship deck in the eye of the storm so as to "hear the fierce wind tearing past the vessel and to see the ship not swaying in the least one way or the other."[15]

Possessing an insatiable appetite for the wonders of the natural world, Alexander insisted on sharing this passion with others. "Mama" observes in one letter that, beholding the majesty of Niagara Falls in the moonlight, "Papa calls me every minute, 'Oh do come, this minute; I do not believe you have yet seen the Falls!!!'"[16] In an amusing account of a railway journey along the Susquehanna River, Mama describes "Papa's restless state of mind":

> *I counted that he rose from his seat to look at the view from the other side of the car, thirty times in the space of an hour and a half, making a move, therefore, upon an average, of once in every three minutes; and this he afterwards continued to do as often as the road crossed the river. I foolishly, at first partook of his locomotive propensities, but my exhausted frame soon gave way, so that he declares I only saw one half of its beauties, namely, the half on the side where I was seated; but this half was ample to satisfy any reasonable mortal. I am at a loss to imagine what our fellow-travellers could have thought of him, as they lounged on their seats, and scarcely ever condescended to look out of window.*[17]

Alexander's enthusiasms were tempered by a disciplined and scholarly mind. An avid reader, he considered booksellers "his favorite lounges" from which he added volumes to his personal library. A Fellow of the Geological Society, he was keenly interested and knowledgeable in natural and technological science, and cultivated similar interests in his children, several of whom, as adults, would pursue scientific endeavors professionally or avocationally. Lilias was strongly influenced by her early exposure to science experiments at home as well as holiday excursions to lectures at the Royal Institution and would, throughout her life, avidly read scientific journals such as the *Invention.*

She would see in the laws governing natural phenomena, object lessons of things "unseen" in the spiritual realm. Almost a half-century later she recalled an incident that reassured her concerning the "dim light" of the fragile young Algerian Christians:

> *A memory comes of the far off years when I was a child at the children's lectures that used to be given by Tyndall at the Royal Institution in the Christmas holidays. I can see the great dim lecture hall with tier on tier of boy & girl faces, & in the centre the table with a lighted*

candle & a jar of oxygen alongside—& then the transfiguration of the dim yellow flame, when plunged into the new element—instantly it was a great radiant star. We have the "dimly burning flax" here. All it wants is the intensity around that will make it, in its turn, intense. (26 January 1908)

Letters to Lily contain many technical descriptions of canals, locks and engines, for which Isabella defers to Alexander, writing that

many parts are of your father's dictating. I leave you and others to judge which these are. Without his help I never could have sent you such full accounts of the engine of the Newport steamer . . . and you will, I know, like the letters all the better for his having a part in them.[18]

The scope and depth of Alexander's scholarship is manifest in his own book, *The Financial Position and Credit of Such of The States of The North American Union as Have Contracted Public Debts,* published when he was twenty-five years old. In addition to extensive charts and tables and comprehensive exploration of topics, the book offers views about the dangers of democracy without a religious faith to anchor and assure the character of its citizens, revealing the spiritual paradigm through which young Alexander viewed the world:

To what extent, therefore, religious feelings prevail in the United States, and are likely to form a principle of action, must be a question of deep importance, if viewed only in connection with the subject under discussion; for in deciding whether, in times of difficulty, the states will keep good faith with their creditors or not, the existence of such an influence or of an opposite one must infallibly be found to throw its weight into one side of the balance or the other. Being without the means of forming an opinion on this subject, and wishing neither lightly to deny it, I shall content myself with pointing out the importance of it.[19]

Alexander's religious practices were not confined within the walls of the Church of England. He had a personal faith which found expression in humanitarian endeavors and in a special concern for the condition of public institutions. Isabella's letters to Lily record visits he took while in America with his close friend Lord Radstock, a leader in the newly formed Young Men's Christian Association (YMCA), to prisons, schools, orphanages, insane asylums, and schools for the deaf and dumb, as they were called in his day, to study various philosophies and practices, with the view of reform in their English counterparts. He followed religious trends with interest, such as the revivals of the Great Awakening of the late 1850s, measuring eye-witness accounts against his personal standard of "decorum and sobriety." He, himself, was ever ready with a word of witness or encouragement, admonishing, for example, a young black husband—a freedman—on his domestic duties.

Alexander was a devoted father, bringing to his children the same gracious qualities of personality and temperament which endeared him to his colleagues and friends. He engaged his children in challenging discussion; he encouraged their interest in art and science; he made a delightful companion for his older children and a playful presence for his younger. Years later, Lily would liken her Heavenly Father's generosity to that of her earthly father, referring to "the drawer of what used to be the table of my father's dressingroom—the drawer he used to call my garden—the other one alongside being Alec's—He used to hide in our respective gardens any little gifts—picture books or toys—that he had picked up on his way home from the city."[20]

The letters from the New World reveal a fascinating play between the complementary personalities of Alexander and Isabella, which through the alchemy of marriage doubtless provided balance to the family. Isabella's lighthearted sense of humor relieved her husband's serious intensity. She coaxed him out of his occasional "melancholy mood" with her playful teasing. Alexander, on the other hand, offset Isabella's fears, shoring up her courage by his steadiness and wholehearted abandonment to the moment. His penchant for detail corrected Isabella's spontaneous assumptions or generalities about people or places—a playful argument about the length of the tail of a comet is a case in point. Isabella writes, "I say it looks two yards long, but papa says it is difficult to tell this, but that it is really about a degree and a half in length, or about six diameters of the moon."[21] She was solicitous about his health, headaches, and "figetty states" appearing as a nagging undercurrent of concern; he was caring about her comfort and general well-being. A union of contrasting personalities, they shared a true partnership of heart and mind, based on common values, friendships, interests, and faith.

Lily thrived in the warm embrace of her home and family. She relished the society of her elder sisters, Jaqueline and Emily, and the stimulation of big brothers in and out of the home, bringing tales from their broadening worlds of school and travel. Her nurturing instincts, lavished on dolls and kittens, found a more compelling focus with the additions of a real life baby brother and sister, who would grow into daily companions and life-long friends. Among Lily's childhood memories would be the walks in Regent's Park with brother Alec, talking in a secret language of their invention, building "scientific castles in the air" while little "Minnie" tagged along.

High points for Lily were holidays with the extended family, in winter at Epping Forest in Essex, in summer along the eastern coast at Cromer, where she formed her first chosen friendship with her cousin Edith Chapman (later Barclay). Excerpts from her mother's letter to Lily's grandmother, Lady Louisa Strange, give glimpses into summer days of childhood:

> *I took the children for a delightful day among woods and ferns on Saturday in a donkey cart, Minnie sometimes driving, and Alec sometimes riding postillion. Coles and Taylor came too. We were absent from 11–7.30, and the carriages together only cost 12/-, and they go like lightening! We took our food with us, and you may suppose how they enjoyed it, bringing back quantities of ferns and blackberries.*[22]

Another account discloses aspects both of gracious country living and of the personality of Lily:

> *Lilias and I had a very pleasant evening at old Lady Buxton's at Northrupp, three miles from here last week. She is a sister of Mrs. Elizabeth Fry, and is a most charming old lady, and very kind to me.*

> *It was a thé dinant, twelve or fourteen people there. Her granddaughter married a grandson of Daniel Wilson, Bishop of Calcutta, and they are just now staying with her. There was a long, narrow table in the dining-room, capable of holding more than fourteen. Mr. and Mrs. Wilson sat at either end, he handing me in, and Lady Buxton sat in a centre seat. Mrs. Wilson had the tea at her end; and large dish of eight or ten partridges, stewed beef steak, and roast fowls. Tea, wine, and claret cup were handed round ad lib. It was such an easy, pleasant, pretty repast, and one she frequently gives. . . . I enclose Lady Buxton's note that you may see how kindly it is worded, though Lilias kicks at the designation "sweet"!*[23]

A formal portrait of Lily at age ten, dressed in a long-sleeved frock with a hoop skirt and gazing solemnly into the camera with soulful dark eyes, captures the gentle seriousness of her character. Already her "young friends held her as one a little apart and above them in her tastes and ways."[24] Yet her ebullient spirit and merry sense of humor balanced this aspect of her personality, and her warm, sympathetic nature made her a winsome confidante even at an early age.

Nature had endowed Lily with a bright mind, logical and orderly. She had the heart of an artist, with an innate sensitivity to beauty in color and form, and a rare artistic talent. Birth had provided her the benefits of place and privilege. She was nurtured by parents, each exceptional in their own right. Many of Lilias's extraordinary characteristics, evidenced at each stage of her life—strong values, high ideals, heartfelt empathy, inborn talents, even rigorous mental discipline—were acquired from her family by nature and nurture, laying the foundation for the remarkable woman she would become.

It is hard to imagine a more ideal childhood—or a better start to life. But a shadow was slowly gathering over Devonshire Place House. In the winter of 1864, Lilias's twenty-five-year-old brother, William, became a partner in his father's firm. That same year, Alexander began a battle with an illness that claimed his life two years later. Isabella was inconsolable. Prone as she was already to "variable spirits," this was a blow from which she never fully recovered. Widowed at the age of fifty, with three young children to raise and older children still at home, she faced formidable challenges. Without her beloved husband and companion, life would never be the same again. And life would never be the same for twelve-year-old Lily either. The death of her father left a vacuum that could be filled by no other person. With that loss came the close of her childhood.

3
A SOUL INTO BLOSSOM
1866—1872

Take the very hardest thing in your life—the place of difficulty, outward or inward, and expect God to triumph gloriously in that very spot. Just there He can bring your soul into blossom.

—*Parables of the Cross*[1]

Lily was devastated by the loss of her adored papa. The secure predictability of her world was now shattered. A move from Devonshire Place House was inevitable. The older sons were out of the home, each at the start of a careers in which they would distinguish themselves. Coutts, the eldest, was in Germany studying experimental physics, just before his appointment as a lecturer at Trinity College, where he eventually would become vice-chancellor. William, a partner in his father's brokerage firm, was already moving into positions of responsibility at the firm and in the Stock Exchange. Henry was in India with the Royal Engineers at Bengal, launching an adventurous and prominent career in military and diplomatic services. Edward was studying at King's College, preparing for Christ College in Oxford, after which he would take holy orders and devote his life to pioneer work in Trinidad and Venezuela. Lily's "much loved" elder sisters, Jaqueline and Emily, remained at home, along with Alec and Margaret (Minnie), who were now nine and six years of age.

Lily, on the threshold of adolescence, was developing into an attractive young lady, tall and slender with beautifully expressive brown eyes and a firm, sensitive mouth. Her father's painful illness and death had made an indelible mark on her sensitive nature, bringing a new gravity to her personality, and with it the evidence of a deepening spiritual dimension. She was not a stranger to suffering as observed in the lives of others. She had been raised in a family of faith, instructed in biblical stories and precepts. She had witnessed Christianity expressed in the lives of her parents. But here and now, in her "place of difficulty," the precepts would be put to the test.

In the void left by her earthly father, she turned in a new way to her heavenly Father. Family members, years later, recall thinking Lily at play only to discover she had withdrawn to her room, where she was found praying. One can but speculate as to the nature of those prayers in one so new to suffering as well as to the faith. Was there anger in her prayers? Despair over the loss of her beloved father? Fear of what the future would hold without his strong presence? Or did she simply go to her heavenly Father, crying out her need and loneliness—and letting him hold her close to his heart, speaking to her pain with his love?

Her family remembered that from this point there was a distinct change in Lily's character. Always warmhearted, she seemed now to have a great gift of love and sympathy, boundless in its expression. No trouble was too small or too great for her concern. She manifested a quality of selflessness unique in one of any age. Her sister writes, "She simply shed a constant light over her home."[2] She took, it appears, the "very hardest thing in her life," and there God brought her "soul into blossom."

In 1867, the year after Alexander's death, the Trotter family moved to 40 Montagu Square, six blocks from Devonshire Place House and a brisk five-minute walk north to Regent's Park or south to Hyde Park. The tall four-story terrace houses faced onto a garden park the length of the square, shaded by leafy trees and guarded by an iron fence and gate. When writer Anthony Trollope moved next door into 39 Montagu Square several years later, he wrote "it is not a gorgeous neighborhood but one which will suit my declining years and modest resources,"[3] an assessment which understated both his income and his surroundings. Residents of the square could enjoy a "London season" in town; theirs was a convenient base for the round of parties, balls, and cultural events which peaked while the Houses of Parliament were in session. Trollope himself hosted dinners in his home at which Robert Browning, Wilkie Collins, and the American humorist Mark Twain were guests.

Number 40 Montagu Square, like each of the adjoining houses lining both sides of the square, was a four-story terrace built of brown brick and a facade of white stone on the ground level, brick steps leading to the landing and the handsome black wooden door capped by a fanlight. Kitchen and servants' daytime living quarters in the basement were approached from the front by means of a circular staircase concealed behind an iron fence; reception rooms were located on the ground floor; a double drawing room filled the first floor; and bedrooms occupied the second and third floors. Sleeping quarters for servants were in the attic; stables for horses and coaches were in the mews behind the house. Bay windows framed by white stone on the first three levels distinguished the Trotter residence from its neighbors, while an indoor central well, open to all levels from ground to roof, set apart the interiors of Montagu Square from other Regency terraces.

Life, in time, resumed its rhythms and routines. Lily's education continued at home, guided by German and French governesses who instructed her in their respective languages. She also received private instruction in singing for the cultivation of her soft contralto voice. With the exception of one short course in landscape drawing—and that, indoors!—Lily's art education was derived from exposure to great works of art and architecture, at homes and museums, in Britain and abroad.

Summer trips to the Continent continued to be an integral aspect of her education. The family traveled by stagecoach, absorbing the variety and richness of countries and cultures, as they slowly worked their way through France, Germany, Switzerland, and Italy, inculcating in Lily a life-long love of travel. "None of those who were with Lily when plans for holidays were made or journeys begun, will forget the look that came in her eyes, the keenness of the born traveller,"[4] recalled her sister Margaret. "You see I was always a tramp,"[5] Lily would explain, years later, when after a serious illness her doctor gave his grudging consent for yet another desert venture in Algeria.

The zest for travel and the lure of adventure were whetted by Lilias's love of the natural world. Like her father's, her response to beauty was intense—she was so overwhelmed by her first sighting of the snow-covered Alps on a trip to Switzerland, that she burst into tears. And throughout her life nature always would be for her the Creator's primer, instructing her in his mind and his dealings.

Like her mother, Lilias was compelled to record what she saw. Independent of any instruction, she was acquiring the facility to capture rapidly on paper a faithful and convincing representation, a skill that John Ruskin would commend in her to his students at the Oxford School of Drawing: "what skill is more precious to a traveller than that of minute, instantaneous, and unerring record of the things that are precisely best?"[6]

Qualities innate in Lily as a child were being developed and honed in her teenage years, emerging into strong traits of character: discipline, distinct from expectations of tutors or parent; a mind accurate and orderly; and a passionate spirit tempered by love. "'Ask and it shall be given unto you' is one of God's nursery lessons to His children," Lilias would write two decades later. "'Give and it shall be given unto you' comes further on."[7] Open and receptive to her heavenly Father, she had asked of him and had received. Nearing the end of her teens, she was ready for something more.

4

A NEW WORLD:
THE JOURNEY INWARD

1873—1875

And so the Spring-time expands, till it passes once more into the shadow of Calvary. For the blessedness of receiving is not all God has for us: a new world lies beyond—a world of giving: a giving first to God in surrender, then to man in sacrifice.

—*Parables of the Cross*[1]

There was great excitement in the air. Stagecoaches delivering guests from the far reaches of Great Britain and the Continent were arriving in Southampton at Broadlands, the great country estates of the Rt. Hon. William Cowper-Temple, property inherited from his alleged birth father, the late Lord Palmerston. Guests filled the one hundred plus rooms in the stately home overlooking the River Test, spilling as well into the attics and the inns at nearby Romsey.

The guest list was impressive, including a wide range of notables such as the great statesman William Wilberforce, Scottish cleric and writer

George MacDonald, French theologian Theodore Monad, biblical expositor Andrew Jukes, golden-voiced singer Antoinette Sterling, and former American slave, Amanda Smith. Lilias and her mother were among the one hundred invited guests.

Each of the individuals had responded to an invitation "to have a few days of quiet prayer and meditation upon the Scriptural possibilities of the Christian life as to maintain Communion with the Lord and victory over all known sin."[2] Some who attended would acknowledge later that they had come with an uneasy curiosity, even skepticism. Most came with a spirit of anticipation, yet they could not know—nor did Lilias know—how profoundly affected they would be or that they were on the ground floor of a movement which would grow into a worldwide institution, the Keswick Conference, vital to this day.

This extraordinary event, to be led by Robert Pearsall Smith, was not without context in the society of the day. During the early 1870s, there was considerable interest within religious circles in a so-called "Higher Life Movement." Originating in the United States and taking root in pockets of England and the Continent, this movement was stimulated by speakers and writers who explored the possibilities of a Christian life incorporating greater vitality, even intimacy with God, than presently experienced by most. Spiritual interest was also quickened by the presence in England of a young ex-shoe salesman from the United States, Dwight L. Moody, who was creating a stir across the British Isles with his innovative evangelistic campaigns, which would soon become an important part of Lilias's life.

England was ripe for such a fresh wind of spiritual vitality. Dissatisfaction pervaded the established Church of England, with the status quo being challenged by dissenting churches outside the state church and by three distinct parties within. The High Church party, Tractadians, was attempting revitalization by a return to Roman Catholic ritualism. The Broad Church party was attempting to make the established church as comprehensive as possible, departing from traditional church orthodoxy and adapting and absorbing some of the liberal tendencies of the day. The Low Church, or Evangelical Party (to which Lilias's mother adhered) was advocating involvement with the social concerns of the day along with an emphasis on the simplicity of worship, the centrality of the Bible, and the primacy of the preached Word. Yet, even with its admirable combination of orthodoxy and outreach, there was among the most committed in this group, a longing for something more in their personal experience.

This longing and interest was heightened in 1873 by the arrival in England of the handsome, charismatic Robert Pearsall Smith, who had left his lay-ministry in America for a much-needed rest in England. Fame preceded his arrival through Smith's and his wife's spiritual writings, which were widely circulated on both sides of the Atlantic. Before long, Smith's rest was interrupted by invitations to speak in drawing-room meetings in London, followed by a series of breakfast meetings in the city for Christian workers, eventually reaching more than 2,400 preachers. His unique ability to present abstract religious concepts in a practical manner led to yet more speaking engagements in London, as well as in other parts of England and on the Continent.

Enthusiasm grew to extraordinary proportions the following winter when Hannah Whitall Smith and her children joined her husband in England. Hannah's classic work, *The Christian's Secret of a Happy Life,* published three years earlier, had been well-received and much-discussed among the Quaker Friends. A woman of exceptional beauty, gaiety of spirit, and wit, her presence served to heighten people's interest in her lucid presentation of practical spiritual precepts. The great statesman John Bright would comment after a later meeting that she was "one of the few people who could preserve a natural conversational manner"[3] in a formal speaking situation. Within weeks of her arrival, drawing rooms of London's elite were opened to the Smiths, for Hannah's Bible lessons and Robert's preaching. At the same time, well-known members of England's aristocracy sought the counsel of the celebrated couple at their temporary home in the London suburb of Stokes Newington.

It was in this context that the Cowper-Temples (later Lord and Lady Mount Temple) conceived the idea of a conference at Broadlands, their country estate, with Robert Pearsall Smith both chairman and keynote speaker. The Cowper-Temples, given their great wealth and position, were by far the most influential of the England Friends—"that highest sphere of the Quaker world, . . . the plain but brilliant world"[4] of country houses and opulent tables—that embraced the American Smiths. Mrs. Cowper-Temple, a noted beauty immortalized in Ruskin's autobiography, *Praeterita,* was a hostess extraordinaire and later friend to the Pre-Raphaelites, entertaining the likes of John Ruskin and painter Dante Gabrielle Rossetti and his poet sister, Christina. Mr. Cowper-Temple, uncontested leader of the evangelicals, was both a politician of high-minded views and a patron of the arts. Their invitation to Broadlands for a six-day convention in the summer of 1874, could not have been better timed for greater interest or effect.

This was an extraordinary opportunity for twenty-one-year-old Lilias to be challenged and nurtured in her pilgrimage of faith. The setting alone would have nourished her beauty-loving soul. A half-century later, Logan Pearsall Smith would include in his memoir, *Unforgotten Years,* an account of this event, recalling the "beauty of Broadlands with its park and shining river and the great house, full of history and portraits."[5] Meetings were held throughout the day in settings of unsurpassed beauty: The eighteenth-century orangery, with portico, columns, and creeper-covered walls; among the beech trees by the River Test, which bordered the lawn in front of the great house; the grand dining room, which had hosted dignitaries of state and where, one day in the future, Queen Elizabeth and Prince Philip would dine on their honeymoon.

Lilias, of naturally wide outlook, would have been stimulated by the mix of like-minded men and women from diverse backgrounds and locations. Spiritually receptive, she undoubtedly thrilled to the scholarly expositions of Andrew Jukes, the devotional thoughts of Theodore Monad, the inspirational singing of Antoinette Sterling, and the testimony of the black former slave, Amanda Smith. During intervals between meetings there would have been opportunity to discuss varying topics with people of insight or simply be alone to study or to pray. The world of nature was always, for Lilias, a holy book, and the secluded woods along the river would have held lessons well-worth reading.

In the orangery in the park, she attended the Bible readings delivered daily by Hannah Whitall Smith—reportedly the undisputed highlight of the convention. As a Bible teacher, Hannah Smith was considered "second to none"[6] and her expositions, presented with candid gaze, flowing command of expression, and disarming simplicity of manner, attracted by far the largest audience and made the gathering famous in the religious world. Beautiful in Quaker dress, with clear-cut features, wide-set blue eyes, and wavy golden hair, Smith won the endearing title, "Angel of the Churches."

One can only imagine her impact on Lily. Hannah's captivating personality alone would have made her at the very least a compelling role model. Indeed, it is tempting to see parallels between the Hannah Whitall

Smith of Broadlands and the matured Lilias Trotter of later years, in the simplicity, sincerity, and loving conviction with which they each presented their message. Presentation (and speculation!) apart, Hannah's message was arresting as she practically, plainly, and personally unwrapped "secrets" from Scripture which gave life to the premise that "the Christian Life is the happiest of all lives."[7] The life she described as "the only true Christian life" was characterized by "an entire surrender to the Lord, and a perfect trust in Him, resulting in victory over sin and inward rest of soul." She further said that this life "differs from the lower range of Christian experience in that it causes us to let the Lord carry our burdens and manage our affairs for us instead of trying to do it ourselves."[8]

Hannah's message, along with the others to which Lilias was exposed at Broadlands, was not new. Nor was any novel form of doctrine or ecclesiastical system revealed. The speakers were careful to underscore the scriptural foundation of their teaching and to refrain from employing gimmickry or impassioned emotions to attain any desired effect. Prayer and the singing of simple hymns alone supplemented the messages. Years later, Logan Pearsall Smith, although then a religious skeptic, recalled the dignity in which the meetings were conducted, "unattended by the wilder phenomena of American Camp Meetings"[9] of his youth.

The meetings did, however, place distinct emphasis on practical theology: the application of age-old scriptural truths in the arena of everyday living. Not content to merely present the promises of God's provisions—victory over the power of sin as well as the penalty, joy and peace in the present as well as anticipation of a future glory—speakers provided a format in which participants could engage in soul work, then and there.

The Broadlands Conference was, in fact, more a "spiritual clinic" than a conference in the traditional sense. The key elements presented at Broadlands, and in the conferences soon after at Oxford and Brighton, would eventually be defined and refined in the Keswick Convention in the Lake District, the permanent home and parent of similar programs throughout the world. At the core of the program was a progressive, step-by-step format that addressed fundamental issues of the soul. It began first with the negative aspect of Christianity, the renunciation of all known sin (anything which could block a free and open relationship with God), and then moved on to the positive step of surrender, or abandonment to Christ, for his wonderful purpose: the empowering of his Spirit to equip the believer for the challenges of everyday living and for service to others.

One cannot overestimate the impact of this conference on Lily and the other participants, or, for that matter, on the spiritual life of England. Professor Warfield of Princeton Seminary wrote, "There is nothing more dramatic in the history of modern Christianity than this 'High Life' Movement,"[10] as it was called.

The witness of changed lives convinced critics as well as passive observers of the validity of the Broadlands Conference, and individuals liberated from the bondage of past failure were eager to propagate the teaching and focus of the conference. The last evening at Broadlands, Sir Arthur Blackwood, head of the post office in England, proposed that these meetings be repeated on a larger scale so that all who desired could attend. One thousand individuals gathered in Oxford later that summer, and six thousand attended the Brighton Conference the following spring. Lily was present at both.

There is no record of Lilias's response to any given speaker or message, and it is likely that more than any single meeting, the cumulative effect of all the events, teachings, testimonies, personal interactions, and opportunities for involvement in follow-up missions stirred and stretched her soul. The unmistakable imprint of the teaching and the method of the conferences would be reflected in her life and in her ministry to the end of her days. A practical theology was shaped and honed during these months and was eventually articulated in her classic work, *Parables of the Cross*. Here Lilias, using watercolors to illuminate her work, clarified spiritual concepts through parallels in the natural world.

In addition to the spiritual disciplines she acquired during this time, Lilias formed friendships that would sustain her throughout her forty years in North Africa. Indeed, Keswick Conferences in England and elsewhere would become, in a real sense, a spiritual haven to which she would return for refreshment and at which she would inspire prayer support and recruits for the ministry she began in Algeria.

This was undoubtedly a "Spring-time" of the soul for Lilias. Hungry for nourishment which would draw her closer to her heavenly Father and his purposes for her, she tasted freely from the rich sources provided. At the core of these teachings, however, was the conviction that the Father's gifts were never intended to be ends in themselves, that they were provided solely for personal growth or enjoyment. Rather, such provisions were meant to prepare the Christian for her true vocation: a life of service to others, in the name of Christ. As Lilias said in *Parables of the Cross:*

> *We ourselves are "saved to save"—we are made to give—to let everything go if only we may have more to give. The pebble takes in the rays of light that fall on it, but the diamond flashes them out again: every little facet is means, not simply of drinking more in, but of giving more out.*[11]

Lilias's understanding of Christian faith and practice was clarified and solidified in her early twenties by these exceptional conventions of 1874 and 1875. In the metaphor of Hannah Whitall Smith, "the rudder of her will was set" toward God's purposes. Another great gust of God's Spirit would blow over the England of the 1870s, sweeping many Christians into the mainstream of his service. Once again, Lilias would be at the very center of this movement.

5

BEYOND ONESELF: THE JOURNEY OUTWARD

1873—1875

A flower that stops short of its flowering misses its purpose. We were created for more than our own spiritual development; reproduction, not mere development, is the goal of matured being—reproduction in the lives of others.

—*Parables of the Cross*[1]

Lilias's journey beyond herself fit right into exciting nation-wide events in 1870s England. London was abuzz with talk about the dynamic thirty-five-year-old Dwight L. Moody, who, after almost two years on the British Isles, was winding up his evangelistic campaign with a series of meetings in the city. Reports of packed houses and changed lives preceded his arrival. People flocked to his meetings, out of sheer curiosity if not spiritual concern. Tireless, innovative, and unconventional, the uneducated layman from Chicago drew audiences in the tens of thousands to hear his straightforward presentation of the gospel. Before the end of the summer of 1875, Moody would preach to no less than two and a half million people during the Great London Campaign alone.

Though he was at first jeered by the press and mocked by the educated elite, Moody's muscular Christianity, communicated in the vernacular of the common person with his characteristic rapid delivery (a rush of 230 words a minute!), his quick wit, and his sincere passion soon captivated the hearts of the sophisticated and the simple alike. He caught the attention of Queen Victoria, who acknowledged his sincerity but allowed, "It is not the sort of religious performance which I like."[2] Queen Victoria notwithstanding, Moody soon penetrated the higher ranks of society, enlisting the support of the redoubtable Lord Shaftesbury, among others, and at the same time engaging the interest of the urban worker.

The closing evening of his May 1875 campaign in Covent Garden, the first of four in the Great London Campaigns, was likewise the opening day of the Brighton convention attended by Lilias. Moody said to his audience, "Let us lift up our hearts to seek earnestly a blessing on the great Convention that is now being held in Brighton, perhaps the most important meeting ever gathered," and sent to Brighton the following telegram message: "Moody and 8,000 persons at the closing meeting at the Opera House have prayed for the Convention, that great results may follow." Robert Pearsall Smith, the Convention chairman, responded by addressing the people at Brighton, "Let us ask an answering blessing upon our beloved brother, Mr. Moody, a man who walks with God."[3]

When the Brighton chairman dismissed the six thousand people gathered at the final meeting of their convention, he said: "The Brighton Conference has now ended and the blessings from the Convention have begun."[4] The Great London Campaign provided a perfect opportunity for participants to link renewal with revival, newly kindled faith with action. A great number of the Brighton delegates were swept into the volunteer forces of the remaining of Moody's campaigns, and Lilias was among them.

She already had become involved in several areas of service during the preceding year. She was active in the mission work that her father's friend Lord Radstock had organized in the local towns after each Higher Life conference. She also had helped in a mission being held in Cromer the previous summer, an experience noted for the formation of her life-long friendship with Blanche Pigott, her future biographer. An indication of Lily's spirit at that time is provided by an incident related by Miss Pigott:

I do not think I saw much of her during the mission but soon afterward she came over to luncheon with us. We walked across the Park to the edge of the wood, where the stately trees stand like a solemn cathedral isle. . . . I had come to a turning of the ways in my life, and was sorely perplexed, realizing that to follow what I felt was God's will for me would be the breaking of the most precious ties. I told her my difficulty, and, in great distress, cried, "What must I do?" Without hesitation she answered, "You can only obey God."[5]

This advice was not glibly offered. Lilias's spiritual sensibility, quickened by the Higher Life conferences, was deepening with her increased experience of the person and presence of Christ. During the Cromer mission, while attending a local church, she was preparing to place a coin in the old alms plate when she noticed etched in the center a drawing and the words, *The Pierced Hand of Christ.* "One could do nothing but empty one's purse into that pierced hand,"[6] she remembered forty-seven years later. Such was her life response as well. "Utter faithfulness in all her dealings manwards and Godwards was the distinctive feature of her life," one friend recalled of that time. "She set her face steadfastly to follow her Master."[7]

After the 1874 summer mission work, Lilias had been presented with a new challenge, best stated in her own words:

It all started, as His ways are wont to do, from a very small beginning, the being asked to take, as stop-gap, the Bible-class for a few weeks at the Welbeck Street Institute, to which the rooms in Bond Street had been moved. I recall the gasp of helplessness of that first Sunday afternoon, facing rows of grown-up and intelligent faces, instead of the usual Sunday-school children, but God helped and drew us together, and somehow it drifted into permanence.[8]

The work of which Lilias wrote was, in fact, one of the many institutes (or clubs) founded in London by Mary Jane Kinnaird (later Lady Kinnaird), wife of the senior partner of a powerful banking concern. Mrs. Kinnaird's work originated with a home in Upper Charlotte Street for

Florence Nightingale's nurses on their journeys to and from the Crimean War, and, after the war, the work evolved into hostels and institutes throughout London for working girls. This endeavor would eventually merge in 1877 with the prayer unions of Emma Robartes to become the Young Women's Christian Association (YWCA). Lily's involvement with the "stop-gap Bible-class" of Welbeck Street Institute, composed primarily of business girls from the West End of London, would likewise evolve into a full-time career.

But now, in 1875, at the close of the Brighton Convention and follow-up mission, Lily along with her younger brother Alec and her close friend Emily Kinnaird (daughter of the philanthropist) joined the choir which practiced each afternoon at the Kinnaird town house at Pall Mall, where Moody's songleader, Ira D. Sankey, resided during the Great London Campaign. It was not long before Lilias's involvement in the meetings at the Haymarket Opera House extended beyond her participation in the choir. She joined the volunteer force, personally trained by Moody, to counsel those who gathered after each meeting in the "inquiry room" to grapple with soul questions. This involvement plus associated mission work in the city, served to inflame her heart with what would become a lifelong passion for leading people to Christ.

This whole-souled commitment that was to mark all Lily's involvements is reflected in a letter written by her sister Emily following one mission—a supper for omnibus men, drivers of the horse-drawn buses.

> *What do you think L. and I were about from half-past ten last night until 3 a.m.? A rare good time it was. It was a very wet night but they came 180 in number; some could not arrive till 1 a.m. They had a splendid supper, quantities of singing, very short telling addresses. I do trust there may have been much blessing; many of them never go anywhere. Lily and I slept at Kilburn, creeping into lodgings at three, without our boots. We were pretty stiff and sleepy. It was rather hard work of course, at that time of night you can't get unlimited workers. I wished you had been there. E. Trotter.*[9]

In her participation with the Moody/Sankey Campaigns, Lilias could hardly have found a more compelling mentor to guide her beyond herself into the outside world. Moody insisted that sound Christian character would by its very nature lead to charity to others, and it was a mark of his ministry to leave in its wake practical social reforms, beginning with his inner-city ministry to immigrants in Chicago, continuing in the creation of refuges for the destitute of Glasgow, and now, in services for the needy of London. "The reward of service," Moody would say, "is more service."[10]

At the same time, Moody recognized the limitation, even impossibility, of changing society without a fundamental change in the individual. Thoroughly Bible-based in his beliefs, he said, "Here then is our guidebook, our textbook the Word. If I utter a syllable that is not justified by Scripture, don't believe me. The Bible is the only rule. Walk by it and it alone."[11] Nonetheless, he scrupulously avoided battlefields of doctrinal controversy, keeping to the basics, what he called The Three *R*s of Scripture: Ruined by the Fall; Redeemed by the Blood; Regenerated by the Spirit. His focus on essentials of the Christian faith allowed him the range to establish a broad base of interdenominational church support. Unintimidated by the wealthy, Moody did not hesitate to solicit their support to underwrite campaign costs; at the same time, of humble origin himself, he never lost his touch with the common person.

Lilias, revitalized by a deepened understanding of the Christian life and newly immersed into a life of service, soaked in this new experience. Where she was not specifically instructed by Moody, she was inspired by him. Four decades later, Lilias would challenge her coworkers in North Africa with a detailed account of Moody's compassionate address to 5,000 men at a meeting expressly for "atheists, sceptics, and free thinkers of all shade."[12] The confidence and boldness with which he preached, on this occasion as well as the others, and the receptiveness of the people to his message, reinforced all the lessons of the past two years and demonstrated what God could do with one willing life. Moody himself maintained, "I know perfectly well that wherever I go and preach, there are many better preachers known and heard than I am; all that I can say about it is that the Lord uses me."[13]

Moody's innovative methods alone would have provided for Lilias a study in strategy. He intuitively recognized the shift from the rural to an industrial-urban age, and he effectively adapted the tools of evangelism to reach a more sophisticated audience. Many of his techniques newly implemented in the United Kingdom—advance organizational preparation, house-to-house visitation, avoidance of direct appeals for money, joint ministry with a songleader, and arrangement of a separate inquiry room—changed the very character of evangelism and introduced methods practiced to this day.

Moody, by example and by teaching, provided training for Lilias and many others in relating the life of faith to the unbeliever. He personally presided over the volunteers whom he trained to counsel the hundreds of people who flocked to the inquiry room at the conclusion of each service. "You must ply them with the Word of God," he insisted. "Work patiently until you see that they have grasped the truth and are resting on Christ alone for salvation. Don't be in a hurry; think, oh think what it means to win a soul for Christ and do not grudge time spent on one person."[14]

While it is, of course, impossible to determine fully the direct influence of Dwight L. Moody on Lilias, it can be stated with certainty that many of the approaches and attitudes which marked Moody's work would be evident later in Lilias's ministry—first with women in London, and later with Arabs in the slums of Algiers, in nearby mountain villages, and in the desert oases of the Sahara. Innovative, thoughtful, and practical, she, like Moody, would pioneer new methods and materials while never compromising the essential message.

In 1875, at the age of twenty-two, Lilias had no prescience of this future ministry. She still had much to absorb and assimilate from the extraordinary experience of the past two years with her parallel journeys—inward, to a life of surrender to God, and outward, to a life of service to others. Lily stood on the brink of a world, rich and full of possibilities. Little did she know the dazzling prospects which lay ahead for her in the arena of art, or how those prospects would test her at the very core of her being.

6

AN OLD PORCELAIN MAKER, A BIT OF CLAY

1876

The true, ideal flower is the one that uses its gifts as means to an end; the brightness and sweetness are not for its own glory; they are but to attract the bees and butterflies that will fertilize and make it fruitful. All may go when the work is done—"it is more blessed to give than to receive."

—*Parables of the Cross*[1]

It was October of 1876. Lilias and her mother had recently arrived in Venice by way of Switzerland, having taken in a spiritual renewal convention at Maderana Thal, then worked their leisurely way across the Alps over the St. Gotthard Pass, then down into Italy, through the frescoed villages to their final destination—the enchanted city of water and light. They settled into their luxurious accommodations at the Grand

Hotel, a baroque-inspired palace banking the Grand Canal, the main artery of the ancient city.

In Lucerne, Lilias had purchased a sketchbook in which she recorded the journey along the carriage roads to Venice. She sketched and painted her way through the Lepontine Alps, capturing in deft pencil strokes and delicate watercolors quaint village scenes, charming chalets, women and children in provincial garb. As they progressed across alpine roads, place names came alive in vibrant images: snowcapped mountain peaks of St. Gotthard Pass and Airolo; azure lakes of Maggiore and Como. And then—Venice! She could not have imagined whose eyes would witness her work there, whose hands would instruct her views of the ancient city!

Very soon after their arrival, they became aware of a fellow resident of note, John Ruskin, the famed art critic and social philosopher. Mrs. Trotter immediately set herself to task. Convinced of her daughter's exceptional artistic talent, she seized the opportunity to seek *the* authoritative evaluation of her work. She sent Ruskin some of Lilias's watercolors, accompanied by a note with the heading *Grand Hotel, Venice, October 1876:*

> *Mrs. Alex. Trotter has the pleasure of sending Professor Ruskin her daughter's water-colours. Mrs. Trotter is quite prepared to hear that he does not approve of them—she has drawn from childhood and has had very little teaching. But if Mrs. Trotter could have Mr. Ruskin's opinion it would be most valuable.*[2]

Then she awaited his response with trepidation, for, though she was a woman of social standing, he was a man of immense reputation and influence—one of the greatest figures of the Victorian Age. The sequel is best related from Ruskin's perspective, immortalized in his Oxford lecture, "The Art of England":

> *For a long time I used to say, in all my elementary books, that, except in a graceful and minor way, women could not paint or draw. I am beginning lately, to bow myself to the much more delightful conviction that no one else can. How this very serious change of mind was first*

> *induced in me it is, if not necessary, I hope pardonable, to delay you by telling. When I was at Venice in 1876—it is about the only thing that makes me content in having gone there—two English ladies, mother and daughter, were staying at the same hotel. One day the mother sent me a pretty note asking if I would look at the young lady's drawings. On my somewhat sulky permission a few were sent, in which I saw there was extremely right minded and careful work, almost totally without knowledge. I sent back a request that the young lady might be allowed to come out sketching with me. I took her over to the pretty cloister of the Abbey of San Gregorio and set her for the first time in her life to draw a little piece of grey marble with the sun on it, rightly. She may have had one lesson after that—she may have had two; the three, if there were three, seem to me now to have been only one! She seemed to learn everything the instant she was shown it, and ever so much more than she was taught.*[3]

Thus began a friendship, with Lilias being introduced to the splendors of Venice by the author, no less, of *The Stones of Venice,* the definitive artistic and architectural history of the city. The following days were filled with pure enjoyment as Ruskin escorted mother and daughter throughout the city, exposing them to paintings and sculpture which he thought would best educate Lilias's untrained eye. From their hotel, a few buildings down from the Piazzetta of St. Mark, he guided them along the Grand Canal to the fourteenth-century court of the Abbazio San Gregorio for the drawing lesson of which he wrote, and further on to his studio at The Accademia where he was copying *St. Ursula's Dream* by Carpaccio.

This friendship, as well as the glorious introduction to Venice, was intoxicating to the twenty-three-year-old Lilias. John Ruskin was Victorian England's most brilliant and influential arbiter of artistic taste. For more than thirty-three years he had informed the public of his views on art in particular, and life in general, through his five volumes of the *Modern Painters* along with countless other publications. Champion of J. M. W. Turner and the Pre-Raphaelite Brotherhood, radicals of their time, this "high priest" of the art world could break an artist's reputation by a negative review as spoofed by the irreverent magazine *Punch:*

I paints and paints
Hears no complaints,
And sells before I'm dry;
Till savage Ruskin
Sticks his tusk in,
And nobody will buy.[4]

Far more than a critic, Ruskin was, among other things, an educator, instructing his era in techniques as well as a philosophy of art. He held that the chief aim of art is to "teach you to see,"[5] insisting "the greatest thing a human soul ever does in this world is to see something, and tell what it saw in a plain way. Hundreds of people can talk for one who can think, but thousands can think for one who can see."[6] His early publications, such as *The Elements of Drawing,* established the methods and principles that he taught in the Working Man's College in London and later at Oxford University as their first Slade Professor of Art.

During the decade up to his meeting Lilias, Ruskin had firmly established his prophetic voice as a social critic and reformer, addressing a Victorian people committed to self-improvement and social responsibility. He dispensed his assessment of the evils of the industrial age through his forum of lectures and articles and the monthly newsletter, *For Clavigera.* Though certainly not without his challengers, John Ruskin was an indisputable intellectual powerhouse to his age. He carried enormous weight with a public eager to hear his views and sympathetic to the didactic tone he brought to his pronouncements.

It is obvious what this friendship brought to Lilias. Beyond the sheer effect of his personality was a moral idealism which appealed to her spiritual sensibility. He, no less than Lily, could separate the artist from his art, convinced that noble art could only come from noble people. His social views, many of which were implemented through the Guild of St. George, resonated with Lilias's work among the underprivileged of London. What Lilias hoped to accomplish through a spiritual revival, Ruskin sought to accomplish through a moral revolution which would improve the living and working conditions of the poor while elevating their everyday lives with access to the highest quality of books and art.

Ruskin's broad range of views and interests, rooted in scholarship and articulated with dogmatic brilliance, provided enormous intellectual stimulation for Lily. After reading a work of Maurice, she wrote to a friend, "It is such a help to see that it is possible to be wide and charitable in 'views', and yet to be firm and clear as to what one does hold. It is like the stretch of country one sees from Broadway, not necessarily all in a haze because of its wide sweep."[7] Ruskin's thinking was a wide sweep of country, a bracing autumn breeze. What the conferences and campaigns had been to her soul and spirit, Ruskin was to her mind and intellect.

And then there was art. Both Lilias and Ruskin felt a profound affinity to the natural world, viewing it with "heartsight as deep as eyesight"[8] as Ruskin would say of his mentor Turner. Ruskin insisted on first training the eye to see—"Go to nature, in a singleness of heart"[9]—and then, when one has "learned to look,"[10] teaching the technical skills to replicate what one sees in faithful detail. Believing that art should be taught in the context of a liberal education, he was the liberal educator.

But what had Lily to offer John Ruskin? First, she provided the one essential for any teacher, an able student. She had a rare innate talent: "I pause to think how—anyhow—I can convince you of the marvelous gift that is in you,"[11] he writes her in a letter. Furthermore, she had a teachable spirit, that mark of humility often missing in the very talented. "Not seeing or feeling the power that is in you is one of the most sure and precious signs of it," again he writes, "and that tractability is another. All second-rate people, however strong, are self-conscious and obstinate."[12] Lilias also had a unique facility to hear, assimilate, and transfer that knowledge to other situations, as observed by Ruskin in his Oxford lecture. She was eager and able to be taught; Ruskin was eager and able to do so: "Of all the dainty bits of clay in the hands of the potter that were ever fashioned—I think you've the least grit in you. And you can't think what a delight it is to an old porcelain maker to get a hold of such a bit."[13]

But that was not all Lilias had to offer him. Behind the formidable public figure to whom most acquiesced in matters of art, if not life, was a man who in his own words, was in "withering and disgusting pain."[14] He had come to Venice on a leave of absence from Oxford University to recover from the death, a year earlier, of young Rose La Touche, the focus of an agonizing eighteen-year relationship. Seeking solace in Venice, Ruskin was hoping to recapture the delight he had experienced when he visited the ancient city twenty-five years before, but he discovered that much had been lost. Disappointed in friends whom he felt were abandoning their mutual ideals and frustrated by a society seemingly indifferent to the destructive aspects of industrialization, Ruskin was emotionally depleted and struggling with what would be an on-going battle against depression.

Lily was just the sort of woman Ruskin most admired: young, pure, refined, and untainted by the world. But she was much more than the idealized type of woman who had piqued his fancy through the years. She also demonstrated an unexpected strength in her views; well-read, she, like Ruskin, was steeped in Scripture, yet she was stretched by the thought of the Quaker writers, the evangelistic language of Moody, the mystical nuances of Tauler's *Germanica Theologica,* and the richness of *The Book of Common Prayer.* She was high minded but not naive, her idealism being rooted in a solid faith and tested by practical engagement with the problems of society.

Ruskin, reared by a mother with a rigid evangelical Anglicanism, had long rejected the dogmatism of his roots only to flounder for the next sixteen years in an uneasy agnosticism, unable to reconcile new understandings of geology with the religious beliefs of his background—"If only the geologist would let me alone I could do very well, but those dreadful HAMMARS! I hear the clink of them at the end of every cadence of the Bible verses."[15] He grappled as well with his inability to reconcile the spiritual vision of the religious painters with whom he had identified from youth, with what he had come to perceive to be their inferior paintings and, in turn, unsatisfactory beliefs. Finally, in 1874, while studying a fresco attributed to Giotto, *The Marriage of Poverty and St. Francis,* Ruskin had a spiritual illumination which helped him reconcile not only religious painting with faith but himself, once again, with religion. While toying temporarily with spiritualism and the mystical edges of faith, Ruskin was nonetheless receptive to a personal God. Indeed, he admitted that he needed God.

Though over three decades apart in age, Lilias and Ruskin were kindred spirits. In this friendship which would evolve throughout the rest of Ruskin's life, he would increasingly see in his "St. Lilias," as he would affectionately call her, a steadying source of sympathy and understanding. He would write to her out of his darkness, "you are probably the only person likely to help me in my chief difficulties and lost ways. . . . follow on your own path happily the light I cannot find."[16]

Years later, in July 1899, only months before his death, Lilias would send Ruskin a book from Algiers, *Hymns of Tersteegen,* explaining: "It has been full of light & blessedness to me—& I have such a feeling that it will have some rays for you, that I can't help sending it. Always yours with grateful & loving memories. I. Lilias Trotter."[17] But in Venice, in the morning of their friendship, the two were quite simply teacher and pupil. Lilias was "learning to look," to use his phrase, in a whole new way.

A painting, a portrait, and a photograph together capture the time in Venice. The painting is Turner's *Venice: The Accademia.* The city is bathed in a diffused yellow light, reflected in the shimmering water of the Grand Canal. Bright golden sails grouped in front of The Accademia, one of Italy's finest picture galleries, compose the view of the vanishing Venice lamented by Ruskin. On the other side of the canal is the delicate suggestion of the long row of palaces, one of which is the Grand Hotel. The portrait is of Ruskin at fifty-seven years. His sensitive features are framed by the sweep of hair brushed off his face and by closely trimmed side whiskers. From under long bushy eyebrows, steel blue eyes—clear and penetrating—meet, straight on, the eyes of the viewer. A tip of white collar shows above the cobalt blue of his silk neckcloth. The photograph is of Lilias, in her twenties, her dark wavy hair softly drawn into a braided crown at the back of her head. A lace jabot gathered in the front by a brooch sets off her long slender neck. Her face, in profile, reveals strong classic features—a straight nose, full lips, firm jaw. Her eyes gaze into the distance from a gently expressive face.

These three views bring together magical Venetian hours, an old porcelain maker, and a dainty bit of clay—the making of a friendship.

7
LILY'S CHOICE
1876—1879

Have we learned the buttercup's lesson yet? Are our hands off the very blossom of our life? Are all things—even the treasures that [God] has sanctified—held loosely, ready to be parted with, without a struggle, when He asks for them?

—*Parables of the Cross*[1]

After Venice, Lilias returned to London and to the juggling act of balancing this heady new friendship, the development of her artistic talent, and the increasing demands of her social work. Her teaching of the adult class at Welbeck Street Institute, originally intended as temporary, had become a permanent post, and, as would become a pattern in her life, it was spawning related ministries. The institute, one of several cropping up throughout the city under Lady Kinnaird's leadership, provided a home life based on Christian principles. For a moderate charge, girls who were employed in the city could have low-cost accommodations in a friendly environment. The girls had not only a center where they could form friendships but also opportunities to attend Bible classes and lectures and receive instruction in foreign languages, singing, and needlework.

The role of young single women at that time was strictly defined by the class into which they had been born. For the middle and upper class women, such as Lilias, idleness was considered a mark of gentility, domestic servants absolving them from household tasks. Potential boredom was offset by the seasonal round of social events or by charitable work—until a knight in shining armor rescued her for the bliss of family life. Only the working class women were expected to "work," their choices being limited to the several occupations open to them: domestic servants, farm or factory workers, dressmaking, street traders, and shop assistants. As a result of the industrial revolution many of these women came to the cities where there were greater prospects for jobs—and for loneliness—often separated from their families by considerable distances. The warm, supportive atmosphere of the hostels like Welbeck Street Institute, to which Lilias devoted her time, was a life-line for these girls.

While active in the program of the Welbeck Street Institute, Lilias could not help being aware of the spiritual needs of a different group of women only blocks away, the "first hands" of the principle businesses in Oxford Street and Regent Street—business women employed in the galaxy of high-class shops catering to the fashionable trade of London. Ever strategic in her approach, she began to mobilize the work forces of the Institute to offer "at homes" or social hours and drawing-room meetings at her Montagu Square address, where she could provide spiritual nourishment and fellowship in the comfortable surroundings of a home. Many of the women embraced by her hospitality would become the core support group for the later ministry in Algeria. Though, as yet, Lilias had not the slightest inclination to think in that direction.

The home at 40 Montagu Square was likewise becoming the center for the many other friendships that Lilias was forming through her ever-broadening world. Just as the Cromer mission and the Moody Campaigns had cemented what would be lifelong friendships with Blanche Pigott and Emily Kinnaird, the Maderana Thal Convention that Lily and her mother attended on their way to Venice was the setting for new friendships formed with Blanche Haworth and Mary Clifford. Blanche Pigott, a constant visitor at that time, recalls Montagu Square as "that unique household where Lily lived with her mother and brother and sisters, a place of sunny gladness and laughter, as well as varied work and interest and unstinted hospitality."[2]

Summer travel routinely provided Lily a break from seasonal work, and a trip to Norway the following July and to Venice in September offered her the stimulation and the leisure to practice her art. Lilias's work from that time showed the mark of her master. In a pocket sketchbook recording her 1877 journey from Beatenburg to Venice, twenty little sketches capture in pencil, body color, and an occasional touch of watercolor, wonders revealed at stagecoach pace, recorded with speed and accuracy—a skill Ruskin regarded "precious to a traveler."[3] Ruskin's technical influence is evident in Lilias's use of shading to convey light and perspective and in her detailing of key elements, architectural and natural, to highlight the essence of the composition, leaving the rest in lesser stages of finish. Employing controversial body color—the opaque Chinese white which Ruskin advocated to heighten the effects of light if used with "skill, moderation, and discretion"[4]—throughout, Lilias deftly picked out the snow-capped mountain peaks, a flashing sail of a boat, water cascading from a cliff, or the play of light against a rock, chalet, or mountainside.

Ruskin was enchanted by her Norwegian pocket sketchbook of watercolors depicting quaint scenes of peasant life. He "begged of her" some of its leaves, which he later referred to in his 1883 "The Art of England" lecture as "quite provokingly good." He framed six paintings to accompany the lecture, and set them before his Oxford students as an example of "exactly what we should all like to be able to do . . . [or,] how, if heaven help us, it can be done."[5]

Lilias's friendship with Ruskin was developing, nourished by letters and by her extended visits to Brantwood, Ruskin's home in the beautiful Lake District of England, accompanied by her sister Margaret or brother Alec. Correspondence preserved from that time captures the anticipation of the first of such visits:

I am ready for you both this minute; if you could only come! Oh dear, I'm afraid it's going to rain tomorrow, and now—it's exquisite. But

> *rain or cloud, it will still be beautiful—the woods are in such glory, and laburnum and hawthorne just in prime—not a rose out yet—you will watch them all through their sweet lives. Love to Margaret. Her room's little but close to your turret, and she can skip across in the early morning. This ought to catch you to-morrow just to prepare you not to be disappointed if it rains.*[6]

Some letters included paintings to critique, others, words of encouragement from the mentor: "The drawing is wholly perfect and lovely"[7] or "You're more and more wonderful to me. This lily and the chioroscuro gateway are simply and by far the best lessons I have in their kind in the Oxford Schools."[8] Ruskin opened his heart and his home to Lily, luring her with beguiling invitations: "Stay here, June, July and August and you shall have such children to draw and such flowers—and such thanks, and be sent home as merry as a daffodil. Your loving J.R."[9]

From Brantwood, situated along the waters of Coniston, Lilias had all the lovely views of lake and mountains her beauty-loving soul could wish. The house, like the man, was an education in itself, with its collection of art treasures amassed from his many travels—brilliantly illuminated medieval manuscripts, Pre-Raphaelite paintings, Gainsborough oils, and Turner watercolors, plus fabulous collections of minerals, Greek coins, pottery, and seashells. Life in that place had its particular rhythms set by Ruskin's routines: letter writing before breakfast, writing in the morning, then the lessons in his study or out-of-doors, and reading aloud in the evening after dinner.

On one occasion while at Brantwood, Lilias admitted a dislike for the color purple, calling forth stern rebuke from Ruskin as witnessed by her sister: "Cupboards full of lovely minerals were opened, rock crystals and amethysts of every shade were spread forth, flowers were picked, water-colours of birds by William Hunt, mountain scenes by Turner, were all called into contribution by her master to persuade her of the greatness of the heresy. She never dared to object to purple again."[10] Ruskin's strong influence can be seen as she not only avoided objecting to purple but eventually included the full spectrum of the color throughout her later work, portraying evening skies and shadows of the great Atlas Mountain range.

The teacher-critic likewise visited at Montagu Square from his nearby city home in Denmark Hill. A glimpse of their friendship is provided by Blanche Pigott:

> *I can never forget an afternoon spent about this time at Montagu Square with [Lily] and Mr. Ruskin—Mr. Ruskin leaning back in an arm-chair, his sensitive face and blue eyes full alternately of pathos and amusement as he talked and talked, Lily sitting opposite with her hands clasped, resting on the table, bending slightly forward with a look of restrained eagerness, as she watched and listened to him.*
>
> *The sombre London study was forgotten, all the glory of the lakes and mountains seemed round us, and we could see the light upon the grasses and bramble leaves from the sunshine streaming across the road, and hear the children's voices and laughter as he described his meeting a band of village children with a hand-cart, and getting into it and letting them drag him helter-skelter down the hill; the innocent joy and beauty of it all!*[11]

And so the pattern continued, Lilias balancing the work at Welbeck Street Institute and its related ministries with the development of her art guided by her fascinating friend and mentor. Her 1878 sketchbook, from a Cromwell vacation in July and a trip to Wales in September, record the scenery as well as her growing skill as a colorist: golden skies bathe rocks and hills in radiant glow, and purple slopes of Snowdon in Wales rise above waters of delicate eggshell blue.

Even as Lilias reveled in the stimulation of art and the satisfaction of service, a deep shadow was cast on her joy. Her mother, suffering for some time from a degenerative disease of the heart, died from lung complications on 22 January 1878. Through the following months, Lilias, no doubt grieving the loss of her mother, found it increasingly difficult to balance the development of her art with the accelerating demands of ministry. A crisis loomed on the horizon, and Lily knew no way around it.

Ruskin himself brought the issue to a head. In May 1879 he invited Lilias to Brantwood, where he was nursing his own wounds over his defeat in the widely publicized *Whistler v. Ruskin* libel case. This was the occasion when he put before her the brilliant future that undoubtedly would be hers—if she were to give herself fully to the development of her art. And it was at this time that she experienced the great crisis of her soul.

A letter that she wrote from Brantwood to Blanche Pigott at that crisis time reveals both the dazzling prospects and the dizzying pain. She quotes Ruskin as saying that if she would devote herself to art "she would be the greatest living painter and do things that would be Immortal," adding, "You will understand that it is not from vanity that I tell you, at least I think not, because I have no more to do with the gifts than with the color of my hair—but because I need prayer to see God's way more clearly."[12]

However untested Ruskin's belief in her potential, this is certain: he saw in Lilias a unique artistic gift and a teachable spirit; he was laying at her feet, so to speak, his extraordinary resources for the development of her talent and the promotion of her career. Lilias understood as clearly as did Ruskin the condition for the fulfillment of her artistic potential: "to give herself up to art."

Lilias was twenty-six years of age. The prospect was enticing; the offer compelling—it was the opportunity to devote her life to the development of her talent with one who was qualified above anyone of her generation to guide and direct her. Fame and honor apart, the sheer delight of a life given to art and surrounded by art and by the society of minds akin to her own was, at the least, a heady prospect. No one understood better than she what was at stake. She could follow the urging of her artistic nature or, for Christ's sake, choose a different way—a path of hard work, certain discouragement and misunderstanding, and possible failure. Lilias did not want to have to think about it, much less choose. Yet she knew that she must: "I know God will make it all clear and not let me go wrong. I hardly dare think about it all it raises such a storm . . . yet it is by not facing it and getting it definitely settled . . . and sticking to it that I am comparatively wasting the best working years."[13]

The tension built, pressed as she was by Mr. Ruskin's challenge. She continued to write out her anguish, determined to settle the conflict in her heart once and for all:

> *It seems as if I had lived years and years, at first I could only rush about in the woods all in a dream, and it was all like a dream for the first day or two. Since then an almost constant state of suffocation half intoxication so that I can hardly eat or sleep except by trusting the Lord about it, if I had not Him to hide in deeper than ever before, I don't know what I should do. . . . I do believe Christ will win in the end.*[14]

So it was that in May 1879, in Coniston, challenged by the persuasive powers of John Ruskin, Lilias made the choice: "I see as clear as daylight now, I cannot give myself to painting in the way he means and continue still to 'seek first the Kingdom of God and His Righteousness.'"[15]

Some may wonder now, as many did then, at the necessity of such a choice. Could she not have pursued the development of her art and still continued her work in the city? A strong case could be made—one that Lilias doubtless considered—that her range of influence and usefulness for the kingdom of God could be wider as a result of a life devoted to art.

But Lily, whole-souled as she was, knew that she could not continue to do both and give either what it would require of her. The rudder of her will had already been set, so to speak, toward God's purposes—whatever they might be. Ruskin's proposal served to test that resolve at her deepest core. In essence, the most compelling person in her life placed before her the most tantalizing possibility life could offer and said, "Choose."

There had been other choices in the past, as there would be in the future, but this one, deciding the role that art would play in her life, was the great challenge of her soul. It went beyond any question about art or ministry; rather, it penetrated to the issue of obedience, following God's way.

Lilias was careful not to generalize her decision as a pattern for everyone to follow. She would later address this very point in *The Parables of the Cross:*

> *Does all this seem hard? Does any soul, young in physical or in spiritual life, shrink back and say, "I would rather keep in the springtime.*

I do not want to reach unto the things that are before if it means all this pain." To such comes the Master's voice. "Fear none of these things which Thou shalt suffer." . . . It may be that no such path of loss lies before you; there are people like the lands where spring and summer weave the year between them and the autumn processes all, hardly noticed as they come and go.[16]

For all people, however, as for herself, Lilias believed that the fundamental issue in life remained the same: a need for total abandonment to God's purposes. The ultimate test, if not the specific path, would likewise ask for that same willingness to renounce anything—person, place, possession, plan—anything that would stand in the way of God's design. Here was the lesson of the buttercup: "Are our hands off the very blossom of our life? Are all things—even the treasures He has sanctified—held loosely, ready to be parted with without a struggle when He asks for them?"[17]

Few may ever have the options spelled out so vividly, or the choice so decisively, but for Lily the issue and the stakes were clear that spring in Coniston. One decade later she would testify from life experience what she earlier could only trust by faith: "It is loss to keep when God says 'give.' "[18]

On the surface, life continued as always after this crisis, as is often the case in momentous matters of the soul. Lilias returned to London, and later that summer she took a much-needed holiday in Norway with her brother Edward and sister Margaret. She also continued to paint.

On her return from Norway in August, Lilias visited Brantwood, as anticipated in a letter, "I shall probably go to see Mr. Ruskin for a few days, which I rather dread,"[19] and there reiterated once again her decision. Ruskin records that visit in his diary, noting on 24 August 1879, that he took a walk in Yewdale, "Whilst Lilias painted the white rose cottage."[20]

The friendship would continue, and the visits, throughout Ruskin's lifetime—and Ruskin continued to hold out hope for Lily's future in art long after the matter had been resolved in her heart. During a visit in June 1885, Ruskin records, "I have some hopes for Lilias."[21] In a 25 February 1886 letter to the Duchess of Albany, he included a sketch "by my best of pupils, Lilias Trotter."[22] As late as November 1886 he would expound in a letter to Kate Greenaway his ideas for a girl's drawing school in London: "I have a plan for organizing a girl's Academy under you . . . Lilias Trotter & Miss A. [probably Allingham] for the Dons, or Donnas, of it."[23]

Lily could now enjoy her friendship with Ruskin, and her art, with the abandonment that comes from soul release. Yet it would be a serious omission not to acknowledge the loss which accompanies such a decision. Constance Padwick, a long-time friend, wrote of Lily admitting that

> *the ache of desire was with her to the end, not so much on the many days when she did no drawing, as on the days when she took up her brush to make a cover for an Arabic tract. Then when fellow-Christians spoke, with joy of "the consecration of her beautiful gift" she was most conscious of the pain of the artist who takes up an unpracticed tool and knows full well to what beauty he might bend it if he could but give to it his strength and life.*[24]

The pain of which she spoke was the inevitable sense of loss any human being experiences when recognizing the toll of giving up something good for something he or she deemed better.

The full implications of Lily's choice in 1879 were not clear to her then, nor even now to posterity. Did the choice have direct bearing on the place of marriage and family in her life? Only one reference of a friend (and that before her final decision) so much as touches on the subject: "It was with pain mingled with pride that Mrs. Trotter watched her daughter turning her back on fame, marriage, and pleasure, to follow the steps of the Master."[25] We do know that her choice to work, as she did, among the most despised of society had the effect of separating her and her mother from friends who held to a more moderate (and fashionable) view of "social work." Indeed, philanthropic enterprises and charitable volunteer organizations were not only an acceptable pastime for women of leisure but also the main service institutions in a society which had not yet developed the mechanics of law and government to deal with its social problems. Yet, in this work, like every other venture to which Lilias would devote herself, she went far beyond the circumscribed boundaries—both in the nature and the extent of her efforts—for a woman of her class. Her involvement, like Florence Nightingale's before her, went beyond pastime to passion. One wonders if her decision regarding art, made after her mother's death, was deferred until then to spare her the pain of the finality of her daughter's choice.

How God would use her life and her art—for his eternal purposes, if not for the "immortality" promised by Ruskin—Lilias could not fathom at that time. Nor did it matter. "The one thing is to keep obedient in spirit," she would write, "to do otherwise would be to cramp and ruin your soul."[26]

On the surface it was the same Lilias who returned to Welbeck Street Institute the autumn of 1879. But she returned with a grand independence—"the liberty of those who have nothing to lose, because they have nothing to keep."[27]

8

A GRAND INDEPENDENCE OF SOUL

1880—1888

Look at the expression of abandonment about this wildrose calyx as time goes on, and it begins to grow towards the end for which it has had to count all things but loss: the look of dumb emptiness has gone—it has flung back joyously now, for simultaneously with the new dying a richer life has begun to work at its heart.

—*Parables of the Cross*[1]

Returning to London, Lilias threw all her energy into the work at Welbeck Street Institute. This hostel, along with the other homes of Lady Kinnaird, had united recently with Miss Robartes's Prayer Unions to become the YWCA, with Lord Shaftesbury as its first president. The vigorous young association held the lofty aim to "unite young women in prayer and evangelism, to promote Christian friendship and mutual help, and to promote the moral, social, and cultural well-being of its members."[2]

Lilias became the honorable secretary of the Welbeck Street center, a voluntary position usually filled by women like herself from wealthy families. *The Secretary: Her Book,* a small volume later published to provide direction to the women filling this position, includes qualities the association hoped would be manifested in their social and spiritual leaders: "A sense of humor—a gay natural manner—good need not be associated with primness or gloom."[3] The broadness of goals of the YWCA allowed great range for the local secretaries to respond to the particular needs of their residents, and Lily, without a trace of "primness or gloom," devoted her time and talents to maintaining the program and developing it in her own specific areas of interest.

Her responsibilities included a fair amount of teaching. A glimpse into her growing mastery of pedagogical methods and philosophy is given through her *History Lessons for Junior Classes,* published in 1884 by the Church of England Sunday School Institute. She provides a comprehensive presentation of biblical themes, tracing "God's promise of the Day dawn" from the creation in Genesis to the new creation in Revelation. Her "Introductory Note to Teachers" explains "that the topics chosen have been those which would be likely to leave the most distinct impression on [the students'] minds, and in which the teaching is most plain."[4] She challenges the teacher to consider the nature of the student, then proceeds to offer two practical suggestions clearly gleaned from her own classroom experience: "in most in such a class, the imagination is beginning to be developed and delights in fresh food; therefore anything in the way of word-picturing or illustration proves attractive"; and "the line of teaching should be fixed from the beginning and worked up to throughout, that the children may have one definite idea to carry away with them."[5]

She reveals her heart and the philosophy underlying all her teaching—for adults as well as children—in her concluding challenge: "our object as teachers is infinitely more than giving the children a clear knowledge of Bible history, being nothing short of pointing them in God's name to the Good Shepherd, who 'shall gather the lambs with His arm, and carry them in His bosom.' "[6]

A triptych of the parable of the lost sheep drawn by Lilias during her early days in North Africa and used throughout her ministry depicts in one panel the Good Shepherd, wearing a crown of intricately woven thorns. He is holding close to his heart an obviously shaken little lamb who looks up into his face, upon which is an expression of infinite tenderness. The image of her heavenly Father as the loving shepherd was the one dearest to her heart—the One to whom all her endeavors pointed. And Lilias was unceasingly drawn to the "lost lambs." Just as her heart had gone out to the women employed in the fashionable shops of nearby Regent and Oxford Streets, her heart was drawn to women of more questionable employment, streetwalkers.

It is one of the paradoxical aspects of Victorian society that prostitution was practiced blatantly. For some of the women, it was perhaps the preferred form of trade, but for many young girls stranded in the city without skills or means of employment, it was a tragic recourse. Whether they were victims of folly or circumstance, Lilias's heart was moved with compassion for these "lost sheep" so profoundly in need of a loving shepherd. At a time when it was unacceptable for a young woman to be out alone in the city, Lilias fearlessly traversed the streets to rescue these streetwalkers, many of whom haunted the neighborhood of Victoria Station. She brought them back to the hostel for a good night's sleep and for training in an employable skill, and she introduced them to the Good Shepherd.

Friends remember the lengths to which she went to help these girls, planning and providing for them, but often simply listening and offering a word of counsel. On one occasion, a friend recalls her staying up all night with a "half-crazed girl" to save her from taking her own life. John Ruskin, well aware of her activities and missing her visits while he was fighting his own increasing battle with depression, wrote:

> *Am I not bad enough?*
> *Am I not good enough?*
> *Am I not whatever it is enough to*
> *be looked after a little when I'm ill, as*
> *well as those blessed Magdalenes?*[7]

And, on a more conciliatory note he wrote, "You are the most provoking creature I ever knew in this unutterably naughty world and yet I'm always your loving J.R."[8]

Lilias did continue her visits to Coniston, as indicated in Ruskin's *Brantwood Diaries,* and she continued to paint, sending him her sketches. He responded with concern that the life she had chosen was affecting the character of her art:

> *The power in these drawings is greater that ever—the capacity infinite in the things that none can teach; but the sense of color is gradually getting debased under the conditions of your life—the vileness of all things visible in London, and the labour and sorrow of your usual occupation. The greys and browns in which you now habitually work are merely a part of the shadow of death which buries the nation deeper and deeper according to its folly. Technically you are losing yourself for want of study of the great colour masters.*[9]

In fact Lilias's "labour" and "usual occupation" were exacting a toll on more than her art. In 1884 she underwent surgery, slight in nature, but given her physical and emotional exhaustion, it left her very ill. She wrote to her friend, Blanche Pigott from Broadway, a village in the Cotswold Hills,

> *I think I have been rather at a standstill lately. Dr. Bennet can't quite make out what is wrong with me. I seem to have started some original device of my own, but I am to be consulted over again in a day or two, and will let you know the result. It all seems to matter strangely little, whatever conclusion they come to, and meantime the quiet is so good and I can get about in cabs and wheeled chairs.*[10]

She was forced to give up her work for a time of convalescence and, though the exact nature of her condition was never specified, her heart was permanently affected—a consequence which would have direct bearing on her future.

Such overextension in work, followed by a period of enforced rest, would become an observable pattern throughout Lily's life. One might wonder at the lack of moderation in a person whose very life was distinguished by discipline. Surely she was driven by a higher purpose and, perhaps like Moody, even a sense of urgency based on a belief in the imminent return of Christ. She had great respect for the value of time, and her temperament and inclination no doubt encouraged her toward good stewardship of it. But underlying all her action was sheer joy in her vocation; caught up in the task at hand, and without any outside forces to monitor her, she simply lost sight of her physical and emotional limitations. Indeed, she lamented those very limits!

After this first period of convalescence in Broadway, Lilias returned to her work at Welbeck Street and to a challenging pioneer work. The committee at the center was responding to a need of London working girls who at that time were forced to eat bag lunches on the sidewalks, since expensive hotel dining rooms were their only alternative. Lilias and her fellow workers opened a dining room at Welbeck Street—the first public restaurant in the country just for women—which provided hot meals at low prices.

She recalls the fun of "sitting at the desk and seeing pennies turn into shillings, and shillings into sovereigns on the busy days of the week."[11]

So successful was this first restaurant, in fact, that they outgrew their space and opened another within the year. Yet, Lilias, concerned with reaching the outsider, was disappointed that boarders at the center did not mix with the girls who came in for meals. She longed for a neutral ground to which the latter could come freely. How this came about was a challenge of ingenuity and faith, recalled by Lilias in Emily Kinnaird's *Reminiscences:*

> *Day after day, from the back windows I remember looking out over the glass roofs of some unbeknown buildings, used as a not too reputable club, longing and praying that they might be given to us. Suddenly there came the news that they were falling vacant; then a battle of faith, first for the funds, then at the final critical moment, that they might be given to us rather than to "a school of cookery" that was bidding for it. And at last came the joyful day when we could hear the crash of the masons' tools, breaking through the wall between the big halls and our dining-rooms, and see the sudden gleam of blue-green light as the opening was made, and they passed into God's service.*[12]

Thus was born Morley Halls—conceived from Lilias's longings and her prayers—a larger place in which the ministry could be expanded to address the special needs of girls from the most unfortunate circumstances as well as those of their more conventional boarders. Here in the spacious rooms at 101 Mortimer Street, Lilias's leadership gifts found full range for development and expression. The work prospered, backed by a committee with influence and means, and supported by colleagues of common purpose and views. At Morley Halls there were rooms and meals, Bible studies, and programs designed to meet the areas represented by the YWCA's symbolic triangle: body, mind, spirit. Morley Halls, situated strategically off Regent Street, evolved into a base from which they could reach out into the city, and into which they could welcome it.

Lilias was in her element. Living independently now in a flat on Regent Street, she was at complete liberty to concentrate her energy into the work. At Morley Halls she could integrate all her past teaching, training, and life experience into a vocation of caring. Qualities which would mark her ministry throughout life were apparent in this work: wideness in viewpoint, inclusiveness of spirit, and fidelity to the fundamentals of the faith, all combined with a far-ranging vision. Here among friends, solidly rooted to a place, she had no other thought than to spend her life loving London.

Meanwhile, a great new movement was sweeping both sides of the Atlantic as interest was being kindled in the challenge of foreign missions. Countries which only decades before were inaccessible because of political or ideological obstacles, or the logistical barriers of distance and language, had been penetrated by the dedicated, often courageous efforts of pioneer missionaries. Early in the century, Livingstone and Moffet had built bridges, so to speak, to Central Africa, and Carey and Wilson to India. Hudson Taylor had made his inspiring walk through inland China in 1854, distributing Bibles and tracts in villages which had never heard the name of Christ. By the mid-1880s, more than 165 men and women had joined him in his venture to bring the gospel to China's millions.

Popular interest in missions reached a high water mark in 1885 when, as a result of the Moody and Sankey Mission in Cambridge, seven distinguished students at Cambridge University announced their decision to go to China as missionaries. The "Cambridge Seven," as they were labeled by the press, were "one of the grand gestures of nineteenth Century missions"[13]—a "dream team" composed of athletes, military officers, people with wealth and intellect. Their story, *The Evangelization of the World,* was published and distributed free to every YMCA and YWCA in the British Empire and the United States. The public press, fascinated by these talented young men forsaking their bright prospects for obscurity in a remote land, covered their meeting at Cambridge with two thousand undergraduates the night before their departure and the send-off by hundreds of students the following day from the platform of the railway station. Hundreds of young people joined the Student Volunteer Movement in Britain and abroad, pledging their lives to work in foreign missions.

While the YWCA opened its own department of foreign missions in the mid-1880s, to Lilias, consumed with her work at Morley Halls, the whole missionary subject seemed "rather dull," and "altogether beyond the horizon"[14] as she would later confess. She had two special friends, however, Lelie Duff and Adelaine Braithwaite, with whom she was involved in various kinds of work, and she was aware "that they had a fellowship with Christ over His work in the dark places of earth" of which she knew nothing. At length, Lilias says, "the cry rose unbidden, with a curious persistence, 'Lord, give me the fellowship with Thee that these two have.' "[15]

She testifies that soon after that prayer she sensed two inner developments, which at the time seemed to have no bearing on the direction of her life. First, she felt a yearning begin to spring up over needs in non-Christian lands, though without a thought of personal service in them. A little later, the words *North Africa* began to awaken strange vibrations in her heart. If she came across the words in print, they seemed to stand out in letters of light. Yet, even then, they did not seem to be a matter of personal importance. The London work was prospering. At the same time, her sister Jacqueline was invalided and Lilias was committed to be available to her for six months of each year.

In May 1887, Lily and her colleagues arranged a three-day missions program for Morley Halls. The third evening Edward Glenny spoke on North Africa, beginning his address by saying that this was Thursday and that the Sunday before he was out in the Kabyle mountains where Christ was unknown. The rest is best related in the words of Lilias: "In that first sentence God's call had sounded. If Algeria was so near as that, I could spend half the year there, and the other half at home, then it was for me and before morning there remained no shadow of a doubt that it was His plan."[16]

Interestingly, just one month before her "call" to Algeria, Lilias had had an article, "Making A Venture," printed in the April YWCA monthly letter. She had written the article without the slightest idea of how it would anticipate her own venture. Picturing an eaglet on the outermost stick of a disassembled nest, the article tells of the mother bird calling the baby to take its first plunge out into the air:

> *The face of the cliff goes sheer down—how can it venture into that great gulf, with untried wings? But it gathers up its courage at last, and dashes out. There is the giddy depth below, its strength is failing already; one or two feeble flaps, and it drops down—down—a moment more, and, all unseen, it knows not whence, strong warm wings are beneath, and it is being borne along up into a place of safety. The mother bird has swooped underneath it. There was not risk after all! Now see our Father's explanation, written, as it were, below the picture. "As an eagle stirreth up her nest, fluttereth over her young, spreadeth abroad her wings, taketh them, beareth them on her wings; so the Lord alone did lead him" (Deut 32:11-12).*[17]

On the surface, it is nothing short of remarkable how quickly Lilias "took the plunge" after that fateful May evening of the missions program at Morley Halls. On 14 July, her thirty-fourth birthday, she sent in an application to North African Mission. She was unable to pass their health exam most likely, though unstated, because of her weakened heart. So they arrived at the understanding that she would "work in harmony with this mission but not connected with it."[18] She then spent several months in training at the Mildmay Hospital, leaving the leadership of Morley Halls to Lelie Duff, ironically one of the two colleagues whose "silent flame" had kindled in Lilias the fire for missions. On 5 March 1888, less than nine months after she felt God call her, Lilias along with Lucy Lewis left the Waterloo Station platform with the chorus "Crown Him Lord of All" ringing in their ears and hearts. Blanche Haworth joined them at Southampton, where the women began the first leg of their journey toward North Africa by ship. As the paddle wheels gave their first throb, Lilias records "a strange glad feeling of utter loosing and being cast upon God."[19]

In truth, thirty-four years had gone into this culminating event. The resources of the English clime—rich, well-drained soil, moist air, sheltered site—provided the ideal environment for the cultivation of the "garden lily." Heredity, environment, intellectual and artistic stimulation, spiritual nurture, training in service and leadership, even inherited wealth, which provided the essential funding of her ventures in ministry as well as travel and extended periods of rest and recuperation—all this would become the stored energy requisite for survival in the harsh Algerian soil.

This dandelion has long ago surrendered its golden petals, and has reached its crowning stage of dying—the delicate seed-globe must break up now—it gives and gives till it has nothing left. . . . There is no sense of wrenching: it stands ready, holding up its little life, not knowing when or where or how the wind that bloweth where it listeth may carry it away. It holds itself no longer for its own keeping, only as something to be given: a breath does the rest, turning the "readiness to will" into the "performance"(2 Cor. 8:11). And to a soul that through "deaths oft" has been brought to this point, even acts that look as if they must involve an effort, become something natural, spontaneous, full of a "heavenly involuntariness," so simply are they the outcome of the indwelling love of Christ.

—*Parables of the Cross*[20]

Part Two

The Algerian Age

1888–1928

Sand Lilies

Sand lilies grow wild in arid sand. They draw life from stored energy in bulbs underground.

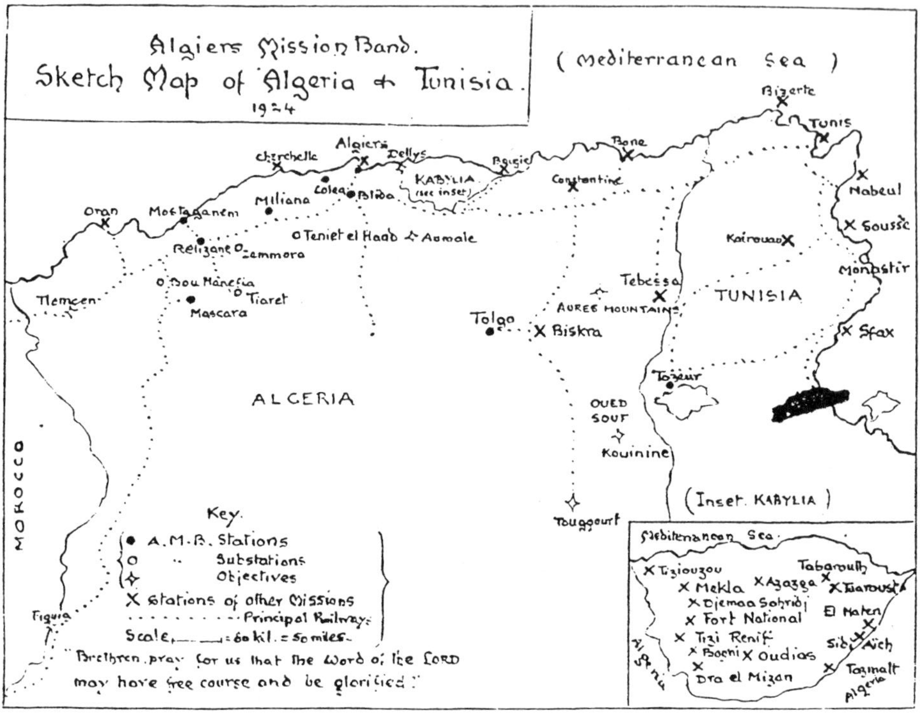

Map of Algeria and Tunisia

9
FOOL'S ERRAND:
KNOCKING HEADS AGAINST STONE WALLS*

1888—1890

At sunrise . . . the first peaks of land came into sight, dim and purple, and as the night darkened, the phosphorescence became wonderful, making a firmament of green starry flashes on the water beside the silver ones overhead. We went below for a time, and on coming up again there was another far-stretching cluster of golden stars, the lights of Algiers!

—Journal Letters[1]

*The reader is strongly encouraged to refer to the historical and religious setting to part two, found in appendix B.

Exhilaration continued to mark each successive stage of the journey from England to Algeria. Traveling by night mail to Marseilles, Lilias felt "a fresh flood of gladness."[2] On 9 March, as they sailed into the Algiers harbor, "the evening all a-sparkle with stars above and light on shore,"[3] the women were almost beside themselves with joy. Alone on the upper deck, with the noise of the steam being let off of the boat as cover, they sang once more "Crown Him Lord of All."

The next morning they awoke to their first daytime view of Algiers. Lilias responded in these words:

> *I shall never forget the loveliness of our first sight out of our port-hole of the Arab town rising tier above tier in a glow of cream colour against the blue-grey western sky, the water glimmering in blue and gold below, and a flock of gulls sailing and wheeling alternately between us and the land.*[4]

They disembarked and continued by carriage to their pension on the outskirts of town feeling like "children on holiday" as they took in new and wonderful scenes, arriving at their lodging "almost exhausted by delight."[5] There they held their first prayer meeting in Algeria, timed at the same hour as the missionary prayer meeting at Morley Halls in England.

The euphoria continued right into the next day as the women worshiped at a service conducted by a small group of English Christians who were at once amazed and delighted at the presence of the adventuresome women.

The hallowing phrase that ran through each new experience was *In His Name!* These words came to Lilias, and to Blanche as she later discovered, when they first stepped from the boat to the quay. Lilias ends her first Sunday in Algeria writing, "I could cover sheets if I tried to say how happy we are; my heart just goes out to, and clasps round the natives; we do love them."[6]

Lilias's first impressions of Algeria over the next few weeks are captured in a little pocket sketchbook painted in a glowing range of hues which would have delighted the color-loving Ruskin: sunrise in golden shades of coral; hills of emerald green against teal blue skies; a bit of blue bay with billowy white clouds banked above purple hills; dark green cypress trees and olive groves; white-washed houses stacked against hillsides or nestled within valleys. Plants and flowers, familiar and "unbeknown," are painted in delicate detail—clumps of leathery prickly pear; long lavender spikes of thistle buds; golden yellow bloom and exquisite sage green leaves of a sea poppy. Nationals of Algeria are captured in white robes and headdress—a woman balancing a water jug on her shoulder; men seated in a local café; a child placing flowers on a white-domed tomb.

Lilias and her two colleagues, Blanche Haworth and Lucy Lewis, would need far more than exhilaration of spirit and delight of the senses, however, to carry them through what she would later concede to be "a fool's errand."[7] They were totally unprepared, by any objective human measure, for the enormity of the task ahead: There were health issues for all three—not one of them was fit to pass a medical exam for any mission society. They knew little about the country, Algeria having been open to missionaries for only a small number of years, with current mission activity being concentrated mainly among the Berbers in the Kabyle Mountains. The three women knew neither a living soul in Algeria nor a sentence of Arabic. They had not a clue for beginning a work in untouched ground; they only knew that they had to come.

Where to begin? They had neither masters nor methods to advise them. No one could help them into a single native home—or tell them what to do when they got there! They determined that the focus of their concern must be access to the people, and so they began by concentrating on this three-fold prayer: that doors might be opened; that hearts might be opened; and that the heavens might be opened. They then proceeded, by trial and error, to find the means to hurdle what they considered "stone walls" that separated them from the people.

The first and most immediate stone wall was finding housing. Initially, the three lodged at the Pension Anglo Suisse, a base from which they could explore more permanent accommodations. The very first evening in Algiers, they made the acquaintance of four English women, Mrs. Kemp and her three daughters, who took their meals at the Pension while residing in a nearby villa. This family instantly embraced the missionaries, inviting them to a small weekly Bible study and becoming their first friends in Algeria. One of the daughters, Alice, found the missionaries' venture so compelling that she gave a generous gift, year by year, which became the backbone of their small mission fund.

On 5 May, they moved into their own flat, 39 Rue Dupuche, in the French part of town. That evening, at their first little "missionary prayer meeting," the three women determined to dedicate one room of the house each day to God, beginning with the sitting room. The first item they removed from their wooden packing cases was a text that had been prepared for them by Adelaine Braithwaite, a colleague of Lilias's in the YWCA work at Morley Halls, as a reminder of God's promise about Mohammed's power: "He shall be broken without hand."

Letters relating the events of the next few weeks give the impression of grown women "playing house." Because of a series of snags in securing consistent household help, the women were consigned to doing their own domestic duties, a habit unfamiliar to all of them. Lilias, who at Montagu Square was accustomed to beginning each day when the chambermaid drew the blinds, placed a cup of tea at her bedside, and announced, "Your bath is ready, Miss," noted with obvious delight that the housework was "capitol practice." She writes, "Blanche proved to be a capitol cook & I was house & parlour maid, Lucy helping us alternatively."[8]

The housework, while draining in the increasing seasonal heat, proved to be as much therapy as practice for their new way of life. On Ascension Sunday, not many days after her arrival, Lilias received a telegram that her sister Jacqueline had died after what had earlier been reported as successful surgery. Although Jacqueline was an invalid (the cause of which is not given), her condition was not regarded as terminal. In fact, Lilias's full intention, upon coming to North Africa, was to divide her time equally between Algeria and England in order to devote half of each year to the care of her beloved elder sister. Jacqueline's death was a stunning blow and the singular event which severed England's last hold on Lilias's life, allowing her now to focus entirely on her work in Algeria.

Lilias was immediately comforted by the tender care of her two friends, Blanche and Lucy, who after the initial shock accompanied her to the Communion Service at the English Church in Algiers: "It was so beautiful to go straight to that, before anything of realization began to come. They have been *so* dear & tender, these two—& it has been a help having all this household work to do as the bodily tiredness made one sleep." (Journal Letter, 15 May 1888)*

---

*Excerpts marked either "journal letters" or marked solely with the dates 1888–1890 are taken from circular letters Lilias wrote for friends in England. Excerpts marked "diary" or marked with a post-1890 date are taken from Lilias's diaries and journals.

It was also "a help" to throw her energy into the preliminary aspects of ministry. The three friends wasted no time in attempting to scale the second stone wall: language. For someone born into an Arabic culture, twelve years of study is considered requisite for mastery of the Arabic language. To start with, the vocabulary includes some eighty thousand words, each having its many forms and variations. Six pages of a French-Arabic dictionary, for example, is devoted to the verb *to walk*. Each verb is conjugated in singular, dual, and plural, as well as masculine and feminine, with up to ten forms of the infinitive. Furthermore, the women found, with all the richness of expression in the Arabic tongue, there were significant omissions: there was no word for "holiness" nor for "humility"; the only word for "home" was "house." Moreover, when it came to the written language, not only did they need to learn an entirely new set of characters, but their only study resource was in French, as opposed to their native English tongue.

Within the first month of their arrival the women began to tackle the Arabic language—word by word! They embraced the challenges of the language and proceeded in a self-prescribed study. With the aid of a French-Arabic dictionary, they set to work on the first chapter of the Gospel of John, writing down each word and memorizing it as they went along. They enrolled, mid-session, in a local Arabic class which met two evenings a week until it was discontinued because of the teacher's illness. Undaunted, they invited a young Algerian boy to come and read with them three evenings a week—he having taught himself sufficient French to be their common ground. After two weeks, he "took fright," alarmed by the distinctives of the English women's Christian faith. Several months into their endeavor, they acquired a professional tutor, M. Fabsal, who directed their study, which they supplemented with the now resumed bi-weekly Arabic classes.

Considering the enormity of the assignment, it is amazing to read Lilias's journal at that time: "it was nice to get a good spell at Arabic again. We love it so—& only can do it when too tired to write or do anything else, & only feel rested by it—When once we begin we don't know how to stop, till we are cut off by some meal or other."[9] Their love for the language was whetted, unquestionably, by their motivation to master it sufficiently to communicate with the Arab people. "Oh we do so long to speak," Lilias writes, "the power of talking can only come by being among the people—but time will shew God's plan."[10]

The women did not wait for mastery in Arabic to begin ministering. They immediately began to climb the third stone wall—contact with the people. On the more familiar French turf in the city, they immediately began to volunteer their services to the McCall Mission, helping evenings in the French-conducted meetings. But now, with a place of their own, they were ready to initiate a ministry in their neighborhood. Printing handbills on a typograph, a primitive copy machine, they went door to door with invitations to a Sunday meeting at their home. Then, clearing the largest room of the flat, they moved in Blanche's harmonium, strung up lights, stocked the room with rushbottom chairs, and awaited the response. Over twenty neighbors showed up and expressed a desire for further meetings. The next two meetings—Wednesday night and Sunday afternoon—no one came, but, in time, the meetings were so well attended they were forced to consider a larger meeting place.

The much-desired contact with Arabic people was limited by language, but Lilias prevailed upon their Arabic teacher to translate bits of Scripture into the colloquial form of expression, which the women, in turn, worked out as best they could and printed off the trusty typograph, hand-coloring the decorative borders. They then sallied forth in the Arab town with one of their few sentences, "Canst thou read?" With a small boy leading the way, brandishing a stick to keep them from being crowded by the men who with outstretched hands pled "Papier, papier," they distributed the texts in the streets and shops. Often they were able to initiate conversations among the French-speaking men, but access to the women sequestered within the homes was still beyond their reach.

Another point of contact was in the quay and in the public squares where the missionaries distributed literature: their own hand-printed French and Arabic text cards, as well as Spanish and Italian translations they had acquired from England. The tireless trio found through this "polygot seed-sowing" many openings for conversations and, on occasion, opportunity to practice their Arabic. Saturday evenings were devoted entirely to visiting cafés in town where the printed texts were eagerly received—sometimes the waiters helped them with distribution, even reading the papers aloud. As they became better acquainted with people and the language, the three women attempted to read the texts aloud themselves, to the delight of the men who assisted them in their stammering efforts.

By the end of May, the missionaries' lives had assumed some semblance of routine as indicated by Lilias's journal account:

At 6 a.m. Amonciade, our new little servant, rings to be let in. At 7 she has breakfast (French fashion, bread & coffee) on the kitchen table, & we arrive in various stages of toilette, to take it off to our rooms, which gives us a good bit of unbroken time to ourselves. . . . At 8.30 we meet for prayers . . . ending about 9.15. Then come small household duties & if possible a bit of spare time for letters till 10.30—when Arabic comes on till "dejeuner" at 12. At 12.30 we have another short time of prayer. . . & then go for siesta—this & the gradual process of straightening up the house, takes till teatime at 3.30—After that we go out till 6 or so—then comes the getting supper & washing up . . . & an hour or so of letterwriting is generally about all that we get before cocoa at 9.30 & at 10 we go off to bed. (22 May 1888)

The routines and activities of the first months, with an occasional excursion to Pescade on the coast, set the pattern of the months to follow. Early elation was tempered by certain discouragement. The growing attendance at their meetings invited the interest of local "roughs" who repeatedly disrupted their gatherings. These French lads, in their late teens, with little to do and on the lookout for action, found irresistible both the uniqueness of these events and the women who sponsored them. Some individuals with whom they made inroads backed away. The climate could be oppressive, so much so that it would lead within a year and a half to the departure of Lucy Lewis. Yet, in an October 1888 update published by the North African Mission, Lilias sums up their early experience: "The whole place gives one the impression of being 'White unto the harvest.' May God Himself put in the sickle and gather the souls into His garner, to be made in their turn seed for future sowing."[11]

The dawn of 1889 brought a new venture: a New Year's Day tea at the women's flat for the Arab water-carriers with whom they had made contact during their forays into town. The young lads were at first uneasy about this novel adaptation of an English tea party—"eggs, dates and oranges, nuts and breads, some French sweetmeats, and jam of their own making"[12]—but after refreshments, they settled down with Blanche's first chords on the little organ and the singing of a few French hymns. Then, in the perfect quiet, Lilias for the first time presented God's plan of salvation through a wordless book improvised out of pieces of calico, explaining it in halting Arabic, an early linguistic effort, the result of infinite toil and preparation.

The immediate yield was the receptivity of their guests: "The Arab water-carriers who came to the tea are so warm in their greeting & shower a volley of Arabic upon us whenever we pass, evidently having formed a high-opinion of our powers in that direction."[13] Over the long term, this would be the seeding for their first regular Arab meeting and the fueling of their desire to live closer to the native Arab town.

Meanwhile, the dominating challenge was the French meetings at the women's home. Having outgrown their space—and having raised the ire of their neighbors with the disturbance created by their two weekly gatherings—an independent meeting place was no longer a wish but a necessity. The pages of Lily's journal letters for 1889 record their lengthy efforts to find a place to meet. After the women secured a deserted corn warehouse near the center of town, Lily writes of the need to control the growing crowds and manage the increasing disturbance by local onlookers.

They must have been a tremendous novelty, three English ladies holding meetings in the large hall near the main thoroughfare of the town. They were lavish and utterly undiscriminating in the distribution of invitations: neighbors and strangers met in house-to-house visitation; even soldiers in nearby terraces and sailors in ships at port. The problems were manifold, and outwitting the irrepressible troublemakers tested the very limits of their ingenuity—they employed local lads to guard the doors, brought in police protection, temporarily issued admission cards, and restricted attendance on occasion to women only. Repeatedly and often, however, they were forced to close down until the trouble had subsided, and then they started in all over again. One obvious solution was to completely and permanently bar all the ruffians from the premises, but to that alternative, Lilias, who always saw the potential in these young lads, would respond, "they are just the kind of people that one wants to get hold of."[14]

Two words characterize Lilias's first years in North Africa: *inexhaustible* and *indiscourageable.* When meetings were suspended, she used that time to visit the outlying suburbs and villages in the nearby foothills. When no one showed up for a factory girls' tea, she went out on the streets and invited the market porters and shoeblacks; forty Arab boys appeared at that "feast"—from which evolved a weekly Bible class of twelve students.

Lilias was visionary with the ability to see much farther than her own vested interest. A year after her arrival, she invited the handful of English-speaking Christian workers from the several small organizations in the city to the flat for tea and prayer. The time was so encouraging that they determined to meet weekly and to include French workers of whom they were aware. "It comes over me," she writes about these times, "that God has far greater thoughts towards this place than just blessing our little meetings—so much so that prayer for them had got almost swallowed up in prayer for the whole town."[15] Visualizing a united effort to visit every house in Algiers, Lilias concludes with this divine strategy:

> *It came so strongly that our present work was just to sow broadcast, as far & wide as we could, in preparation for the coming harvest. The sowing beside all waters must mean such unselfish sowing—not calculating what will take root on our little plot; but letting that just take its chance of sharing in the future harvest—& scattering meanwhile far & wide.*[16]

And scatter broadcast she did, far and wide, without calculation. Lilias's heart reached out and clasped Algeria, and just as she learned Arabic word by word, she loved the country house by house, café by café, person by person. How, one wonders, did she spend so liberally without herself being spent? How did she proceed with so little direction and against so many obstacles without faltering? Lilias offers only hints in her journal letters, rather than explanations on this topic, and the answer is found buried within paragraphs recording the early years. Almost every morning from 7:15 to 8:30, Lilias would retreat with her Bible to a corner in Fortification Woods, five minutes from the house, out of sight and sound of the city:

> *it is so delicious in these hot spring mornings. And God rests one through it for the whole day, & speaks so through all the living things. I sent in the last journal a drawing of a little plant through which His*

message came the first day I was up there. Each leaf fringed with tiny balls of dew—but day after day something comes afresh. (May 1889)

"Knocking our heads against stone walls"[17] would be Lilias's summation of those early years from the hindsight of twenty-five years. Yet, alone with God, Lilias was given the strength and the sight to hurdle seemingly insurmountable obstacles and to scale stone walls that would have deterred a less intrepid traveler. She returned for the first time to England after almost two-and-one-half years with unabated passion: "If only one had twenty lives! But I suppose that to have the power of God concentrated on the one that we have would be better still!"[18]

10

OPEN DOORS, OPEN HEARTS:
ALGIERS AND BEYOND

1890—1893

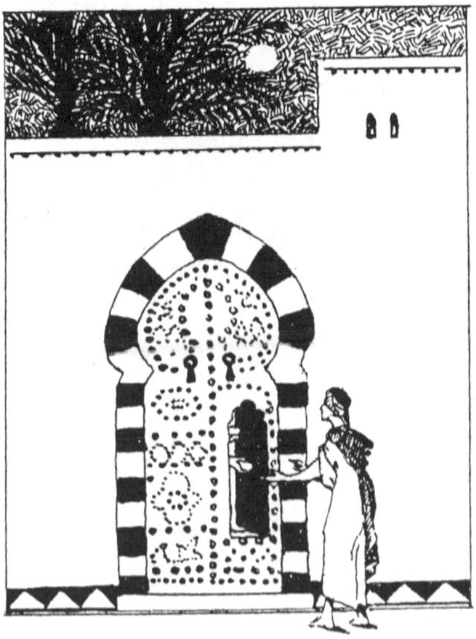

It is so lovely to watch how one door opens after another nearly every day; of course one knows that "in favour with God and man" is only an early stage, and a passing one, in any work that is really of God, but we can take the gladness of it while it lasts.

—Blanche Pigott, *I. Lilias Trotter*[1]

Lilias's return to Algeria in October, after a four-month rest, is marked by gravity, in distinct contrast to the ebullience of the initial venture—"When one left England again those left there seemed dearer and closer than when we first came away."[2] Now, as she sighted the first lights of

Africa, she knew of the difficulty and resistance they meant. She reminded herself of the underlying motive in being there at all, apart from emotion or results, quite simply, "God wants us under a southern sky, not under an English one."[3]

If Lilias returned somewhat subdued in spirit, she was met with exuberance. The Europeans and nationals with whom the women had made friends were elated to see her, and welcomed Lilias and Blanche back with open hearts. The Algerians, in particular, must have been surprised at the return and sustained interest of their new English friends, given the separatist mentality, at that time, of both European settlers and French colonists. The welcome heartened Lilias, although she recognized the capricious character of such good will.

A great boost to the work was the arrival of Helen Freeman, Lilias's close friend and colleague in the London work, who joined them in Algiers in 1900, after the death of her mother. Helen, like Lilias and Blanche, was able to support herself and the various ventures in ministry through her own independent means. Together the three woman—Lilias, Blanche, and Helen—would make an indomitable team (later referred to as "the seniors" by their younger colleagues), bonded in spirit and purpose, remaining in Algeria to the end of their lives.

From the beginning, Lilias's heart had been particularly drawn to the Arab people with whom there had been virtually no evangelistic effort. Now, with increased staff and skill in the language, she could concentrate more fully on her ministry to them. Her first endeavor was to start up the weekly classes for Arab boys, begun shortly before her departure, in which she introduced Old Testament battles and heroes to their adventure-loving spirits. Contact with the Arab men continued in the streets and cafés, and the women were encouraged by evidence that their earlier limited efforts were not in vain: "An Arab stopped us and asked, 'Was it you who used to give away books three years ago?' We said 'Yes.' 'Then you give me another—the biggest book you have. I'm looking for a religion.'"[4]

To their great joy, Ahmed, the first of their Arab friends to become a Christian, was baptized in the river the following April by Mr. Lambert, a missionary friend. The persecution that followed his public witness brought home forcibly the cost of following Christ in an Islamic society. Several days after his baptism, Ahmed appeared at their home covered with blood, the result of being attacked by eighteen Arab men.

The decision was made to send him to Tunis until things settled down a bit, for his sake and in the best interest of missions efforts in general. The women were only beginning to experience the extent of the familial and social hold that the Islamic community held over the individual, and to witness the opposition—overt and subtle—for those individuals who chose to separate themselves from that solidarity. Indeed, Islam permeated every aspect of society—legal, civil, educational, domestic—virtually defining the weeks and months of the year with its feasts and fasts.

The religion, itself, held a powerful attraction in its doctrine of a powerful and majestic God—albeit fundamentally distant from and disinterested in man. The very simplicity of its creed—"There is no God but Allah, and Mohammed is his prophet"—rotely recited for the salvation of one's soul, while giving little *to* them (salvation, in the end, being dispensed at the whim of an arbitrary God), likewise demanded little *from* them beyond outward observances.

Islam worked itself out in the daily life of its adherents through its duties or practices—legalistic and external—as observed in the Five Pillars of Islam: confession of faith—the witness or creed (Sheheda); prayer—repeated in Arabic five times daily preceded by ritual purification; fasting—keeping of the thirty-day Ramadan fast; almsgiving—a mandatory giving of one-fortieth of one's income to the poor or to a religious cause; pilgrimage—to Mecca, or holy places of Mohammed, which could be done by proxy. Yet, while the people were bound together by their common experience, it did little to change their lives.

The position of Muslim women, for example, was difficult at best. The slave of her father from birth, she then became the slave of her husband till death. She was raised to have one goal: to serve men. After the few short years of childhood, around the age of ten, she was to wear the veil and enter the paternal harem until sold into the conjugal harem. Once married, she remained cloistered in the harem where she remained until her death—competing with the younger wives or as was often the case, divorced and tossed from husband to husband before even reaching the age of twenty.

From their earliest days in Algeria, Lilias felt uniquely called to this sequestered group, recognizing that such a ministry was the sole domain of women. Now, with her and her coworkers' greater facility in Arabic, came their much-desired access to these women cloistered within the fortress of the homes in the Arab section of Casbah, the old city built upon a hillside crowned by the ancient citadel. And what they discovered was that the *children* were the keys that opened those locked doors. As they befriended the little urchins on doorsteps or in back alleys, they made contact with the hidden world of Arab womanhood.

Lilias writes,

> *Their ways are so curious. The women all mix freely, and do their cooking together in the court on the lower floor, but if a man comes in, he clears his throat violently in the little vestibule inside the street door, and instantly all the women and girls run helter-skelter into their rooms, like rabbits to their holes, and pull down the door curtains, and the place is cleared of all except his own woman, for they recognize the throat of their lord and master. As soon as he has passed in his room they all pop out again. In every house there are four or five families, and in the lease of a room it is entered that unless in illness or urgent need, the men must not come into the house between 7 a.m. and 7 p.m., except for their midday meal, which leaves the ground much freer for us. The women shut up so when the men are there. We often divide and go into different rooms. (9 November 1890)*

Names appear and reappear in Lilias's journal pages, first friends among the national women—Yamina, Fatima, Hatique, Taitum—as the workers win access into homes through little gifts of bonbons and pincushions, and into hearts through small home remedies, kindly attentions to children, and mostly through their loving presence. Partaking of the couscous that was the staple of the daily diet and listening to the chatter that was the substance of the Arab women's closely prescribed existence, the English women told their new friends how Christ loved them and blessed the little children. Lilias summed up that experience: "it is worth anything to tell the story for the first time, helpless though one feels."[5]

The Arab women delighted in the friendships and, no doubt, in the novelty of these three foreign ladies. They listened to the stories about Jesus, sometimes prayed to Sidna Aissa (Jesus Christ), and even in their own limited way, witnessed: "I gave Taitum my story-book to show the pictures. 'Come and see Him,' she said to a strange girl, 'our Lord Jesus.' How glad that 'our' made one's heart! It is a strong word in Arabic—*'Our possession.'* "[6]

Yet the challenge remained: how to bring the Arab people to the point of accepting Christ. They listened and, after a fashion, even assented to the message but without a real understanding of what was involved in the teaching. For example, they readily accepted Jesus as a great prophet, second only to Mohammed, but when confronted with the claim of Christ to be *the* way to God, they would insist: "Jesus *and* Mohammed." The very idea of Jesus as equal to God, indeed *being* God, was blasphemy—the worst possible sin. His death on the cross was not only untrue but unnecessary—sin being less a question of a rupture between God and man than of transgressions of certain rituals, limits, or laws which could be effaced through prayers and alms.

Having hurdled the stone walls of language and of access to their homes and even their hearts, the missionaries were baffled as to how to penetrate the spiritual walls that blocked true acceptance of Christ. Although Lilias believed that spiritual penetration was ultimately the work of the Holy Spirit, she understood the gospel mandate to be one of collaboration with divine purpose. On the human side, their responsibility was to find the most effective way to convey the message to bring the listener to the point of understanding—and decision.

Confronted with the empty legalism of orthodox Islam (which was their primary exposure in the early years), Lilias believed that absolute candor was essential in distinguishing between the belief systems of Islam and Christianity. Her message was basic: the gravity of sin (which separated men from a personal relationship with God); God's plan of salvation (Christ given over to death that we might have life); the necessity of a personal decision—an act of the will—to accept this gift freely given; the promise of a new life in Christ for believers. Her method of conveying this essential message would constantly evolve to reach most effectively each individual. (It is interesting to note that later, in her communication with the mystic seekers of Islam, she first sought to establish the common ground of Islam and Christianity—hunger for God—before addressing the variance of belief.)

For those who, like Ahmed, made the decision for Christ, there were immediate consequences within the family and in society at large. Whereas, for the Muslim, the observance of the duties gave witness to their faith, for the new convert to Christianity, being no longer bound by those rituals gave witness, in part, to their newfound faith. Nowhere was the challenge to Islam more evident than during Ramadan. At this time in the year, publicly breaking the fast—during which "for thirty days no food nor drink may pass the lips during the hours when you can tell a white thread from a black"[7]—would clearly distinguish the Christian from the Muslim.

Then, as now, some would challenge the Arab's need, even more the Englishwomen's right to bring to them Christianity. After all, it is not as if they were without religion. Furthermore, is it not presumptuous to foist on others one's own creed? But Lilias's call to North Africa was based on the two-fold biblical premise: the world is lost without Christ; it is a mandate, not an option, to spread the Good News of God's plan for salvation. Her contact with individual Muslims fleshed out this belief with names and faces of people groping in an abyss of hopelessness, and her conviction only intensified with increasing intimacy. Day after day, says Lilias, she observed a creed "stiff with formalism and slavish fear chilled through and through with meaningless ceremonies and silly superstitions, and a dull morality with no motive power to make it workable. All this is at best: down and down they trend, to depths that are indescribable."[8]

The only valid question, she believed, was how anyone who had experienced the light of eternity "in the face of Jesus Christ" could withhold that light and life and love from those who had not. It was irrelevant what their creed was or was not; whether they were in North Africa or England; the crux of the matter was that they were without Christ. "All that is of dimness and dreariness and hopeless heart-emptiness is wrapped up in those two words—*without Christ.*"[9] The love that Lilias felt for North Africa could be explained in no way other than that God led her to a particular place and people, the vast majority of whom were Muslim, and without Christ.

She attended a special service at the mosque the last week of Islam's month-long fast of Ramadan, feeling there the emptiness of their most holy place during their most holy month:

I wish I could give the feeling of it, the great dim mosque lit by rows of tiny lamps, open on all sides to a court brilliant with starlight, with trees and splashing fountain, and then the rows of these solemn white figures, rising and falling simultaneously in their prostrations, like the waves of the sea. The front row, the strictest sect, joined in the recitation of the Imam and then suddenly the whole crowd went down on their faces, and after a pause of silence there began a kind of wail repeated at intervals of a moment or two by the whole congregation, with their bodies rocked backwards and forwards again to the ground—"Allah! Allah! Allah!"—there was an indescribable moan in the intonation—a crying out for the living God; the echo of it has rung in my ears. (1891)

As the ministry became more focused on the native Arabs, Lilias reluctantly recognized their need to be more selective in expending both time and energy. The French meetings, which had been far more manageable since their return, were eventually turned over to a Swedish missionary. The women determined to actively pursue living accommodations in the Arab section of the old city. At the same time, the influx of Kabyles, from the Berber tribes in the heart of the mountains of Kabylia, in town created an inner crisis for Lilias, who found irresistible any opportunity to share Christ's love. She resigned herself to an occasional visit to the Kabyle houses, where she "just kept the door open" with this thought:

Other workers may come later; meanwhile we can be loving them and praying for them. I have been thinking lately what a work for God it is, just loving people. He says in Deut. 22: "If an ox or an ass has gone astray, thou shalt bring it unto thine own house, and it shall be with thee till thy brother seek after it." I think He gives us sometimes a like service for souls—wandering souls that we cannot bring back to Him; sometimes all we can do is to keep them near us, and show the kindness of God to them, and hold them in faith and prayer till He comes to seek them. (25 April 1891)

So they carried on, three English ladies—Lilias, Blanche, and Helen Freeman—alone amongst the native peoples. There were small gains—the first baptism, the first little communion service with two native men, the classes for Arab boys, and access to the women in the Arab houses. And there were definite disappointments and discouragements. Along with the obvious struggle of pushing against the current of belief and the continual nerve strain of the climate, there was the indefinable pressure in the spiritual domain, the ongoing battle between darkness and light. Each solid advance seemed to provoke spiritual resistance and opposition—some of a nature so perverse, especially in regards to young believers, that the sensibilities of the early biographers restrained them from "publishing details" except to say "the fight was fierce and the enemy strong." In spite of the fierceness of difficulty, Lilias continued to find special joy in the pioneer challenge: "Oh, the beginnings! The joy of them more than counterbalances the hardness of working in an unsown land like this."[10]

With the tiny nucleus of a ministry established in the city of Algiers, the call of the inland stretches began to sound in Lilias's heart. Virtually no one at that time seemed to be drawn to the hill country or the great south lands beyond; Christian work in Algeria was concentrated mainly in the coastal towns and Kabylia. Lilias's dream when they leased Rue Dupuche was to use it eventually as a pied-à-terre, launching pad, and outpost, as well as a station for the new workers they prayed would join them, freeing them to move deeper and deeper into the interior. As early as 1889, Lilias and Blanche had made their first venture inland to the little mountain village of Blida some thirty-five miles south of town. In 1892 they had made serious inquiries about joining a native caravan in order to penetrate the western frontier of Morocco—a plan foiled by political difficulties. Now, with Helen Freeman to carry on the program in Algiers, and the addition of English workers Francis and Reba Brading to their band, Lilias determined the time had come to investigate possibilities for work further inland.

In March 1893 Lilias, approaching age forty, set off with Blanche for Biskra, an oasis some thirty miles into the desert. They traveled by rail 288 miles eastward to Constantine, south another 150 miles by horse-drawn diligence, and across the barren tableland that separates the desert from the sea. Two hours short of their destination, they halted at an inn at El Kantara—the great gateway to the desert, as Lilias describes:

> *Such a strange fairy land of a new world it is, one looks and looks, and feels as if in a dream. Beyond the primitive inn, the sides of the gorge close in till there are not fifty yards between them, in towering masses of red crags, and then suddenly they open on a great forest of palm trees stretching far into the valley beyond, along the river bed, backed by the purple mountains. (13 March 1893)*

Lilias explored areas within walking (or rafting!) distance from the inn, visiting villages of clay houses and talking to women who gathered around her. Fascinated at their first exposure to a European at close quarters, the women exclaimed, "Look at the skin on her hands (gloves); look how smooth her hair is!" as they drew their fingers gently down the part of her hair, having already taken off her hat![11]

After a couple of weeks exploring outlying villages, the two women arranged for camels to take them the remaining thirty miles into the desert to their final destination, Biskra. Lilias writes this:

> *Looking on and on, the desert stretched away like a great sea, broken only by an island of palms here and there, away and away to the Touaregs and the Sudan beyond. I shall never forget the sight of it. But the sense of rest and silence that lies in the immensity of it grows day by day. (3 April 1893)*

Thus began Lilias's love affair with the Southlands. Her travel journals are filled with words and watercolors conveying the haunting beauty of the desert:

> *Sunset is coming on with wonderful effects of light & colour: as the sun sinks they deepen and glorify beyond any possibility of putting on paper—there comes sudden twilight & an almost visible dying down of the fire in the west, & in half an hour it is night—night so dark*

> *and so clear that the "earthshine" on the new moon a few evenings ago shewed up to the naked eye in the dusty circle.*[12]

The journal watercolors include delicate paintings of desert flowers found about dry water-courses; houses literally of one piece with mother earth, thick clay walls and dark pillared interiors decorated with colorful cloths of blue, green, and gold; women and children draped in a rainbow of color, men in white robes and headdress.

Here in the desert, as in Algiers, Lilias prayed first for access—usually gained through the children—and then for openness, fully recognizing that their path must be one of faith. "It throws one more and more on God for guidance, as to the bits of work, and He does guide."[13] Her approach and her methods were disarmingly direct. When asked "What do you want?" she would answer, "I love the Arabs and have come to have a talk with you."[14] And then, often with the visual aid of the wordless book (a simple tool using colors to symbolize spiritual truths), she explained in the simplest terms the human condition and God's plan of salvation. Sometimes she was invited to the people's huts or tents, where other women would gather around and offer at times little gifts of eggs and dried dates.

Village to village, house to house, Lilias walked, sometimes alone and sometimes with Blanche, seeking entrance into the homes, offering basic medical services, and telling them bit by bit about Jesus—measuring all the while the response for future work. She says:

> *Such faces they have, these women, full of character and intelligence. Forcible faces. Oh, they would make Christians! I felt more access to them today, more touch with these souls, and they are so sweet and friendly; they pressed us to stay to supper or to come back and spend the day, and we got two or three more houses.*[15]

Word about the strange European women spread fast among village residents, preceding them at times to the next village. Sometimes the travelers were approached with interest, and other times with resistance. On one occasion, their words were met with a chorus of "Mohammed is the one who saves us." One Muslim woman pled with them with an intense spiritual earnestness seldom seen in a Christian: "Witness to Mohammed. Say 'La Ilaha illa Allah' or 'Mohammed Rasoul Allah.' Say it once; we will never tell of you and it will get you to heaven."[16]

Six weeks into their desert venture, the women received a telegram from Algiers informing them that the landlord had consented to the terms of lease they had offered for a home in the Arab quarter of the Casbah in Algiers. So, with a tug of heart and the determination to revisit these desert places, they straight away began the journey homeward, choosing fresh halting places along the way, "places where no one ever stops, and one can always leave little glints of light."[17] And the Gospels they left as they went were received gladly, a new book being a rare thing to the people they met.

Number Two Rue du Croissant was a huge fortress-like house in the Casbah. Three hundred years old, with an aristocratic past, the house had evolved through the centuries into a rabbit-warren dwelling for fourteen families. It was located at the end of a long flight of stairs, or *street,* and entered through a heavy nail-studded iron door which opened into the *skiffa,* or entrance hall. At the end of the skiffa, yet another door opened into a mosque, the prized remnant of lost glory, which in turn opened into the large open courtyard, around which were located the maze of many rooms.

It fell to the three women to make sense of the endless holes and corners, to distinguish huge cupboards embedded in the walls from tiny, windowless rooms. With characteristic gusto they tackled the domestic challenge. First, they explored their new domicile, discovering twenty-five rooms (including stable, cellars, and mosque), of which only eight were inhabitable given the lack of air and light; then, they moved and settled their possessions into their first Arab home. "It is just the right time for flitting," writes Lilias. "This is the [customary time] for everyone to move, so we could not do much visiting, and the people are delighted that we should change houses at the same time they do."[18]

Lilias's dream of five years was realized in that May 1883 as they moved into their own native home—"The House of the Turk's Son, in the Street of the Crescent," its name by interpretation. Lilias writes of the experience:

It was good to turn our backs on the long French streets and plunge down among the crowds, first through a street thronged with Jews, then a little bit up again through the native quarter, and then down the flight of steps that led to our door. I was praying all the way for some word of God for our coming in, but it was silence till the moment of crossing the threshold, and then came the word, "In this place I will give peace, saith the Lord." It was sealed by a lovely verse that Miss Cox had for us, "The remnant of Jacob shall be in the midst of many people as a dew from the Lord."[19]

Lilias was thrilled to wake up in the morning and find herself in the Arab town, to go out in the afternoon and in two minutes be in the thick of the Arab people. From her window she could literally reach out across the narrow street and touch the hands of the women who crept along a rooftop parapet to a projection opposite where they would sit and talk to their remarkable new neighbor. Here were some Europeans, people who normally separated themselves from Arabs, choosing to live among them in the native quarters, considered by most a slum area!

In July of that year Lilias prepared for a three-month break in England. Although sorely in need of a physical and emotional respite, she felt torn, she writes, at leaving: "just as we have got down to the place we have so longed for among the people."[20] But she could leave this time with the encouragement that God was opening the doors and the hearts of the people in Algiers and now beyond in the interior of Algeria. She placed her faith in God:

It is no harder for Him to open the heavens. What we want is to have our faith brought down to the uttermost simplicity, to the absolute transparent childlikeness of those words. "I believe in God." It can be so when, as some one said the other day, "there is nothing between our bare hearts and Jesus."[21]

11

BEYOND THE SKYLINE WHERE THE STRANGE ROADS GO

1894—1895

The special vocation wherewith we are called (so we feel) as a Band is the evangelisation as far and as fast as we can of the great unreached stretches that extend back of the coast line.

—A Thirsty Land[1]

In October Lilias returned to their own native home in Algeria with high hopes. When she had left Algiers in July, feeling "mown down in body and soul," she claimed the scriptural promise "He shall come like rain upon the mown grass." Now, upon her return she could affirm, "And He has made it true, Hallelujah!"[2]

Now, with a home in the midst of the Arab town in Algiers, the missionaries possessed not only a base for ministry among the native peoples but a launching pad for ministries beyond. Their small ranks had increased to five workers—Lilias, Blanche, Helen, Francis and Reba Brading—making the early dream to penetrate deeper and deeper into Algeria's interior ever more viable, since they could maintain the program at the Rue du Croissant while sending out rotating teams to unreached stretches beyond Algiers.

Lilias's most immediate concern was to revisit Biskra, and from there to distribute literature to nearby villages and assess possibilities for future work. In March 1894, Lilias and Helen Freeman traversed southeast to Constantine, then south over the tableland to Biskra, thirty miles into the desert. Torrents of rain prevented their camping in the area as they had intended. "We held our plans before God," Lilias writes, "and the conviction grew that we were to go to Touggourt, a large native town 120 miles south."[3]

Hiring a little horse-drawn *trap,* they began the four-day journey down the rough road, stopping nights at a *caravanserai,* a crude unfurnished room provided by the government, or setting up camp along the way. Lilias relates the scene:

> *Touggourt was reached at last, and such a sunset over the desert! Real desert here, the sand so fine and soft and deep. The streets are strange places, roofed in till they are twilight tunnels at the brightest and often quite dark for a bit in broad daylight. We got into a good many houses by the help of Abdulla the guide who had come with us from Biskra. (March 1894)*

After several days in Touggourt, they hired camels and a mule and set east for the Oued Souf, a cluster of oases, eighty miles deeper into the desert. After a two-day march over a roadless stretch of sand dunes with bits of level land between, they arrived at El Oued, the chief oasis town. Lilias writes:

> *It is a strange country; the palms look half buried in the sand, for they plant them in deep pits where the roots reach the watery stratum below, and the towns look like a sea of tiny domes, built of grey concrete. It is utterly out of the way, and we were very curious objects; so much so, that it was a work of time and patience to get a hearing. Their dear, wild-looking women, and still more the children, were intensely excited over us; there were more houses clamouring for us than we could possibly visit. It did, indeed, need a miracle working Lord who used the loaves and fishes to make anything of it. The men everywhere in the desert were eager for the books—"I am reading and reading," one man said, "we are all reading—we have never had these books before." (March 1894)*

The journal narratives of these early ventures are so unassuming that it is easy to overlook the difficulty and the danger for any traveler of that era, much less single women. Consider this particular journey: The initial trip to Biskra was an almost 450-mile stretch achieved by primitive arrangements: rail, diligence (rickety horse-drawn carriage), and camel. Penetration deeper into the desert, four days south to Touggourt by cart then two days east by camel, was long, fiery hot, and risky. Two women traveling alone with an unfamiliar native guide were at the complete mercy of humankind and the elements. They were in a place where thieves made it their business to profit from unsuspecting Europeans. Deadly scorpions, disease, and ferocious dogs were the gamble of any given day.

Then there was the desert. Beyond Biskra, it is said, the Sahara starts in earnest—flat, scorching, and difficult to navigate. The Great Eastern Erg, the sand sea covering 120,000 square miles, includes some dirt- and gravel-supporting patches of grass and small bushes; large flats of salt (or *chotts*); and the occasional oasis. But mostly it is sand—great dunes at times nearly four hundred feet above the basin floor with endlessly shifting sand.

Miscalculations by a few degrees can result in missed destinations by miles, and navigation through the unmarked expanse of sand, under the best of circumstances, is a test for the most skilled guide, requiring an encyclopedic knowledge of the land and stars. As one old Saharan explained, "Yes, by the stars at night. In daylight by local knowledge of the desert—this soil, this tree, this ruin, these tracks, these shadows before sunset. It is passed down from father to son, and spoken of among friends."[4]

Yet even the most experienced veteran could become victim of the elements. By afternoon in the desert, the very air can sear the lungs, and the reflective sun can burn the traveler from the ground. An unexpected sandstorm could overpower a person anytime, erasing a subtle marking at a critical point. Survival under such circumstances becomes a contest between time and water: In the Sahara, it may take only a half a day to reach the point of dehydration. The Arab recognizes the unsubdued desert as god and accepts its supremacy with characteristic fatalism: "If you die you die," or "It is written."

Even so, Lilias loved the desert. She loved its inhabitants who lived out their lives in the most basic battle for sustenance and survival. It broke her heart to think of these people braving the scorching sun of the Sahara without so much as one ray of light from the Sun above. She rejoiced at the privilege of being the first one to bring the light of God in the name of Christ Jesus.

Lilias loved as well the desert's brooding beauty: the cream-colored sand of impalpable fineness; the afternoon light on the dunes with "exquisite and unpaintable delicacy of dimple and curve and shadow"[5]; the rapidly changing hues of sunrise and sunset painting the gleaming canvas of sand; the tiny population of desert insects burrowing in the subterranean coolness. She loved to travel the spaces between town and oasis by camel, camping at night in a tent under the stars. In the desert, far from the stench and squalor of the Algiers slums, her soul was rested and revived:

> *Oh, the desert is lovely in its restfulness—the great brooding stillness over and through everything is so full of God. One does not wonder that He used to take His people out into the wilderness to teach them. (1895)*

So intense was the lure of the desert to her that Lilias would, through the years, subject the pull of the Southlands to a special test of the Spirit to ensure that it was of God. In her diary she once wrote:

> *Such a cry has awakened these last days to get down to the desert again . . . a great deal of attraction to all that . . . I don't suppose He can let me go until it has been dealt with & supplanted with a fellowship with Himself about these places. (1899)*

In May, Lilias and Helen returned to Algiers to the work being carried on by Blanche and the Bradings. They had their first Arab prayer meeting at which they specifically prayed that God would bring new native men to them, believing this now to be the necessary focus in the ministry. The next evening eight new men showed up at the meeting—a sign and seal, they felt, of God's direction.

Throughout the summer and fall, the workers carried on with the struggling nucleus of believers—black Belaid and his wife, Yamina; young Taitum, with her growing brood of children; and Mohammed, Dahman, and Mahfoud, young Arab boys from Algiers, who during the summer "crossed over into the light." They continued with the ministry of loving the Arab people, through identification and involvement in their lives and through the house-to-house visitation.

At the same time, the conviction that they were to evangelize the great unreached stretches beyond the coastline—"as far and as fast as we can" —was strengthened by the addititonal workers in Algiers and by the receptivity of the Arab people. Lilias records, "There is hardly ever a day now that we do not get a link with some place outside Alger—We feel that the inland places are opening just as the Alger houses opened three years ago."[6]

On 20 November 1894, Lily and Blanche set off across the plain in a "country diligence" toward the mountain villages surrounding Tablatt, a small French town some seven hours inland. They were going to a people who had never heard the name of Christ. They visited village after village, distributing Gospels along the way, seeking access to the people, and when they could get a hearing, telling the story of the Cross. "It is so beautiful to be allowed to tell it for the first time!"[7] Lily's writes. "If only we could sleep in their huts and just go on! Oh, to get down amongst them as Jesus did!"[8]

Mountain travel, like desert travel, had its own peculiar perils—including long tramps along steep mountain trails when donkeys were not available, and when they were, the risks of faulty harnessing and shoeing, riding on saddles without pommels or stirrups. Ever present dogs, heavy rains, and swollen rivers (across which they were literally carried by their mule driver) were only a few of the obstacles they faced, but the welcome Lilias felt from the people more than compensated for any danger or discomfort. She reported:

> *Oh, it is wonderful to be allowed to break the silence in which God has been loving them all the time. We believe there will be a real work of the Spirit among these mountains, there is so much more sense of sin than in Algiers. "Oh, we are bad!" the people say. "We lie, we quarrel," and other words I don't understand.*[9]

Lilias found touching the way the people would pick up and pass on the little bits of truth they did understand:

I saw one sad-faced woman with her arms round a chubby, dark-eyed child. "You love that little girl," I said. "Yes; I am a widow," she answered, "and she is as my eyes." "That is the way God loves you," I said. "He tells us we are as His eyes," and passed on. In the next group we came to, I overheard one of the lads telling a new woman that we had come to tell them that God loves them as His eyes. Oh, that they may know and believe the love that He hath to us! (1894)

When they reluctantly prepared to take leave of the mountain people, Lilias and Blanche did not know when they would, if ever, return. In her journal, Lilias painted a man scattering seeds along a hillside from a basket slung over his shoulder, backed by blue sky and indigo mountains, and beside this she wrote: "& so the seed scatters, & we know not which shall prosper, like the seedsowing that is going on before our eyes on every hill side."[10]

Back in Algiers they celebrated Christmas at Rue du Croissant, decorated with evergreens, "keeping Christmas for the first time in [the house's] life."[11] Lily concludes a memorable 1894 with the words, "And now the year is dying out. Will next year bring the dawn?"[12]

With the dawn of 1895 came the most ambitious journey yet undertaken: an expedition, almost five months in duration, by camel caravan to the Southlands. Informed now as to the requirements of travel over plain, mountain, and desert, Lilias had a clear plan and a purpose. The plan was to follow the string of mountain villages stretching eastward along the desert edge of the Aures mountain range, then south into the desert to the district of Djerid to visit Tozeur and Nefta, two large towns just within the borders of Tunisia. If time and strength held out, she hoped to revisit the Oued Souf and Touggourt, traveling southwest across the desert from the Djerid. Their aim was to follow up previous contacts, to advance the penetration of the gospel within the mountain villages further inland, and to assess the land for possible mission stations.

Lilias and Blanche set off in mid-January from Biskra with their caravan (three camels, a mule, and a donkey), Edgington tent, trestle hammocks, and native camp outfit of iron cooking things and colorful goatskins holding their provisions. Accompanying them was a camel driver and Abdulla, their guide of most dubious qualifications. Lilias wrote: "We have a strong suspicion that Abdulla does not know the way, and wants someone to guide him![13] What transpires on their journey is as much a story of God's guidance as a travel tale. Lilias concluded that

> *one learns slowly that one can do nothing mechanically in this itinerating work—that one cannot choose a place, or settle to stay long in it, or push into many houses in it, simply because it is large and important—we want to learn "whithersoever the Spirit was to go they went—thither was their spirit to go" [Ezekiel 1:20].*[14]

The adventures that follow the fearless twosome (recorded in a 186-page illustrated journal) could easily make an epic adventure movie. They were two English ladies dressed in long woolen skirts, mounted on camels in caravan hugging the mountain edge by day, or camped by night in a tent pitched on the outskirt of a village. They brewed coffee over a little camp stove heated by glowing wood-ash and slept on hammock trestles within the folds of a tent while gusts of wind threatened to literally raise the roof.

Day after day, they worked their way along the desert edge, facing the caprice of the elements—rain and wind—and the whim of their guide, who was prone to displays of temper and heavy drinking. Once they found themselves prisoners of etiquette, stranded for days as guests of an aristocratic Arab *caid* (or chief). Another time they were followed day after day—untouched—by the most noted thief in the region. Everywhere the presence of these strange women with "books and medicine" drew a crowd, and often an audience, especially among the men.

In late February, the travelers caught the first glimpse of their intended bit of desert:

> *Then at last at a sudden turn the desert opened before us afresh, with its blue sea-like horizon line and as we got out into it a dim line of low hills came into view beyond the Chott to the left, which we knew instantly must be the Djerid, the centre of our hopes and longings for this expedition, the goal of our struggling on. (22 February 1895)*

Turning their backs to the mountains, they began the three-day march south along the great chott that lay between them and their hopes. Upon arrival, they first visited oases along the northeastern edge of the Djerid chott, then worked their way westward, where they camped at last at Tozeur.

> *The fortnight we had there we shall thank God always, I believe, right into eternity. From the first we felt that the Spirit was brooding over the place and that His word had a strange power on the hearts, simply His word, with very little of explanation or comment of our own. We did not get into a single house in the town, only in the villages round, and in them there was a lovely spirit of listening and, as always when the hearts are opened, such a spirit of giving—more eggs and dates and oranges than we knew how to carry. But, as before, it was chiefly among the men that we felt God's door stood wide; they would be round us in groups of six to twenty or more, every hour of the day, till sometimes for the sake of the time with God that one felt one must have, we had to send them off and take refuge in the lovely palm forest that stretched away behind us. They were touchingly eager for the books. "There are 4,000 in the town who can read," they said. "If you had a pile as big as your tent they would all go"; they knew our store was running low, and would ask so gently, "Could you exchange this Gospel for another; I swallowed this last night!" And the questions they asked showed how thoughtfully they had read—in no cavilling spirit for the most part—only wanting to know and glad to get an answer.*[15]

Two men impressed them in a special way with their hunger for God's Word—a schoolmaster named Si Taher and a blind marabout (or holy man) named Si Mohammed—and they longed to stay on and talk further with them. It was getting late, however, for going farther south, and they felt strongly that they needed to get to the Oued Souf to pick up the threads of their past visit. They also hoped to meet some Touraregs (the masked camel riders who dominated the mountainous core of the deep Sahara) who occasionally visited El Oued, the chief Souf village in Oued Souf. So, after a short and unresponsive visit to Nefta (an oasis twenty miles west of Tozeur), they packed and provisioned themselves for the next vast stretch of desert travel.

In late March the unique caravan—Lilias, Blanche, Abdulla the guide, and their cameldrivers Keroui and Aoun—began the five-day trek southwest across the great Eastern Erg toward the Souf villages of Oued Souf. From Lilias's camel-top vantage point she recorded the sights and sounds of the Sahara: "the first creamy drifts of the real desert sand, soft and deep," the "exquisite notes of two mokkars [desert birds] answering each other like boy angels trying their golden pipes," the "delicate tracery of tiny tracks—beetles, lizards, Jerboa rats and birds."[16]

Abdullah did not find the journey quite so poetic, and Keroui, the camel driver said pathetically, "Tomorrow I shall die," so hot was the weather and parched their lips. The third evening the sun set in "lurid streamers of brown cloud that augured ill, and in the night came the wind in gusts that tried the strength of . . . tent poles and cords to their utmost." And thus began their battle with a true Saharan sandstorm as recorded by Lilias:

> *The next day was a battling on in simple endurance through a blinding blizzard of sand—Every trace of footprints round our tent had been swept away, and the track was invisible as we journeyed on, to our eyes at any rate. A knotted head of broom now and then proved that the men knew what they were about and that we were keeping right.*
>
> *We camped early as the wind was getting stronger and stronger, and it seemed doubtful if we should ever get up the tent. "The world is wind" poor old Aoun observed wearily as we struggled with it, all six of us together. At last we got it secure and crept thankfully into its frail shelter. Toward evening the gusts lessened, and the stars came out of the brown sand-clouds, and the next morning dawned clear and calm, shewing round the western half of the horizon range after range of snow-like sand-hills, rose-tinted in the sunrise: and we knew that buried among them were the villages for which we were making—villages where "the True Light" had never yet dawned.*
>
> *How the angels must watch the first day when that light reaches a new spot on this earth that God so loves—and the great wall of dark-*

ness is pushed back one tiny bit—and oh the joy of being allowed to go with His message that first day. How can His people hold back from that joy while one corner remains unvisited by the Dayspring! (March 1895)

In the Oued Souf—that region of desert oases along the buried river bed—the two women brought "Daylight" for the first time to Souf villages of hidden palms and beehive dwellings. The general response, however, was disappointing. Though in El Oued, their great hope was realized: they met for the first time a Touraget from the great nomadic tribes of the deep Sahara, a man who gladly took the Scripture portions they bundled up for him, promising to bring them to his people and giving Lilias and Blanche "little treasures" in exchange.

The last halting before heading northward was in Touggourt, where they revisited people from the previous trip. One woman with a wide-awake face listened intently to the story of Jesus and responded with earnestness. Lilias records the event this way:

"We have had no news of this: we are getting old but we have never heard this before—no one has come to tell us except you!" Dear soul, one little short half hour's telling was all that she could have after the life-long delay. "You will come back next year?" "We cannot tell"—I wonder in how many places they have said "Why do you not stay—why do you not come and live with us?"(1895)

No, they could not stay, but they left the desert with the strong determination to return and to stay longer, perhaps in one of the dome-shaped dwellings of the Souf. As one last Souf present to themselves, they took roses fresh and sweet out of the sand—"a pledge of the blossoming that is coming to the desert when the Lord is king."[17]

12

ENGLAND INTERLUDE: A SCENT OF SPRING

July 1895—January 1896

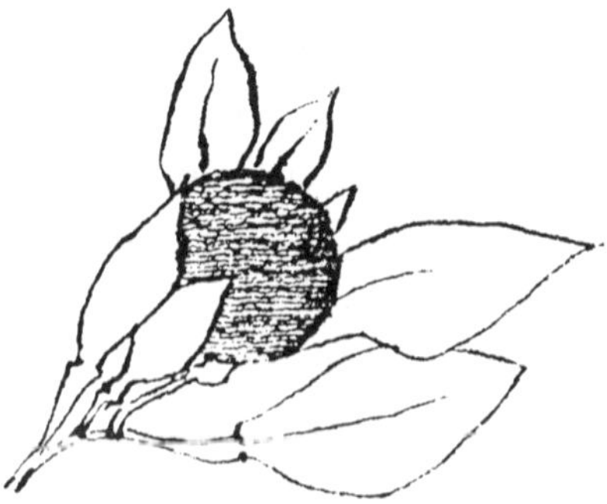

My eyes feast on the clear emerald green in its grey setting of rock and stone wall. One sees how it would be garish in our African sun, and how our dull blue-greens are what are needed there—God's harmonizings are so beautiful—but the vividness of it under these cool skies is a joy.

—Journal[1]

There was good news and bad news awaiting Lilias and Blanche upon their return to Algiers. On the positive side, Hamdan, who was the first boy they had made friends with in the old Arab town, and who with self-appointment had made himself their protector, had reappeared on the scene. He came with the same eager, fearless spirit that had marked him when but a "scrap of a boy." The three Arab converts, Mohammed, Dahman, and Mahfoud, had survived the perils of Ramadan, resisting the pressure to comply with the annual thirty-day Muslim fast, albeit secretly, and were struggling on as best they could in the small weekly meetings, as were the handful of women in their respective classes.

A great blow, not unexpected, was the Brading family's decision to leave North Africa for health reasons. Lilias reported, "The doctor had said months before that he could not answer for the children's lives if they stayed on in the Arab town and now Mr. Brading too was flagging more and more." The women remaining in Algiers could only concur it was best, yet Lilias's heart was revealed in her poignant comment, "'They leave a missing' as the Arabs say."[2]

Lilias did not want to return to England for the summer, leaving the fledging souls alone even for a few months, yet all pointed to that necessity: Blanche was still suffering the effects of the sun, and even Lilias admitted to being "rather good for nothing since we got back" as well as to "longing to get away alone somewhere for a month."[3] So, putting Belaid and Yamina in charge of Rue du Croissant, Lilias left Algiers for what she believed would be a few summer months.

It was a totally depleted Lilias who arrived in England. The strain of unbroken months of travel with no significant rest in between, to say nothing of the sheer wear of the climate, had taken its toll on her already weakened heart, leaving her on the verge of breakdown. In her fragile physical state, the emotional strains of ministry weighed heavily upon her. She ached for the struggling souls left behind in Algiers: "There are times when their feebleness weighs down upon one and human hope and courage flag—and only the God-given indwelling 'faith of the Son of God' can overleap the difficulties and discouragements and land down with both feet on the promises of God."[4] Sad and discouraging letters from the "dear baby souls" in the region of the Southlands left her wrestling with their plight: "How one's heart aches for them standing alone with no human sympathy or help within hundreds of miles of mountains and desert."[5] And Lilias bore an overwhelming sense of the enormity of the mission—"more and more one sees that everything that is done, put together, barely touches the outermost fringe of what is left undone."[6] On top of all that was the shadow of an *interpellation*—a formal representation in the French Chamber in Paris—against all English missionaries in Algeria—the result of a growing French antagonism against England.

Alone at last, in Rosthwaite, in the Lake District of England, she writes resignedly,

At present I don't seem to have sense for any concentration in praying or anything else, and am just vegetating and writing up this journal and drawing its pictures, for in its present form it had to come to a dead stop about the end of January, and will have to be disentangled from very promiscuous notes in tiny notebooks, written and drawn on camel-back or in stray moments while supper was cooking or while the beasts were lading.[7]

Lilias began to adjust her vision from a sun-parched North Africa to a lush-green England and to feast her eyes on "God's harmonizings" for the refreshment of her soul. Given her literal desert experience, it is not surprising that God spoke to her through water—first in a dew drop, then in a stream—as recorded in her journal.

He maketh small the drops of "water." I have never seen how literally true that is till I began studying the dew these mornings. Let a drop fall from your finger and you will see its natural size: but that would be too heavy for the frail little blades to bear—it would slip off them from its weight—so He weighs out to each the tiny measure that it can bear without even being bowed down, yet enough to "drink into" in abundance. On one wee filament of moss I counted through a magnifying glass forty-six little globes of water in what just looked like moisture to the naked eye—on one side only, without turning it. (30 July 1895)

Another thing—the grass has to stand very still as it holds its precious "weight of glory"—and so has the soul on whom the dew of the Spirit comes—literally easily as this dew, His dew is brushed off—some of us know it to our cost—an impulse of impatience—a sense of hurry or worry allowed to touch us—a mere movement of the self-life against His checking, and He is gone, and our soul stands stripped and bare. Noiseless must be His Holy Habitation within us—still with the stillness of the Holiest Place of old, with all the camp sounds shut out by the four-fold curtain and the very footfall of the priests hushed by the desert sand. (30 July 1895)

"Out of him shall flow" comes afresh these days, brought home by a landlocked backwater in the little river here, that only lets its stream filter slowly through a bank of stones instead of running free. The still pool of living water lies in every saved soul, keeping life within that little plot of a river. A river is wide open to its source, and as wide open to the needs lower down. We need barriers down, man-ward as well as God-ward—to believe for the outflowing as definitely as the inflowing. (3 August 1895)

Lilias's intended month in Rosthwaite was cut short by rains and subsequent flooding from the mountains. She divided the remaining summertime in England between Crowthorne (in the southern county of Berkshire) and London, enjoying visits with old friends and family, but not gaining either her "month alone" or physical strength. Finally, in October, for what she described as "the pacifying of my dear people," she submitted to seeing a doctor who prescribed "that I should stay in England till the end of November, not get over-tired for about two years, and meantime go to the sea for a fortnight—alone if I didn't mind!"[8]

The resulting seaside visit at Eastbourne could not have been better timed, for it was here that she received the news that the dreaded "interpellation" would, in fact, take place in November, putting in jeopardy the work in Algeria, and more immediately delaying their return. She went down to the shore to "spread it before the Lord" and to hear what "He had to say about it."[9] She writes,

I was watching vaguely the breaking of the waves while listening for His voice. Suddenly there came, clothed in His living power, the words—"Fear ye not me, saith the Lord, which have placed the sand for a bound of the sea that they cannot pass; though the waves thereof toss themselves yet can they not prevail: though they roar they shall not pass over it!" Oh with what joy it came as one watched them hurling themselves in with all their might and succeeding in doing nothing but washing a few tiny pebbles a few inches and dragging others back in their place—such power, and such impotence! (5 November 1895)

Another sea message came on Sunday in Church, through the morning Psalms—"Thy way is in the sea and Thy path in the deep waters —Thy footsteps are not known." There is no trace of His path after more than before—but He has reached His end! And seen from above "Thy way is in the sanctuary" all the time; clear and calm and visible: it is only on earth that it seems in the storm. (18 November 1895)

Looking back, it is clear that God used these delays in their return to Algeria for His purposes. Most immediately, Lilias needed a radical complete rest before resuming the work ahead. She writes, "It has begun to look as if I were meant still to stay on in England, for sleep will not come back, and the only thing left to try, as far as means go, seems a "rest cure" of a month or so of bed and no visitors or letters." And she adds ruefully, "Perhaps this is to be the month with God that I have been trying for ever since getting to England!"[10]

In the even bigger picture, all evidence indicates that during the many delays of the autumn and winter months, Lilias wrote her great devotional classic, *The Parables of the Cross,* born, no doubt, out of her own travail of soul and tempered with her breadth of life experience. Undated, the first of her two parable books falls within the window of 1892 to 1896, and, given her activities, this is the only plausible period in which she would have had the time to write a work of such comprehension and scope. Furthermore, there are within her journal at this time repeated references to the "dying to live" theme that is the thesis of *The Parables of the Cross:* Via Crucis, Via Lucis—"Death is the Gate of Life." She writes,

There came such a lovely sense—not through anything that was said specially I think—of what it means to be "buried with Christ"—not only dead but buried—"put to silence in the grave"—"I can" and "I

can't" put to silence side by side—the lovely silence and stillness of "a grave beside Him" with God's seal on the stone and His watch set, that nothing but the risen life of Jesus may come forth.

"Give me a death in which there shall be no life, and a life in which there shall be no death"—That was a prayer of the Arab saint, Abed-El-Kader—I came upon it again the other day—is it not wonderful

And all nature here is full of such intense quietness, these autumn days. A solemn quietness, with the sense of the spring behind it, like Easter Eve—the dear living things are going into their graves—and one sees how the grave is a must-be. "Fall into the ground and die"—not upon it. The road outside our lodging is strewn with acorns that will never come to anything because they are just lying on the ground, not in it. "Fall into"—not "struggle into." (6 October 1895)

As Lilias was resting her body and soul, she was continuing to learn lessons of release—"dying" even to the finest of intentions and purposes, particularly in regards to the people of Algeria: "It has come with a sense of utter rest, these last days, that God expects nothing from us in all this or in anything else for that matter—and it is when we have got to the point of seeing that God expects nothing from us, that we can expect everything from Him."[11]

It is interesting to note that she dedicated the *Parables of the Cross* to "B.A.B." (probably Blanche Bannister from the Training Home at Olivage) and to "A.C."—Amy Carmichael of Dohnavur in India. While Lilias and Amy never met, they were kindred spirits, coming from similar backgrounds in Britain and having both been deeply influenced by the Keswick Conferences. Each woman possessed that rare combination of pioneer and poet, developing ministries in their respective countries while writing devotional literature of depth and grace. They would, through the years, keep informed of each other's work through their published writings and personal correspondence. Inspired by the example of this woman fourteen years her junior, Lilias later would encourage the children in Algeria to support the children at Dohnavur with their prayers and offerings, as she herself did.

One cannot read about this period of time without asking certain questions. Consider the activities of the previous two and a half years: four major itinerations plus the ongoing program in Algiers. If she were under the care of a modern mission board, would she have been permitted to keep such a punishing pace? Would her activities have been monitored sufficiently so that she avoided a health crisis? In short, was there anything she could have done to have avoided such a state of collapse?

Setting aside the obvious consideration that with her heart condition, she would not be accepted by any mission board—then or now!—one must acknowledge that she appeared relentless in her activity, going the extra mile without, it seems, the slightest concern for her health. Yet, pace notwithstanding, she was equally "relentless" in setting aside significant blocks of time daily for periods alone with God, sometimes early in the morning, other times breaking away from activity for that purpose. And yet her situation is not so unusual: The climate and condition of the area where she lived has retired many a worker, even men of strong constitution.

At that time, and throughout the rest of her life, Lilias would ascribe the "health challenge" for anyone engaged in this work to a combination of factors, both physical and spiritual, a view summed up in a little booklet, *A South Land,* which she wrote to "fellow-labourers" among Muslims:

> *And it may be that our souls have felt the scorching breath—nerves get overstrung in these climates in a way they never did before, and little things bring a ruffle and jar, and cannot be shaken off again; and a sense of exhaustion comes through the body to the spirit, even apart from the consciousness, so vivid at times, that the very air is full of the powers of darkness; and the enemy launches his fiery darts in showers on those who come to attack his strongholds. How many of us have gone through the testing of every fibre of our inner life since we left England—and how many of us have known a bitter breaking down under the tests!*[12]

The solution as much as humanly possible, she believed, was to seek avidly times of daily refreshment with God, and—she would gradually come to realize—to secure times of retreat within terms of service. Still, she believed the greatest battle to be spiritual: Nerves strained by physical stress become a playground for "the Enemy" who would not have his stronghold broken. Increasingly and more fervently throughout the years, Lilias appealed for prayer on behalf of overseas missionaries, recognizing that without a divine call few would survive the first three years in such a work. During the England interlude she wrote a booklet, *A Challenge to Faith,* toward this end, saying in part:

> *A story of the wars of the first Napoleon has often come back to me. He was trying, in a winter campaign, to cut off the march of the enemy across a frozen lake. The gunners were told to fire on the ice and break it, but the cannon-balls glanced harmlessly along the surface. With one of the sudden flashes of genius he gave the word, "Fire upwards!" and the balls crashed down full weight, shattering the whole sheet into fragments, and the day was won. You can "fire upwards" in this battle, even if you are shut out from fighting it face to face.*[13]

Rested at last, body and soul, Lilias set forth for Algeria in late January of 1896. On the train to Marseilles, from which she would board the steamer to Algiers, she anticipates being once again among blue skies and jessamine, observing the last bit of northern winter:

> *One gets more of the breath of spring through the little half-asleep January buds, than through all the wealth of beauty down south. It is something like that with the feebly breaking life in those hearts out there in the darkness—there is a joy over it deeper even than in the summer-tide of the spiritual atmosphere in England. Is it not so that the Lord looks down on the earth, it may be, alongside the radiant beauty of His Kingdom already set up in other worlds? He sees the slowly swelling buds of His dawning springtime here, and is glad.*[14]

With that breath of spring scenting the realm of faith, Lilias writes:

Through all the fogs, through
all earth's wintry skies
I scent the spring, I feel
the eternal air
Warm soft & dewy, filled with
flowery eyes
And gentle murmuring motions
everywhere
Of life in bird & tree & brook
& moss—
Thy breath wakes beauty, faith &
bliss & prayer
And strength to hang with nails
upon Thy Cross.[15]

13
STORM CLOUDS AND STAR GLEAMS
1896—1899

The things that are impossible with men are possible with God. May it not be that the human impossibility is just the very thing that sets His Hand free?—& that it is the things which are possible for us to do that He is in a measure to let alone.

—Diary[1]

Rest, alone, could not prepare Lilias for the storm clouds awaiting her in Algeria. The unfolding events of the next three years, as recorded in her journal, read like the evolution of a worst-case scenario: bad, worse, worst. The story bears telling for its documentation not only of the outer events of her life but also of the inner events of her soul: in the darkest of times God was working, guiding, and speaking, while lifting Lilias's human spirit above the circumstances. What emerges is an account of one woman's journey of faith, of her walking blind, so to speak, under deepening clouds of doubt, disappointment, and discouragement. And it is a story of God's ways, His light shining through the darkest clouds, bringing glimpses of grace and glory.

The shadow of the French investigation, the *interpellation,* continued to hover over the workers in Algeria. It was repeatedly postponed, yet unresolved, and aroused the Algerians' suspicions toward the missionaries as well as the Arabs' fear of being identified with them. With the exception of a few special friends, there was none of the usual welcome awaiting Lilias's return. Attendance at meetings and classes slackened, with only two or three men at any given meeting, and no women at all. Adding to the sense of helplessness, the rigorous and demanding observance of the Muslim fast of Ramadan began soon after her arrival, legislating against any initiative on the Englishwomen's part, visiting during Ramadan being, as a rule, against their local etiquette. They were forced to stand back and watch the fragile young converts falter and fail without their usual supply of nourishment and fellowship.

Then came the report of official developments that "the *interpellation* should be made in the course of a month or two, and that it would be preceded by the sending over of one of the members of the French Chamber for the purpose of making a close and searching investigation into all the sayings and doings of the missionaries."[2] With the political spotlight now trained on all English missionaries, their every movement began to be monitored by police and observed by spies. Newspapers published false stories—most, political in nature—accusing them of treason against the French government. Their work among the Arabs, for all practical purposes of program or advance, came to a standstill.

The morning after that grim news, Lilias opened her shutters at daybreak and watched the sky as the sun rose, writing in her journal: "The pillars of cloud themselves on the horizon melted first into glistening fragments and then sank into the opal sky—and the Word came how God's enemies shall be 'as the morning cloud and as the early dew that passeth away.'"[3] In her journal, she painted the pillars of clouds against a sky golden in sunrise, a visual reminder of God's ultimate victory: *His* Sun rising.

Undaunted, Lilias began to reconsider their work in light of the new developments. First, she reevaluated what their stance should be toward the handful remaining with them: "all one can do is to begin far back, as God begins, with the little feeble beginnings, and learn from Him how to make the utmost meanwhile, of the bits of material that He has given us, poor though it may seem."[4]

Next, she rethought their expectations of the Arab believers:

I have been seeing so clearly lately how they must be trained in every way possible to give, not just to receive—and it has come as the solution at last of the problem of ours, how to fulfil the commands about not shutting up our compassion from them, without weakening their moral fibre—They must learn to give as well as we—that is the plain solution.[5]

Finally, she reviewed the mission workers' strategy. With their access to the Arab people severely limited, she returned to the idea of their early years in Algeria, of reaching the Arab people through the Arab-speaking French, an idea which co-worker Helen Freeman initially deemed sad, as it seemed a step backwards. Ever-practical Lilias observed, however, (and Helen agreed):

There was no use in wasting the evenings in sitting waiting for Arabs who did not come, while there were those glad to take the chance of hearing. To me it was not so sad, for it seemed a returning to "the pattern shewed in the mount"—the dream of the first months out here, eight years ago, that God's way would be to get Arab-speaking French people saved, as fellow-workers among the Arabs . . . workers 'raised off the soil' whom no one could turn out.[6]

Meetings were held for the French, led by a young Swiss worker, Jean Renand, and from that, plans evolved for bringing him and his family from Switzerland to join them in Algiers in order to carry on the work among the French. They secured a little house for them at the edge of the Arab town and rented a hall, as in days past, in the center of town, near the Place du Gouvernement where people of all nations thronged. God's ways were glimmering through the very dark clouds of difficulty.

Lilias, pondering their experiences, writes,

Things still look dark and heavy all round—but "when the clouds be full of rain they empty themselves upon the earth"—it is better to wait as the parched ground waits here, for the torrents that will set life going. And I am beginning to see that it is out of a low place that one can best believe. "Great is thy faith" came to the Syrophenician

In the Garden, a lily (circa 1878), from the John Ruskin Long Cabinet at the Ashmolean Museum. Used by permission.

Photo by Steve Sonheim

Assortment of journals, diaries, and sketchbooks*: (top to bottom) Open journal (1907); closed diary (1899); open diary (1907); sketchbook (1878); sketchbook (1888).

*All of Lilias Trotter's journals, diaries, sketchbooks, and artwork, unless otherwise noted, are used courtesy of Arab World Ministry archives.

(Above) Reader outside a café in Algiers (1888), enclosure in a letter.
(Below) Flower; back view of robed man (1888), Algerian sketchbook.

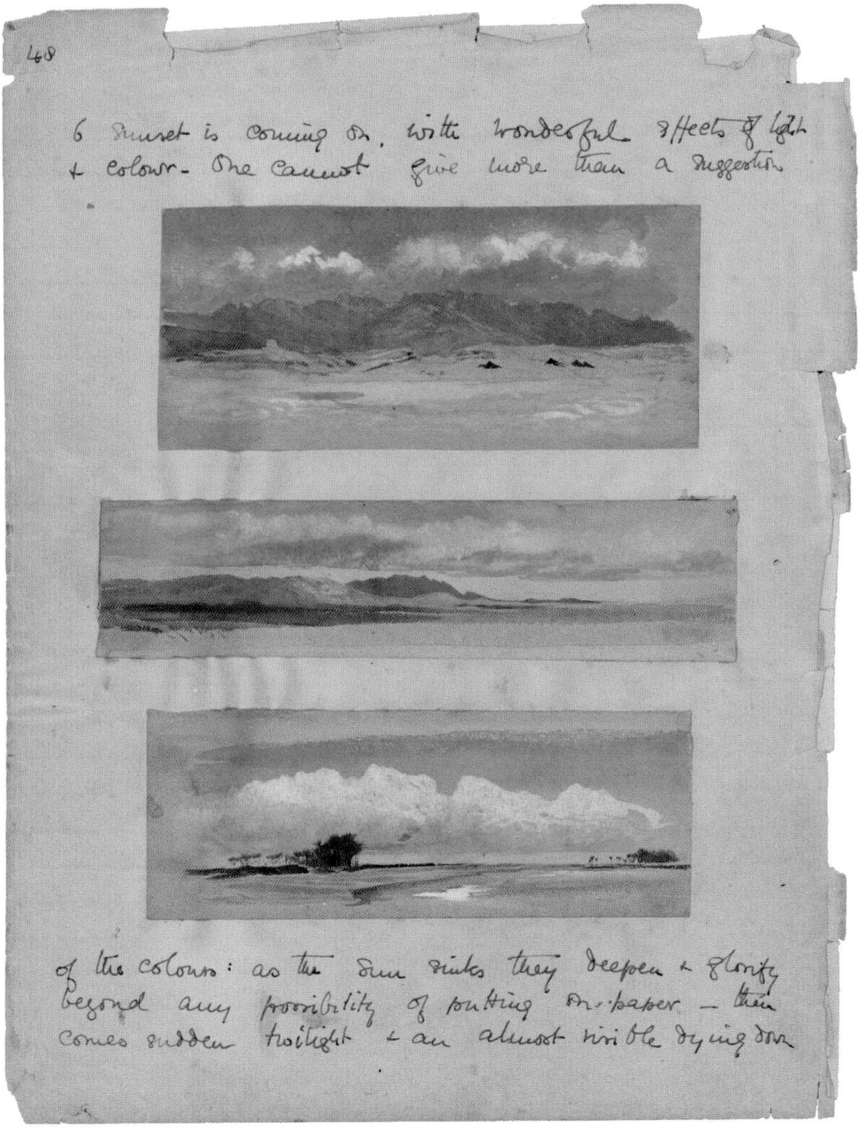
48
6 Sunset is coming on, with wonderful effects of light
+ colour - One cannot give more than a suggestion
of the colours: as the sun sinks they deepen & glorify
beyond any possibility of putting on paper — then
comes sudden twilight & an almost visible dying down

Views of a desert sunset near Biskra (1893), Journal: *Sunset is coming on, with wonderful effect of light & colour—one cannot give more than a suggestion of the colours; as the sun sinks they deepen & glorify beyond any possibility of putting on paper.*

Skylight of latticed palm stalks in a Tolga house, Southlands (1900), Journal: *I don't think anything has ever been quite like that joy of getting back to one of these desert villages—to be living in a real native house of their own building.*

Scenes from Blida, a mountain village thirty miles outside Algiers (1899), Diary.

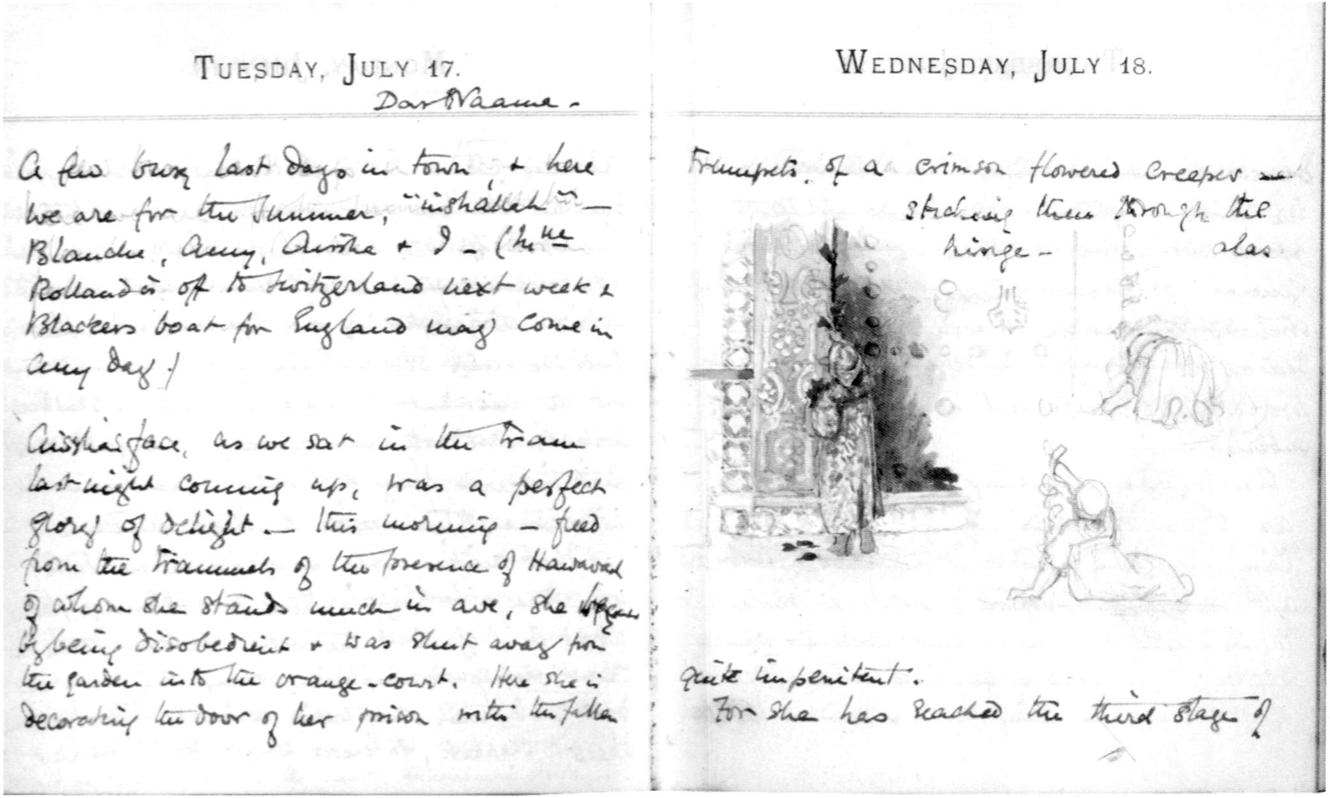

TUESDAY, JULY 17.

Dar Naama.

A few busy last days in town, & here we are for the summer, "inshallah" — Blanche, Amy, Aissha & I — (the Rollands off to Switzerland next week & Blackers boat for England may come in any day!)

Aissha's face, as we sat in the tram last night coming up, was a perfect glory of delight — this morning — freed from the trammels of the presence of Hamwood of whom she stands much in awe, she began by being disobedient & was shut away from the garden into the orange-court. Here she is decorating the door of her prison with the fallen

WEDNESDAY, JULY 18.

trumpets of a crimson flowered creeper — sticking them through the hinge — alas

quite impenitent.

For she has reached the third stage of

Aissha in the Orange Court at Dar Naama (1906), Diary.

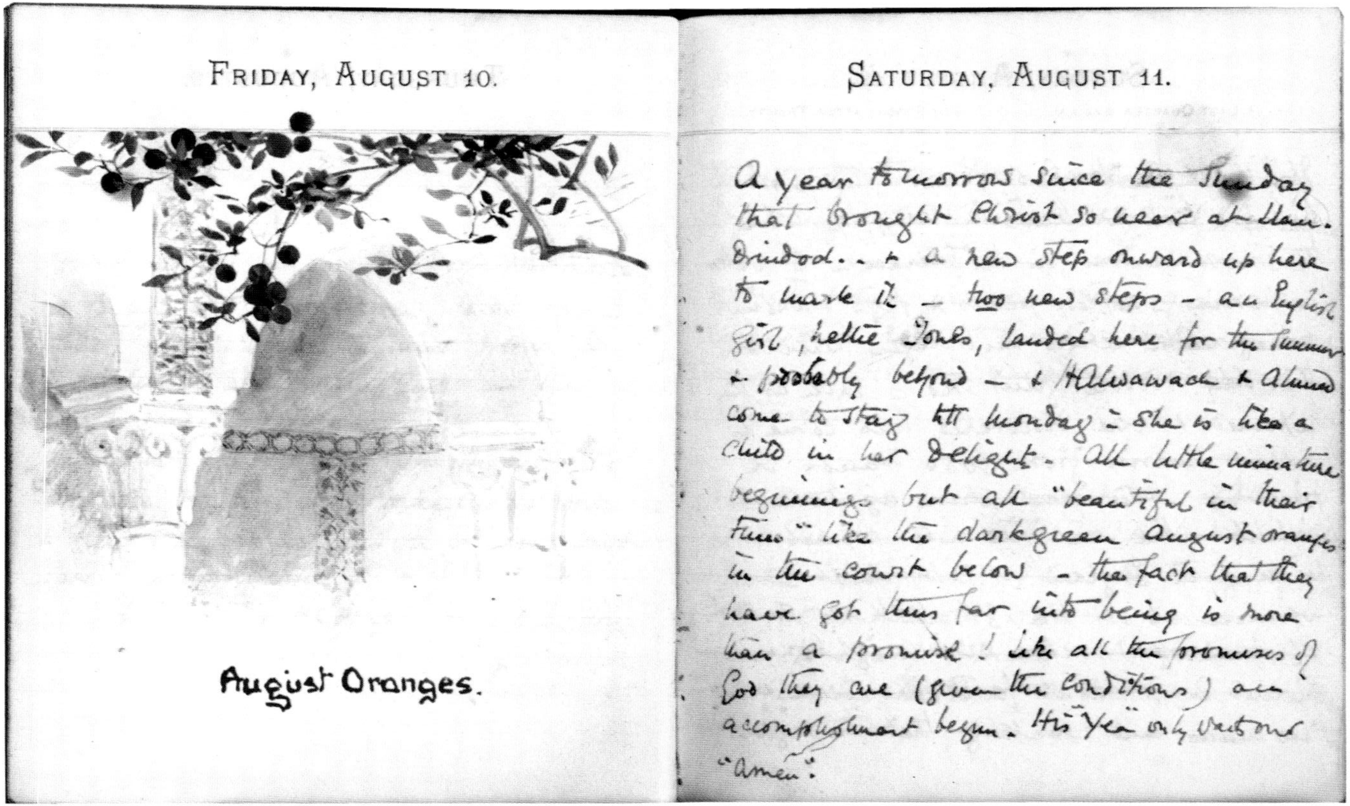

August Oranges, courtyard at Dar Naama (1906), Diary: *August oranges . . . all miniature beginnings but all "beautiful in their time."*

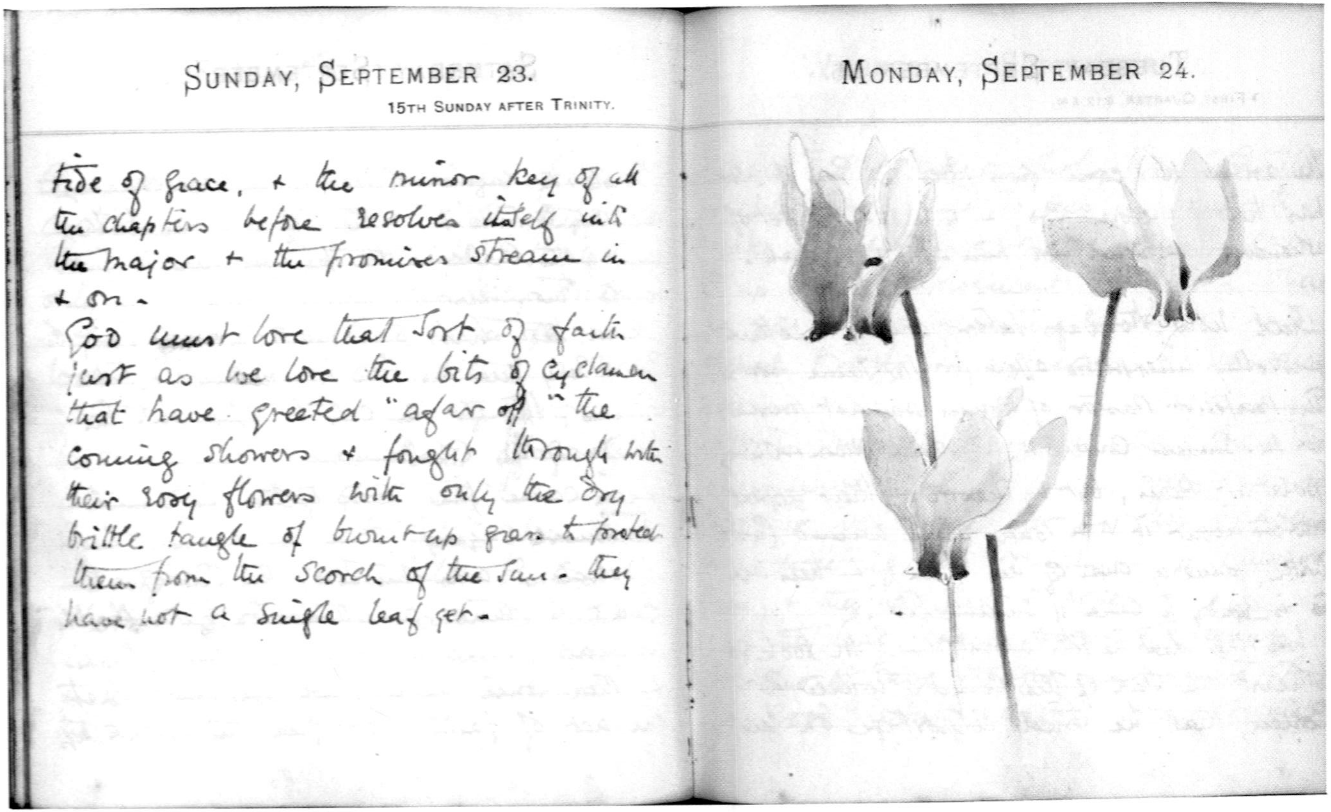
SUNDAY, SEPTEMBER 23.
15TH SUNDAY AFTER TRINITY.

tide of grace, + the minor key of all the chapters before resolves itself into the major + the promises stream in + on.
God must love that sort of faith just as we love the bits of cyclamen that have greeted "afar off" the coming showers + fought through with their rosy flowers with only the dry brittle tangle of burnt-up grass to protect them from the scorch of the sun. They have not a single leaf yet.

MONDAY, SEPTEMBER 24.

Cyclamen (1906), Diary: *Bits of cyclamen that have greeted "afar off" the coming showers.*

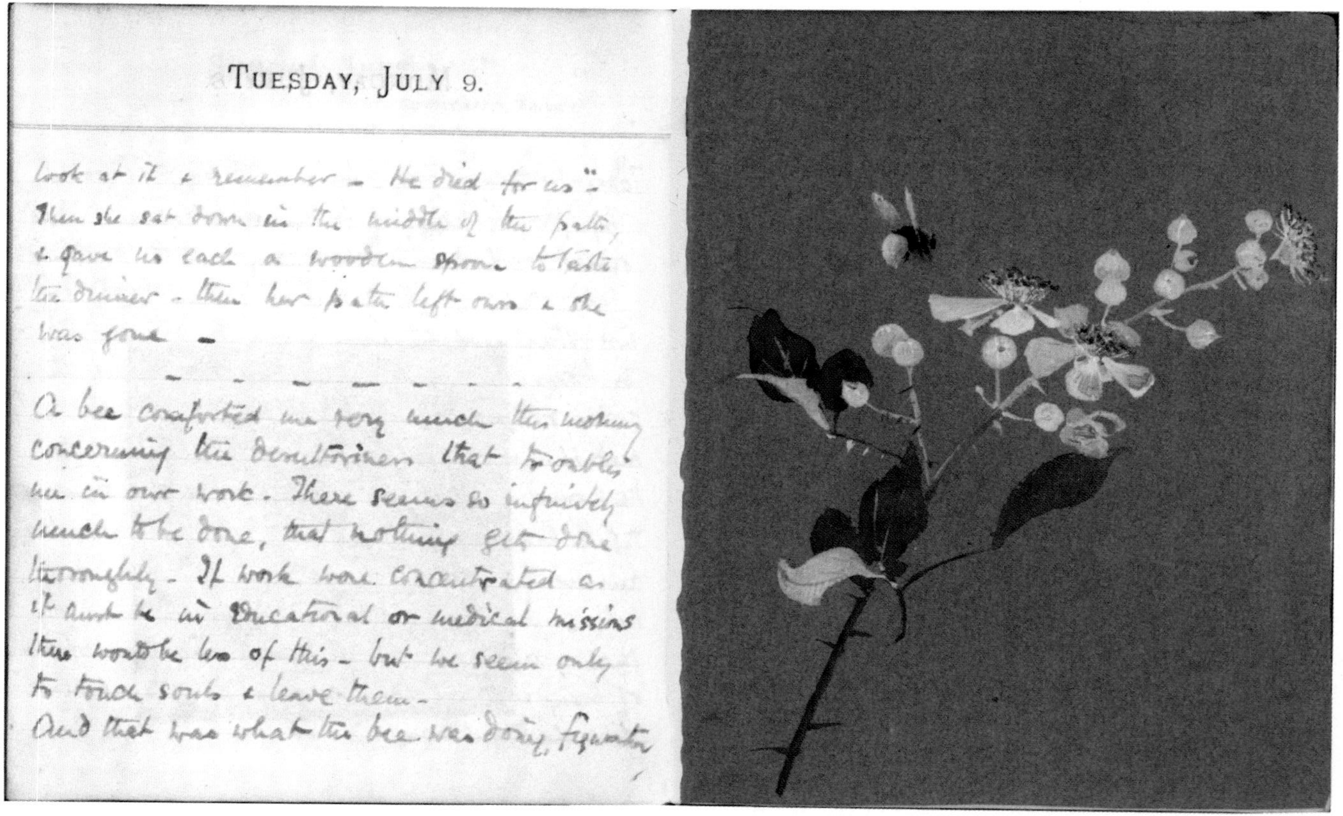
TUESDAY, JULY 9.

look at it & remember — He died for us"—
Then she sat down in the middle of the path,
& gave us each a wooden spoon to taste
the dinner — then her pater left ours & she
was gone —

— — — — — —

A bee comforted me very much this morning
concerning the desultoriness that troubles
me in our work. There seems so infinitely
much to be done, that nothing gets done
thoroughly — If work were concentrated as
it must be in Educational or medical missions
there would be less of this — but we seem only
to touch souls & leave them —
And that was what the bee was doing, figurativ

Bee hovering among blackberry sprays (1907), Diary: *A bee comforted me very much this morning concerning the desultoriness that troubles me in our work.*

Algiers, plate A, from *Between the Desert and the Sea* (published by Marshall, Morgan and Scott, circa 1927).

On the Way South, plate H, from *Between the Desert and the Sea*

Out and Beyond, plate P, from *Between the Desert and the Sea*

Wild iris pods, color plate from *Parables of the Cross* (published by Marshall Brothers, circa 1895): *See in these wild iris-pods how the last tiny threads must be broken, and with that loosing, all that they have is free for God's use in his world around.*

Title page from *The Bird Book* (published by Niles Mission Press, circa 1927).

Cover page for the booklet *Sand Lilies* (published by Marshall Brothers, n.d.).

woman who called herself a dog, and to the centurion who held himself unworthy that the Lord should come under his roof—it was to Jacob halting on his thigh that the Angel said "thou hast power with God." It is water poured down into a low narrow channel that can rise into a fountain—faith that comes from the depths has a spring in it! (10 July 1896)

And then again, in Switzerland, where she rested during the late summer months:

It was a narrow strip of valley, with a distant view of the Breithorn at the end, and lovely firwoods to sit in—and lovelier wreathings of clouds round the crags overhead—All day long they were twisting in and out of the little gullies . . . with one river of blue sky between,—just overhead—wreathing really round the feet of giant mountains unseen above till one got on to the first ledges of rock at either side. . . .

All was wrapped in clouds at first and we could do nothing but watch for glimpses of the Matterhorn—At last by moon light he came out from head to foot with the last shimmer of cloud drifted away—and I don't think I shall ever forget the "watching for the morning" next day—with the whole amphitheatre of snow standing in dead white against the dim blue sky—it came as such a parable of waiting for the sunrise that is coming—to miss the first touch of rose-colour is to miss the whole—"Blessed are all they that wait for Him." (August 1896)

The storm clouds grew ever darker upon their return to Algiers that fall, and 1897 was ushered in with no relief. Lilias summed it up: "January was one of the darkest and toughest months we ever had."[7] There was, to start with, the unrelenting investigation by the French government throughout the winter months. Then, Jean Renand, whom they had brought on to help them, required their help to keep *himself* going, unnerved as he was trying to carry on the work while upholding his delicate wife and three young children. Meetings were canceled and people unvisited while Jean helped his wife, who was overwhelmed with child care and household tasks. Because the family had such a difficult time, they left within six months of their arrival.

As usual, during Ramadan, numbers sheered off from the tiny remnant; programs were introduced only to drop off after a few days. In addition to the invariable social pressure brought to bear on Christians during the special times of fasting and feasting, the women were becoming aware of another force as insidious as it was subtle. Black magic was commonly employed in North Africa: to cure a friend, kill an enemy, or drive a desired woman crazy with love. A sorcerer, by the use of charms (melted lead forms), sacrifice of birds, invocation of demons, hypnotism, or more simply, poisons, could work his or her will upon the object of concern. A foreign concept to the western mentality of the missionaries, black magic was a constant threat to young converts who were becoming prey to the mixture of poison and magic as a means of dulling intellectual faculties and numbing the will. As Lilias became more familiar with these practices, she would come to recognize the sudden pulling away of the young converts as symptomatic of poisoning (secretly administered into their food or drink) which, she observed, made them susceptible to suggestion and satanic influences.

The situation was unspeakably grim. Their very presence in Algeria was jeopardized by the political situation. The opposition that they experienced—overt social constraints and subtle spirit attacks—threatened to shut down the ministry. And yet Lilias reflected that more discouraging than any outward disappointment was the "sense of 'the oppression of the enemy' in the very air," adding,

> *one literally could do nothing but pray at every available bit. One might take up letters or accounts that seemed as if they were a "must be"—but one had to drop them within five minutes, almost invariably, and get to prayer—hardly prayer either, but a dumb crying up to skies of brass.*[8]

And yet they carried on. Lilias's method of proceeding is astonishing both in sheer doggedness and shrewd strategy. Employing the services of two young British workers who had joined them, May Eustace and Gertrude Targgot, she organized a class for the small boys who ran in the alleys about their house; when the boys' lessons had to be abandoned because of their disruptiveness, she used that time for a class of Jewish girls who inhabited the new French street cut directly above them. With the few Arab women and girls remaining, the missionaries visited the *kittars* (cemeteries) in the neighboring suburb of Belcourt, where each Friday (their sacred day) Muslim women visited the graves—bringing sweet-smelling flowers for the spirits of the dead—and enjoyed the liberty of their rare excursions away from home. Lilias, taking advantage of this unique opportunity to build relationships, rented a room for an Arab adaptation of "at homes" for women, whom the government apparently deemed no threat.

Finally the governmental investigation ended, with authorities satisfied that they were doing nothing amiss politically. But suspicion once cast is hard to dispel, and many things remained unchanged. Lilias took heart from the occasional flickers of grace which penetrated the dark clouds. Nothing could have prepared her for the glimpse of glory to come!

What follows is a strange intertwining of experiences between the women's city work in Algiers and the mountain work of others among the Kabyles. In early June, Lilias and Helen visited for the first time Albina Cox and Kate Smith, early friends among the Algerian missionaries, at their North African Mission Station at Djemaa Sahridj—in the Kabyle mountains some sixty miles from Algiers. After a ten-day visit for a much-needed time of refreshment, their ways parted, each eventually to go to other places of rest for the summer, yet connected in ways still unknown to them.

Through circuitous circumstances, Kate Smith took an unplanned trip to Switzerland alone. She waited on God in a unique way during this unexpected solitude. Then, on her way back to Algeria, she experienced a filling of God's Spirit. She returned to Djemaa Sahridj with an overwhelming sense of power and joy. Upon arrival in Djemaa, she shared her joy with her fellow workers who likewise experienced that same Spirit touch, praying and praising together until their hearts seemed melted into one. Lilias later wrote that one after the other, mission workers, French helpers, and the four Kabyle lads living at the mission station "broke down, in confession and surrender, as the sweet breath of God's Spirit swept over them."[9]

Looking back, Lilias noted, "it seems as if simultaneously with this, setting in action as it were of the wheels, a movement began in Alger; for those last weeks before we went away for the summer were very different from those that had gone before. Answers to prayer began to flow in steadily." Meetings and classes were once again attended, and there were other indications of "God's near presence."[10]

In July, a month after Miss Smith had gone to Switzerland, Lilias also left for Switzerland (though they never met up) for a time of rest. She went with a strong sense that God's Spirit was at work

> *and that the showers of blessing were nearing—just a breath here and a breath there. That verse "I will make the showers to come down in their season" kept ringing as an inspiration. The "season" of showers in this southern land is just when everything is at its very dryest and hardest—when the ground is baked and scorched till it looks as if no blade of grass could ever pierce through it again—that is the "season" when the showers come.*[11]

Yet she found no lift in her own spirit. When she went to write in her journal, she felt such a burden of prayer that she could "only lay down the pen and yield to it."[12] The same was true with her drawing, her journal pages bearing only one painting for the summer's harvest. Then, inexplicably, one day near the end of her time in Switzerland, she felt a freedom of spirit she had not known for months: "I found the burden was gone and that I could take out the bundle of arrears and set to work on them."[13] Later, she would discover by consulting her almanac, that the freedom came at the very time "the flood gates had opened" for Miss Smith.

After the quiet summer days, with no outward happening to speak of, Lilias headed back to Algeria, quite unaware that "God was preparing lovely surprizes of blessedness . . . all round."[14] On the train south through France, she began to record lessons that God had taught her from Romans during her weeks in Switzerland, as she had sat with her Bible at the edge of a little woods by the inn. Traveling through France, she received a promise: "The Lord whom you seek shall suddenly come into His Temple."[15]

The rest is best told from her journal:

The next morning—Sunday—God fulfilled to me the word He had given me in the train coming south through France—about suddenly coming to His temple. If I were to write an inside journal instead of an outside one, it would be a wonderful story of His dealings—but I don't think He means this—only now just the joy must break out—this last bit of the way has been just one cry for Him from head to foot—I wondered whether it was some revealing of Himself that would come at Mas, but it was not—only the cry deepening and deepening—and on Sunday He woke me long before morning with such an unutterable sense of light and sweetness and of the thirst of all those days being quenched in Himself—it is no "experience"—just God Himself filling all the horizon in a way I never knew before—as if one's being were just an empty shell for Him. He had suddenly come while I was asleep—oh, glory be to His Name. (12 October 1897)

Prefacing her account of the following weeks—"I hardly know how to write anything—the unfolding of His ways is all so wonderful"[16]—she begins to chronicle the events. The next day a delegation from Djemaa came to Rue du Croissant to tell what had happened since Miss Smith's return. Similar miracles began all round them, amongst the Arabs and the French, signs of the softening of hearts, a sense of "liberty and life and that He has a nucleus here where the Spirit has His way."[17]

Never one to keep the blessing to herself, Lilias arranged for a coming together of the mission workers in Algeria, inviting representatives from missions along the coast—thirty individuals, as it turned out, from a five-hundred-mile radius—for "four days with God." The little inner circle of missionaries at Rue du Croissant prepared for this unprecedented event in closely knit times of prayer and in planning the logistics and practicalities of hosting such a number. Lilias writes: "Blanche Haworth managed all the 'Martha' part . . . no small matter with eighteen people to house and twenty-five or so to meals and only two native boys, quite untrained—but she and the girls got it all into such order than none of them had ever to miss a meeting."[18]

"'Four days with God' was what we had given out," Lilias records, "but it was soon evident that *He* meant more than that, and that the whole thing was just a watching Him and seeing His plans unfold." Acknowledging a time of resistance in some, she adds, "there were those who had come longing for blessing . . . and yet who had not known that God must break down before He can build up—a thawing and melting began."[19]

She concludes:

> *There is no describing the meetings—we were just brought into God's Presence and . . . left to do whatever work had to be done—they were perfectly free—perfectly spontaneous—with the liberty of the Spirit of God. Mostly they lasted nearly three hours each—one in the morning, another in the afternoon, as shown on the paper overhead—but the time went before ever one knew it. The keynote all through was Life—Christ our Life for Spirit and soul and body and everything else to be delivered into the place of death.*[20]

The last Wednesday "there was a sweep of the Spirit through the room—We hardly knew how—just in singing softly again and again the chorus, 'Jesus, Thou art mine for ever.' "[21] Friday morning the slow Algerian trains carried the participants off, east and west, and from the far-off places came testimonies of triumph over old circumstances which before had brought defeat, and of awakened hunger and thirst in other hearts in the various stations.

"The New Year is dawning full of hope and wondering at what it holds in store,"[22] writes Lilias in her first journal entry for 1898. Ramadan was the first thing in store and once again they faced the dull unresponsiveness that accompanied this annual test of spirit. Snare after snare was laid by the Arab families round the feet of those who wished to break Ramadan; some who for years had broken the fast in witness of their Christian faith, reverted to their old practice. The entire town was in an uproar with anti-Jewish riots, and living as they did on the borderline between the Arab and Jewish quarters, Lilias and her coworkers felt the brunt of this unrest on top of all the other "anti" sentiments.

On 9 February, less than three months after the last train had departed from the joyous gathering, Lilias wrote in her journal, "Has that wave of blessing lost its impetus? Sometimes I begin to feel that it has. . . . There is blessing still, but looking round one feels that something has gone."[23] What happened to the blessing? One cannot have felt her profound joy of the previous months without recognizing the poignancy of that question. Seemingly, it left as it came, inexplicably, as often is the way of God. There were lasting benefits to be sure—the lift of spirit for Lilias, a healing for Blanche from the lingering effects of sunstroke, a few new names added to the short list of national believers—but what happened to the blessing?

Lilias pondered that question, fearing it to be blocked by some grievance of their own, but in the end, she concluded, "I am coming to see that our own 'experience' so far as a conscious emotional thing, matters nothing, if He is free in His working all round."[24] The adding up is not ours to know, not now on this side of eternity, but perhaps God gave them one dazzling glimpse of glory to sustain them through the darkest days to follow.

They concentrated on the handful of native Christians in Algiers. Names previously mentioned in the journal now begin to step off the pages as fully developed characters. There is black Belaid, big and gentle, the pillar of their work in Algiers. When they first met him he was ill with typhoid and, to their amazement, murmuring one of his few English sentences, "I love Jesus." He had become a Christian in England some years earlier and, until he met the three women, his faith was nurtured by his Arabic Bible alone. There was his spirited wife, Yamina, the first woman convert among the Arabs. Yamina's daughter Atiqua and her sisters, Fatoma and Aissha, and their many relations become the hub around which spin many familial dramas. There is Taitum, bright and young, married at twelve to a half-crazed man given to fits of insanity, and her increasing brood of children—fourteen-year-old Baiya, "delicious Doudja," and solemn-faced baby Bonalem. And there are the Baija's—called "Wild Baija" and "Tame Baija" to distinguish the irrepressible young girl from Yamina's passive sister-in-law, the mother of little Touma. Newcomers arrive on the scene, young girls—Hanifa and Sherifa—and older lads, survivors from their early classes of boys—serious and studious Dahman, who is preparing to be a schoolmaster, Mohammed the silk-weaver, and Almed, a person vacillating in his zeal. A host of other people walk on and off the pages, each with a story and hopes for the kingdom.

The ongoing challenge for Lilias was to minister in a way that both nurtured the believers and strengthened them to stand up to the test of their young faith. Such was her empathy that she could not merely impose the practices and constraints of Christianity on the tender converts, but would wrestle through the implications of faith from *their* point of view. She was well aware that public witness in particular, which she held to be health to the soul of any believer, had profound ramifications in a culture permeated by the practices and precepts of Islam.

The breaking of the Ramadan fast, in particular, provided the acid, annual test for any convert. This being the ideal, courageous stand, Lilias took every measure possible to strengthen the believers toward that end, having special "coffee drinkings" during the day at their home and then evening Magic Lantern meetings (the precursor to slide shows) for the encouragement of their faith. Yet it was with "pain and perplexity" that she considered the enormous, almost unbearable, cost to the one who chose to take this stand; it might mean loss of jobs and status for the men, loss of husbands and honor for the women. Perhaps even more disturbingly, the act of breaking the fast by the young implied a dishonoring of their elders.

Taitum, who broke the fast secretly, articulated to Lily the plight of the women: "No one can know what it is for a woman to break Ramadan. No one will let a room to her, or buy from her or sell to her—she is hooted like a carnival if she shews herself out in the street or even on her roof: she is looked on as an outcast woman—just that."[25] Knowing the grave consequences young men and women faced, when they weakened in their stance, Lilias comforted herself with the conviction that God understood: "He is so gentle and patient with them, the blessed Spirit of God."[26]

She was tireless in her efforts to find more effective ways to equip the new believers toward independent faith. Consistent with her certitude that giving strengthens the giver, she was ever devising ways to make that possible: providing sewing classes for the women to make *haiks* (long pieces of cloth worn as outer garments) for the poor of Central Africa; encouraging the men to take up an offering for the needy of Kabyle and then to deliver it in person—a most uncommon gesture between Arab and Kabyle.

She took the women with her to the kittar to visit, partnered Algerian men with the French colporteurs (book sellers) on their itinerations, and employed the older boys to assist in the classes for the younger. As she continually adapted and refined the methods employed in reaching the Arab people, Lilias pondered issues of conventionality for both missionaries and natives. No stranger to the hold of custom, she knew only too well the cost of stepping outside its boundaries. She respected always the prescribed etiquette of the culture, yet she continually wrestled with the empty conventions that bound national and missionary alike, suggesting: "For them as well as for us there needs to be a 'loosing' from conventionalities when 'the Lord hath need.' "[27]

Through the pages of her journals, Lilias evolves a methodology, constantly honing her approaches to her increased understanding of the people—a process that would continue throughout her life. She marvels at the "unorthodoxy" of *God's* ways, penetrating through the iron armor of tradition to the very hearts of individuals. In particular, Lilias observed the instances, increasing in frequency, in which God used dreams to communicate with the Algerians. Characterized by unexpectedness and individuality, the dreams occurred, by her observation, only in nonreaders. She writes, "[The dreams] seem to be God's way of teaching just now those who are shut out by their ignorance from having the direct communication with Himself through His word."[28]

These dreams, related to her by the Algerians, are recorded in her journals and diaries throughout the rest of her life—each instance lovingly relevant to the individual and invariably life-changing as it gave the particular light or courage or comfort needed for the person's lonely pilgrimage of faith. For instance, "Wild Baija" related being unable to sleep because a care weighed down her heart:

And I asked Jesus "O, Jesus, take away the care and send me sleep"—and my eyelids dropped down and I was asleep. And in my dream I was in a place full of thorns, and they pricked my face and my hands and my feet. And Jesus came up with a long staff and a hatchet—and He began to smite the thorns right and left with the hatchet—and I said "O, Jesus, they will hurt Thee." And He said "No, they cannot enter into my flesh"—and He smote them and smote them till He had made a road as wide as the road of carriages—and then He turned to me and saw my feet bleeding and He said "Take my staff and it will help you home." And quickly, quickly I got home, and I woke. (14 April 1898)

As the little band labored on under the unrelenting atmosphere of political opposition and spiritual oppression, grace continued to filter through. During the months of 1898, Lilias spent Saturday afternoons at Olivage, a training center outside Algiers, working on a second parable book, *Parables of the Christ-Life,* conceived the previous year during those darkest of days, while she was walking through the hayfield near Olivage. A fresh "seeing" began through the tiny seed-vessels hidden within the withered grass:

The seed-vessels get more wonderful and more full of heavenly meaning every bit that one gets alone with them and God—a new little Parable book is growing out of them—or rather the materials for it are getting together as the glimpses of their meaning unfold and grow into unity.[29]

During her late summer months, when she was in Switzerland, God "spoke" his lessons to Lilias through the mountains:

The milky looking glacier torrent spoke with God's voice this morning—so obedient to its course in its narrow bed,—yet just—tossing with freedom & swing in every motion—such a picture of the rivers "of living water"—bound & yet unbound. (8 August 1899)

> *And another river lesson has come with the words "His voice was as the sound of many waters"—I have never noticed before how such a thing will check the voice of the torrent—a rock, a bush, even water running will dull it from a thunder of power into a mere whisper—where all the harmony of its multitude of tones is deadened & lost—oh we want to live where not one of the undertones or overtones of His Voice is stifled or missed! (8 August 1899)*

> *And today's "first lesson" was in these little mountain paths. I followed mine only a few yards further this morning & such an outburst of beauty came. You can never tell to what untold glories any little humble path may lead, if you follow far enough. (13 August 1899)*

And there were the delightful twists of God's ways, providing just what her spirit needed just when she needed it most. She records an episode in which her plans for "one week alone with God" (preferably in a firwood!) are repeatedly foiled. In a desperate plea to God—"to make me love His will whatever it is"—she resigned herself to yet another change of plan and set off to an untested location with reduced expectations:

> *Away we drove into the darkness—on & on till deeper darkness began closing in—"Oh Lord it really is in the firwoods, I do believe"—it was so lovely—at last a mile out we stopped at a perfectly ideal little hotel—just opened this season—Everything as fresh—sweet—simple as can be—with my window opening on to a great stone terrace with a bay of plain below, stretching right out to Mont Blanc—the firwoods beginning across the road at the back & stretching up to the top of the Eura. It seemed as if the Lord were saying "So I know how to choose!" (13 September 1899)*

The most unexpected "glimmers of grace" came in an unusual form. For some time, a curious idea had taken hold of Blanche that there was, perhaps, some special ministry for her to the little girl-children running wild in the streets. Through a series of unlikely circumstances, two little girls—nicknamed Brown Berry and Pink Shell—came into their lives.

Over a period of time, this led to their adoption by Blanche and opened the door to a parade of other children who danced in and out of their home through the years to follow. Though Lilias referred to them as "Blanche's children," clearly they stole their way into her heart and ministered to her through their quaint ways and sayings.

The pages of her little leather-bound diary for 1899—the page-a-day diary being the way she would, from this time on, report the remaining years of her life with great economy of space—are illuminated with sketches and paintings of these children: wild little Brown Berry, feisty and determined, of Kabyle descent; delicate, frightened Pink Shell, blossoming with the first touch of love. Whimsical and tender vignettes of the irrepressible little girls are interlaced with reports of discouraging circumstances all around. Laughter and tears, tantrums and hugs fill the house and the pages of the diary. Her entry for Christmas 1899 speaks of "Such a 'merry' & 'joyful' Christmas Day as we have never had before."

Days after the merry and joyful Christmas, Lilias witnessed the nineteenth century drawing to a close. Lilias, now in her middle forties, was a study in remaining faithful to God in those things possible, and trusting in God for all that seems impossible.

14

TRAINED FAITH:
FALLING FULL WEIGHT ON GOD

1900—1902

Trained faith is a triumphant gladness in having nothing but God—no rest, no foothold—nothing but Himself—A triumphant gladness in swinging out into that abyss, rejoicing in a very fresh emergency that is going to prove Him true—The Lord Alone—that is trained faith.

—Diary[1]

The new century began with the firing of the Ramadan cannon—and all the challenges inherent in the month-long fasting by day and feasting by night. Brightening the near horizon for Lilias, however, were plans for the "Spring Tournee"—first to Teniet and then to Tolga in the Southlands, a village west of Biskra—this year with the added boon of a reunion with her long-time friend Blanche Pigott. This brought Lilias the heightened joy of companionship and provides posterity with Miss Pigott's delightful inside view:

It was settled that we, i.e., Lily, Miss Freeman, Miss Synge and I, should all four travel together to Biskra, from whence Miss Freeman and she [Lilias] would go south. It was a wonderful journey, Lily enjoying it with the free heart of a child. We seemed to be back in the old days of fun and laughter, in delight at the wonderful revelations of strange beauty around us.[2]

Lilias's diary, likewise, is filled with her happiness in introducing the wonders of the Southlands to fresh new eyes.

Off at last, with such gladness of heart! . . . We crossed the Mitidja yesterday in showers of misty rain, & the snow was all round us as the train jogged up to the long stretch of table land, parrallel to the coast. And today came the joy of setting our faces due south again down the branch line, after all these five years of waiting. It was lovely to reach one remembered place after another—First the salt lakes, then the highest level of the plateau, where the base of the northern hills begins to be cut off—then the plunge down into the basin of El Kantara with its blue-green sea of palms & dear sundried brick houses . . . the desert hills took on their pink & blue afternoon medley of light and shadow & one moment's glory of sunset flashed out between the shower, lighting the desert from the mauve of the distant hills in the flame colour of the cliffs of the river bed in the foreground—a chord of colour that is quite unpaintable & indescribable. (3 April 1900)

Oh it's lovely being south again. Even to the brackish water & the queer half-coagulated tea that it makes, so recalling camping days of the past! Blanche Pigott is so enchanted by it all—& buys all the most extraordinary bits of colour to take home. She says the people have learnt them from their sunsets. Nowhere else could they have learnt to put orange and green together as they do—that their striped tents are an unconscious copy of their curious stratified mountains. (9 April 1900)

The rest of the journey is recorded as pure joy. On 12 April, Lily and Helen bade farewell to their comrades and set off together, to Tolga, a native place untouched by modern ways. They settled into a little house near the main street of town: earthen walls and floors, ceiling of palm trunk with a thatch of palm leaves above them, little rooms opening onto an open court where they pitched their tent for meetings by day and sleeping by night. Lilias wrote, "I don't think anything has ever been quite like that joy of getting back to one of these desert villages—& to be having for three weeks anyway the longing of my heart—to be living in a real native house of their own building—so . . . on their level that they come in & out promiscuously."[3]

The days that followed were filled with a steady stream of visitors, men, women, children, with eager hearts. A blind *taleb* (a mystic student or initiate), Si Ibrahim, who was a strong leader among his people, took great interest in the two women and their message, installing himself as their protector. One of the many men that came to listen pled, "Come & stay always with us & we will come & hear every day & we will give you a house & a garden, or perhaps two!"[4] The idea of returning to Tolga for a longer stay began to take shape. Lilias described it as "a wonderful sense of *possibility*" that God might let them have a winter station there, exclaiming, "oh the total joy that would be! I hardly dare let myself think of it."[5]

A highlight of their visit was an invitation to a *zaouria,* a fraternity house of the Sufi brotherhood (Muslim mystics). Lilias records the experience, a rare honor for women:

> *Up a winding stair we went into a big booklined room, the floor spread with great camel skins—round the skirting boards were solemn white-robed figures, sitting or squatting round. We had coffee & talk & promised them a Bible for their library. And though we could not say very much, because of the time limit, it was a joy to witness to Christ in the very stronghold.*[6]

Summer break for Lilias in 1900 took place in England, with the usual family visits, some time at Keswick, plus a side excursion with friends to Ireland. She records:

> *Oh the joy of being here again—Cornwall has the most wonderful 'attrait' of any place I know on earth—except perhaps the desert—& there is a likeness too in all their unlikeness—the huge illimitableness*

of everything—one's whole being can expand. And then the joy of a fortnight alone crowns it all—oh it is a gift from God.[7]

Paintings and parables were the invariable byproduct of these times Lilias could spend alone, and diary entries give insight into her process of re-creation:

I have been making some first attempts with my "Brownie" [camera] . . . last year's [diary] was a very dull one as regards illustrations, for want of time to get into the spirit of drawing specially in Alger. When one gets away one's storing of mental photographs & incomprehensible scribblings come back against the leisure of a resting time as in Tolga this spring. (17 August 1900)

Oh so endlessly beautiful the days are—& they go so quickly—God has many things to say & one can sit by the hour on the heather with one's Bible and listen. (25 August 1900)

Lilias learned upon her arrival in England disturbing news concerning her sister Margaret's health and of her resulting plan to spend several months in St. Moritz for a "cure"—a strict regime of diet, exercise, and fresh air. Lilias accompanied Margaret, and the sisters spent six weeks together, taking up skiing for exercise, about which Lilias commented, "It looks delightfully like flying when you have got past the preliminaries of getting tangled up in your six-foot shoes."[8] She also absorbed the crystalline beauty of snow and sun:

The peaks are dead white at first against a sky of "old rose"—then creamy again against mauve, amethyst, lavender & deep blue in turn & then again the moon will come out & turn the snow & its reflections in the lake into a land where the angels might be walking. (26 November 1900)

Lily returned in December to heightened political unrest in Algiers, a situation which brought their work to almost a complete halt. Yet through these darkest of days shone two rays of light. The first ray was the town of Blida, located some thirty miles inland at the foot of the mountains that bound their plain. It was a place they had first visited some ten years before and on subsequent visits had found unreceptive—"hard as nails." A change of attitude had come within the community in the last couple of years, and with it came a warm welcome to the missionaries. The women rented rooms at the back of a house in Blida as a base for visiting the outlying villages, and they claimed for the kingdom this new parish of "white-roofed houses below" and "little groups of hamlets above"—each representing scores of women and girls, red-robed in the hill country dress.

The women were methodical in their approach to visitation. Blanche drew out districts, and there being no numbers on houses or names on streets, made maps big enough to mark separate streets and houses—which she named and numbered accordingly! Throughout the next several years, the women and their younger assistants occupied the flat, partnering in various combinations often for shifts of a fortnight. Through this faithful and systematic approach, their tally of visited villages gradually grew to almost eighty, and Blida became, in time, the site of their first out-station.

The second ray of light for the workers was the arrival of reinforcements. French helpers—first a couple, Paul and Philomene Villon, and then Paul's brother-in-law, Michel Olives—began working as colporteur evangelists. Being French, they were at liberty to travel freely to the Southlands in winter and tablelands in summer, selling Scripture portions and later colloquial parable tracts. They also held meetings by the score. Being men, they could work the native cafés and shops of Algiers and play a "big brother" role to the Arab lads.

The women's association with French workers proved to be a lift in unexpected ways as others joined their ranks—Marie Brilland, Mlle. Arnaud—helping them keep the program going and keeping open doors otherwise closed to English missionaries. In Lily's words,

> *God has so given us these . . . French helpers—& given such a sure of heart-knitting with them. And they are all so ready & wholehearted & willing to go all lengths. Oh "blessed are all they that wait for*

Him."—It is our thought of the early days here coming true at last—but in a way so apart from ourselves and our planning. (1 November 1902)

Even as their own activities in Algiers and itinerations in Algeria were severely curtailed, the women continued to hammer out programs and evolve patterns of ministry. As Lilias watched young girls get married at eleven and twelve years of age and get initiated into the hidden—and uncertain—world of womanhood, she became increasingly concerned with equipping women and girls for independence, economic and spiritual. To this end, she engaged the services of Mme. Gayral, the keeper of an embroidery shop, to teach them *girgaff,* the native art of embroidery, so they could produce articles that would be sold in her shop. Lily set up classes in reading, virtually an unknown skill among women, noting, "It will be such a thing when they can get their spiritual food straight from Him through His word, instead of these scraps of oral teaching, so half remembered with their untrained memories."[9] And she encouraged the young converts to hold "cottage meetings" in their own houses, building leadership and a guarantee against a time when association with the missionaries might be prohibited altogether.

Lilias was convinced that the "lads were the key" to the future church of Algeria. Now the Frenchmen, Villon and Olives, could engage in the lives of the young Arab lads, nurturing them in the life of faith and ministry, taking them, one by one, on their colportage trips. The mission workers hit upon the idea of establishing their own café as a point of contact with the Arab men. Lilias writes,

We have had the little cafe opposite whitewashed & curtained & turned into a meeting room where M. Villon can collect the men he gets hold of in two cafes—without their coming under the ban by entering our house. It is just right for them—even to being fitted with the big native store which is the "fitting" of a cafe—so that he can give them whatever is necessary from time to time in the way of hospitality without difficulty. (11 December 1901)

It is nothing short of astonishing to observe how they mobilized the small ranks to maximize their services. Daily, weekly, and seasonal routines fell into patterns as shifting pairs of helpers took their turn holding down the Algiers program, manning the Blida post, carrying out the house-to-house visitations and itinerations to villages along the plateau as well as longer spring and winter "tournees." All of this worked to ever widen their strategic points of contact. And now, with the advent of the Villons, the house at Rue du Croissant in Algiers could remain open during the missionaries' summer breaks—a visible bulwark to the struggling Arab believers.

With all of this strategy in their work, individual *people* remained the focus of the missionaries. This emerged through Lily's diary pages, replete with stories about their struggles and victories—and often accompanied by water colors or pencil sketches. Readers today can watch the unfolding crisis of Belaid and Yamina's marriage, as she returns to her first husband after the marriage of their daughter Atiqua, and Lilias is lovingly involved in the events of their hearts. A new name appears, prancing through the pages and into Lily's heart—five-year-old Aissha, referred to as "my darling little black kitten," who, at the request of her blind mother, spent the days (and nights, when her stepfather was drunk) at the Rue du Croissant. "There are *such* possibilities in the child," Lily writes, "force of will & imagination & power of leadership—but so gentle & biddable."[10]

Lilias had a summer reunion with her family—this time meeting in Switzerland with her brother Edward and his wife after twelve years of separation from them—before she took some time alone. Later, in December 1901, she and Blanche set forth on their winter tournee, back to Tolga, this time with the intent of setting up a winter station. A native house was found, replete with mud walls and palm roofing and pillars—"all fitting exactly we see more & more, to our needs"—and they were received with the same warm welcome and eager audience as before:

> *Tolga—January 1 . . . and the brightest New Year's Day that there has been for a long time—and such a sense that "the pattern shewed on the mount" long ago is beginning to be worked out by Him who*

gave it—for the new beginnings of the old year have both been on the outline hoped for then . . . Hallelujah! Such a day of small things still, but on God's time, & that is enough: size as well as time & space count nothing with Him.

And we feel with hardly a doubt, that our second outpost is given of Him down here—such a real outpost on the verge of darkness—not one spot beyond, held for Christ til you get down to the Congo—or right or left among the desert towns & villages that skirt the country here. (1 January 1902)

Day after day, groups of native hearers came to the mud-walled house—once, twice, even three times in one day—some to argue, but most with the spirit of silent listening. The "Aid" or feast being held in Tolga at that time drew Sufi brotherhoods from the south and mountain men from further north, 1,400 in all. The women were thrilled to recognize the possibilities of Scripture being carried to far-off places by these mystic visitors.

Then came the rumor that the general from Biskra was coming to Tolga on a "tour of inspection," and, with that ominous warning, the listeners backed away. The dreaded order was delivered, in person, by the French military commandant of Biskra. According to Lily, "He was politeness itself, it was *'une affaire tres delicate'* but perfectly explicit. We were doing propaganda & it could not be allowed—we must return to Biskra."[11] She also reflected in her diary:

Oh the sorrow if it—Our heartstrings have just twined into this place—& all around lie the untouched villages that we had hoped to reach—& our hopes for steady work down here wreaked at a stroke—we fairly ache, body & soul with the blow. (24 January 1902)

They were to later discover that at the heart of the problem was an incident totally unrelated to their work, but one which had tremendous ramifications on all missionaries. Nine months previous, in the French village of Margueritte in the Algerian tablelands, a band of 150 Arab assailants, without warning, pillaged and plundered the village. Under threat of death, all the inhabitants who had not taken flight were forced to repeat the *sheheda* (creed) and to put on Arab garb as a sign of becoming Muslim. Even though the incident proved to have been stirred up by one Muslim zealot, it completely unnerved the French colonists, who in reaction ruled out all "propaganda"—from any source—in the Southlands.

Lilias's pain is palpable in the diary entries that follow. She asked hard questions—"Was it all a dream, those hopes of our first days here of a foothold that God would give us? or was it a vision that is yet for an appointed time?"[12] A glimmer of light came through the "post" (an Algerian rider on horseback)—a text from Proverbs with the marginal note, "Surely there is a sequel," which became a promise Lilias claimed of God.

The women loaded the trap bound for Biskra with a crowd gathered round them—great brown hands silently outstretched for a grasp. After passing the palms that had earlier signaled such hope, they ploughed their way, hour after hour, through the deep soft sand. Moving farther and farther away from the place invested with such prayer and dreams, Lilias pondered texts from her little volume of *Daily Light,* writing in her diary, "'Awake thou north wind—blow upon my garden'—that was the day's 'Daily Light' & we believe that this is what it means. The north wind that seems to nip the young buds has only driven back, it may be, the sap unto the roots to do a better work *there* for the time."[13]

At Biskra, Blanche and Lily went to the commandant with their papers of colportage—colporteur, or bookseller, being their official role in Algeria—proving themselves to be within their rights, but this was to no avail. Lilias reports that the commandant solemnly declared, "that wherever we went in his 'little kingdom,' he would have to ride after us and fetch us back, which would be very inconvenient," and then he showed them a map of his forbidden country.[14]

Undaunted, the women redirected their efforts to the civil territory in the mountains above, a place open to them because it was not under military supervision. What follows is a saga of high adventure. Unbeknown to them, word of the women reached the inhabitants of each town before their visit, combined with a threat of fine and imprisonment for anyone going near them or taking their books. Spies followed them each step of their way. Yet, the intrepid twosome forged ahead, by mule and by foot, encountering one episode after another—their tent and book-bearing mules plunging into a water hole; storms threatening, fierce enough to "blow up" their tent; banned access to food and to the use of mules, which they need to aid their departure. The alarm of the natives upon the very sight of these women, the two later learned, was due to the advance report that they were "sorceresses & spies."[15] All this was taking place under the watchful eyes of the two uniformed "gendarmes" whom they came eventually to recognize and even to greet at each new location with a cheerful "Bonjour!"

When the women finally passed through the huge chasm at El Kantara, the gateway between the desert and the plain, quite inexplicably from a human point of view, they found it a time "full of a triumph of joy" in God: "We felt how difficult it would be for man even to shut that gate—& it will be just as difficult for him to close the soul door of access as long as God holds it open."[16]

Arriving back in Algiers, the workers felt the pressure increase on all sides. Blanche became seriously ill with typhoid. Word came from Constantine forbidding all colportage—English and French alike—with threat of expulsion for any violation. Lilias recognized that the battle had moved to a new plane, one with grave implications,

> *I feel no light this time as to how it will all end on the human side. It has never looked more serious, for instead of being newspaper claptraps & a tissue of lies about political designs, it now issues from government & on the true ground of the work itself. (26 May 1902)*

Lilias left for her summer break in England with "too much head-tiredness to write anything or indeed to have anything to write—& only a continual & increase of the soul-oppression of this last year."[17] Family times refreshed her for a season, yet upon her return to Algiers in October, she learned that activity in their one pocket of liberty, Blida, was now under suspicion and police surveillance.

How did she keep going? The demands were enormous; rewards were few; the future questionable. How did she proceed against so many obstacles with so little encouragement? From a strictly practical point of view, she had learned many lessons since her early days in Algeria. First, she had learned to pace her activity. Ever since her health crisis of 1895 she, without fail, took a break during the hottest summer months, usually in England or Switzerland. During her time on the field, patterns of relief likewise evolved: the occasional getaway to Olivage, to Pescade, or to other coastal retreats.

There is, as well, no doubt that disciplined attendance to regular routines kept her focused and directed—sheer faithfulness to duty regardless of results, and attention to the smallest detail. Lilias, self-disciplined by nature, challenged the other workers by her example and by her words as revealed in the "Letter M," an article written later for *El Couffa,* an in-house publication for the growing band of workers. Noting a kind of "amiable wandering round among the people which is not quite doing our service with all our mind though it may well be with all our heart" she urges service "with all the 'mind' represents of thought and care and 'gathered-up-ness.'" She adds, "in the arrangements of our day I think we must . . . not leave the priceless moment just to the impulse of the moment."[18]

Yet pacing and discipline alone could not keep these missionaries going. Humanly speaking, there was very little reason to continue in Algeria, and Lilias eventually would be forced to consider whether their time of service there was over—but not on the basis of outward fact, rather by waiting on God for direction. Their position was succinctly stated in her diary, as was a statement of their only possible means of survival:

> *I am seeing more & more that we begin to learn what it is to walk by faith, when we learn to spread out all that is against us. All our physical weakness—loss of mental power—spiritual inability—all that is against us inwardly & outwardly, as sails to the wind & expect them to be vehicles for the power of Christ to rest upon us. It is simple & self-evident—but so long in the learning. (22 August 1901)*

The walk of faith that she proposed required a fellowship with the Father as current as breathing. This was no vague, mystical "communion" wrought of some secret formula. Quite simply, she put the highest priority on spending time completely alone with God, studying his Word with a heart open and receptive to his voice—an activity requiring utmost commitment from her, given the many demands on her time. Just as she had found, in the early years, a quiet spot in a nearby woods, later she made sure a place of prayer was prepared in a rooftop room, "so beautifully out of the way of all the sounds of the house." It was called the *melja,* Arabic for "refuge," and no one was to be disturbed there.[19] Even within her summer breaks, rich with family and friends, she actively pursued "two weeks alone with God," considering them essential to her soul.

Clearly, Lilias's writing, which seemed to flow out of those quiet moments, was part of the process, not only of synthesizing the outer objective events with inner spiritual realities, but of reconciling the two seemingly paradoxical aspects of her personality: her reflective artistic nature and her disposition for active visionary leadership. As she wrote out her observations from God's Word and his works—whether from the "illimitableness" of Cornwall, the quiet spaces of the desert, or even a pot of snowdrops on a windowsill in Algiers—mysteries of life and faith took on shape and meaning.

A faith language evolves in her writing, honed from the raw material of difficulty, framed in phrases that become trademark Trotter: "Despising not the day of small things." "Obedience is the atmosphere of God's revealing." "God has Eternity to work out His Purposes." The woman who emerges from the pages of her diary is now in the full stride of faith, an embodiment of the very "trained faith" of which she writes:

> *"As an eagle . . . fluttereth over her young, spreadeth abroad her wings, taketh them, beareth them on her wings—so the Lord alone did lead him." Fluttereth over—the early stages of faith are reaching upward, like the eaglets for their food when the mother-bird is overhead. . . . it is an older faith that learns to swing out into nothingness & drop down full weight on God—the broken up nest of former "experiences" left behind—nothing between us & the abyss but Himself—A rejoicing in every fresh emergency that is going to prove Him true—The Lord Alone—that is trained faith. (9 September 1902)*

It was trained faith that kept Lilias focused on the task and not the results or the uncertain future. It was trained faith that allowed her liberty of movement even when all the obvious avenues were blocked. And it was trained faith that would enable her to survive the arid stretch ahead.

15
CLOSED WINDOWS, OPEN DOORS
1903—1905

When God delays in fulfilling our little thoughts, it is to have Himself room to work out His great ones.

—Diary[1]

One blow after another inaugurated 1903. Most immediate and visible was the purchase by the local government opposition of the home directly across the street from 2 Rue du Croissant with the stated intent to draw people away from the mission by offering competing classes plus compelling perks. Their plots to sabotage the children's classes effectively reduced attendance at the missionary school from over one hundred children to five. Twenty women were brought before a civil court to bring false testimony against the missionaries' activities, and even the Jewish community joined the resistance, rabbis arranging an "interdict" against attendance at any Christian class or meeting, then stationing viewers outside the mission door to warn them away. With spies watching their every move, guards stationed at their door, and newspapers carrying false reports about their work, Lilias and her coworkers found that men and women alike shied away from anything associated with them.

The greatest blow of all, however, was a deeply personal one—the discovery that their beloved Taitum, who for over a decade stood firmly with them in faith and ministry, was living a double existence, engaging in the blackest sin. While never stated explicitly, one surmises from Lilias's writings, that she had given in to the sexual promiscuity to which the Arab girls, tossed aside by their husbands, were so vulnerable:

> *We reel simply stunned & paralyzed & as if it were some horrible nightmare from which we must wake up. If there is one among the women of whom we have been sure, it has been Taitum—& now the Taitum we have loved and trusted has been swept out of existence—& this one can have nothing but the utmost dishonour on Christ's name.*
>
> *How can we have been so blinded we ask ourselves—& yet as we saw her standing in the court—(she came for some medicine just as we left, standing in her modest dignified way, with her pure sad face), we felt again can it be true. . . . Our hearts ache & ache for her. (28 January 1903)*

Reeling from these decisive blows, the missionaries were forced to ask if God had, in fact, other intentions for them in ministry. Perhaps he was opening up their hearts to other more receptive countries, such as Morocco or Egypt. Prayer was always Lilias's refuge and recourse in "celestial combat," as she perceived this on-going battle to be.

An incident had occurred several years before which provided her with an object lesson of the power of persistent, coordinated prayers: One of the pillars which supported the gallery at Rue du Croissant fell into the court, carrying with it a block of masonry and a shower of bricks and tiles from the arch above. The architect who came to check the house for safety offered a probable cause of the collapse. Six or seven years previous, a native baker had installed himself in the house alongside them. Every night, for hours, two men swung on a huge see-saw which kneaded their bread, every blow vibrating through the house, resulting finally in the collapse of the pillar.

Lilias then remembered an article she had read in *Invention,* a weekly periodical, in which this same phenomena had been observed in several similar situations—soldiers walking in step over a bridge, the beating of looms, even the sustained sound of a violin on the note which chanced to be a bridge's keynote—each resulting in the bringing down of a structure. She wrote:

> *The words came with a flood of heavenly light.—If that is the power of unison in nature, what must be within its reach when it is translated into the Kingdom of Grace?—Now if we hold together—hold on long enough in the Name which is the keynote of Heaven, a vibration of power will be set up that will end in shaking to pieces the seemingly immoveable mass of opposition round us. (30 January 1996)*

Lilias was convinced that now, as never before, they were engaged in spiritual warfare that needed sustained, coordinated prayers, not knowing which prayer would liberate the answer, but knowing that each one would do its work. She sent off a prayer circular to their supporters in England briefly stating the most urgent needs with this qualification: "I cannot go into detail; I can only tell you that never in all these years have we needed your prayers as we do now—will you help us pray through the crisis that we feel has come upon us. Pray for wisdom how to act, and for a faith that will not fail."[2]

"Things without a lift on the human side," she writes in her diary at the time, "but God keeps up our hope in Him for His 'sequel.' In the face of black sky & cold wind, four little snowdrop buds, the first we have ever had here, have sat for the last two or three days with their chins on the earth—& now today one of them has reared itself up pure & fearless on its little stalk, with all the promise of the Spring."[3]

"God seems keeping silence," Lilias writes during all the heartache, yet she also saw small stirrings of springtime. The village of Blida, in spite of the earlier scare, remained open and eager—seventy-three visits were recorded in the register for that spring. Faithful Belaid returned to their fellowship, after a time of refusing to set foot in the house as long as the parents of his ex-wife, Yamina, were on the premises! Successful efforts to keep any program alive, however small, were all gains of a sort: Villon & Olives opened a book depot in a new location and started up a carpentry class; other classes for Arab girls were opened in several homes. Most significant, in the long term, were political changes: the resignation of the governor who opposed them followed straightway by the visit of King Edward to Paris, ending a decade of vehement Anglophobia in Algiers; the resulting "Entente Cordiale," the agreement between England and France for a policy of cooperation, and the softening of feeling toward the English missionaries in Algeria.

Meanwhile, the work continued, summed up in Lilias's vivid imagery:

There were the fishing boats in the sunrise this morning. They were tacking before the wind, & at each fresh tack came a pause when the sail took an expression of helpless uncertainty & standstill & under which the boat nearly reeled—then it would catch the breezes from the other side & bound off under it in a new direction. I think we are tacking right now! (1 March 1903)

The next two and a half years were fraught with health problems for Lilias—the inevitable effect of over-work on an already weakened heart, compounded no doubt, by the relentless emotional strain—necessitating extended rest periods for her in England and Switzerland as well as times of relative inactivity in Algeria. While the changes in the political climate harbingered hope for the future and provided the heavenly seal that the mission workers were to remain in Algeria, the day-to-day realities were still grim. Lilias was sustained solely by "holding unto the vision and the voice" that she was convinced "came from above for days to come."[4]

She was forced to leave for her summer break earlier than she anticipated because of, in her words, "failure in sleeping powers, & a sudden sense of having come to the end of my strength."[5] Having settled in Switzerland, she writes, "It is never long before God begins to speak when one gets away in His unspoilt world."[6] In the quietness of alpine autumn days she drew assurance from Scripture of God's way of guiding:

The word of the Lord has come these days in the story of the pillar of clouds & fire. The cloud spread for a covering links on with Col. 3:15—"Let the peace of God legislate." There is such a sense of infinite rest in the desert in being under a great shadow—it seems to bring a cool river of peace through all one's being. God's guidance, if our soul's instinct is healthy, tallies with the sense of rest—in a very real way, this sense of rest guides us—legislates for us. Anything that brings a sense of restlessness means that we have got from under the cloud shadow—we have gone off on some self devised path, or we have not kept pace with God. . . . It is the same in cases of perplexity—where there is no clear command in His word to guide us—where the sense of rest falls (always taking for granted that our wills are in His Hand) there is His path—it is there that the shadow of His cloud is falling. (30 September 1903)

After repeatedly postponing her return to Algeria, Lilias speaks of being forced to see a doctor "to find out why 'laziness hath knelt down upon us' as the Arabs express it." She reports: "He puts it down to heart crankiness—says I must take life easily. He has tried hard to impress on me that I am fifty & must behave as such, which I suppose is a necessary injunction, as tiredness & all I don't feel more than twenty-five!"[7]

Yet even out of this very "inadequacy and inefficiency on the human side," God was preparing the way for a new dimension of ministry. Several years previous, Lilias had had a conversation with Mr. Pope, a worker who later left Algeria, about ways and means of reaching the Algerian masses. Many of these were people who would fear attending meetings; others were beyond any personal access by missionaries. At the time of that conversation, he had suggested the method, if possible, "would be to print, autographed in their own handwriting, a tract every month and distribute it through the streets and cafés, that it might be the talk of the town and a means of coming to close quarters with every man you meet."[8]

Lilias recounts that later she read an article in *Blessed Be Egypt,* written by Miss Van Sommer, which told "how struck she had been in seeing the throngs that gathered in the Egyptian cafés round a storyteller, and how they would hang on, listening untiringly, and she suggested, could not the Eastern love of storytelling and story hearing be used for the Kingdom." Lilias continues, "Also . . . she said how the printed appeal takes the Muslim at an advantage—he is not bound by the fear of his neighbours to combat it, as he is bound to refute a spoken argument, he can read—and reread it in silence and in secret."[9]

These ideas lay dormant, but now, with access in Algeria severely curtailed in every direction, they came back with force and were linked together. A plan evolved to write and issue monthly stories in "Arab dress"—in subject matter and outward format. As Arabic parables, they would be means such as Christ used for "wrapping as much truth as possible in a form in which it will not awaken opposition before its time."[10] These parable tracts would be written in the colloquial Arabic, hand-copied in the beautiful flowing Arabic script, and printed off reproducing machines purchased from England. Villon and Olives would then distribute them in the colportage work and among the cafés, shops, and water carrier fountains in the Arab towns.

Lilias, through her unrelenting months of weakness, began to write story parables, with young Sherifa coming in once a week to translate her Arabic into a completely native phraseology. Sherifa, earlier befriended by Lilias and Blanche, had moved to Blida upon her marriage. Now, abandoned by her husband, she returned to Algiers with her young son—and back to the loving friendships of the women at Rue du Croissant. Sherifa was unique among women in her ability to read, having picked up the skill from her brothers, and was invaluable to the writing effort. Lilias explained, "She gives the sentences that delightfully native flavour which none of us can ever arrive at—and is *so* quick at catching the drift & crystallising it with exactly the form you want."[11] Another helper was found to copy out the parables in a good clear hand for lithographing. Speaking of this new venture in her diary, Lilias says:

> *This bit of work has come as such an answer to the cry that God would anoint for some fresh service in these quiet weeks. I never before could tell a story even to a child—now they come pouring in—I don't know how many outlines are waiting for time to write them out, & it needs the quiet hours to be "introduced into feeling" (with the states of mind that need dealing with). (26 May 1904)*

"The Debt of Ali Ben Omar" was her first endeavor, a story parable firmly set in the context and customs of Algiers, concluding with "The Interpretation." This would be one of scores of such parables issuing from her pen and from others, then translated over the years into many languages. Some remain in print to this day.

Parallel to the story parables, another new venture was taking life—a revision of a translation of parts of the New Testament into truly colloquial Arabic. In their earliest years in Algiers, the colloquial Arabic was not a written language. The only Christian literature available for distribution was portions of Scripture and tracts in the classical Arabic. Later, a Swedish missionary-scholar, Dr. Martin Nystrom, devoted his great linguistic gifts to translating the New Testament into the colloquial Arabic of Algeria, and selected passages of his translation were bound into a small booklet for distribution. Yet even this extraordinary contribution proved too formal for their use. As the result of a visit from Henry Summer (with the British and Foreign Bible Society), of Morocco, the missionaries decided to formulate a committee for the revision of Dr. Nystrom's translation of the books Luke, John, and Acts into a yet more accessible translation. Lilias was full of enthusiasm for the project:

> *They are to be lithographed in their own beautiful writing—another great attraction. The "stampa" [or type] is cramped & banal to their beauty loving eyes, to say nothing of the infidel about it, and the doleful association with tax papers and police summons. We want to have it as Arab as possible—their own rough creamy paper and marginal lines and flap covers—and all of the lightest weight that can be for the long journeys. (23 February 1904)*

Lilias later wrote, "In all the withholdings of this year, God, as is His wont, has been 'opening a door' where He 'closes a window.'"[12]

The new year, 1905, brought little relief in the spiritual atmosphere in Algiers or in Lilias's fatigue, resulting in the doctor's decree of "six months brain-rest." She did submit, at last, to bed rest, but hardly to "brain-rest" for "in the dear little prison" of her room, she continued in the spiritual battle as she prayed for various individuals: Sherifa, who remained strong in her new-found faith despite resistance from her family, determined to marry her to a wealthy Muslim man, Lilias records in detail saying, "I think they are 'making history' in a small scale"[13]; Belaid's friend Ali and his wild young bride from the Sudan, Chiradjah, whom Lilias and Blanche took on as a housemaid, for her encouragement instead of the "superior one . . . who really knew her work and could take charge of things without being looked after"[14] for whom they were looking!

A special insight into Lilias's spiritual pilgrimage is revealed as she releases to others ministries especially dear to herself and in so doing redefines her role. The year before, as Villon and Olives prepared to revisit her beloved Oued Souf, she had written,

> *It comes as such a carrying out of last summer's lesson of the old trees setting all aside to give place to the young life around—God is making it such joy to get out the maps . . . and everything that we can find that is not stamped with English origin in our camp outfit, & sending them to those loved & longed for places—a really deeper joy than if we were going ourselves—& that is saying a good deal! (5 January 1904)*

In 1905, as the men journeyed to Tolga, Lilias followed them on her map, tracing their steps daily and discovering in an unexpected flash of recognition, that they were entering Tolga three years to the day that Lilias and Blanche had been expelled: "How wonderful God's timings are. There is such a strange kind of heavenly poetry about them—& it brought such a strong assurance that His Hand is in it all, working out a purpose worthy of His great thoughts!"[15] Though separated by many miles, she visualized their first day of visitation in Tolga and set up "banners" in prayer, claiming spiritual victory in the name of God:

> *He can set them up, just as really—perhaps better than if there bodily—and who can tell what it means in the unseen world that these two men in outward deed & we here by faith, hoist them once more after the seeming defeat of three years ago. (28 January 1905)*

Lilias prayed prayers and dreamed dreams in the little rooftop room in Algiers, seeing beyond the Arab town around them, far along the coastline of Algeria and into the Southlands beyond. In prayer, she claimed five new workers in anticipation of advances they could make in the freer political atmosphere, and she claimed four towns at the points of the compass as "outstations," planning for the time that Blida would become a regular station! She envisioned a day of "short service," short-term missionary work, for girls whose parents would not let them join a society or venture into unknown, faraway places—"such visions of villages reached and outposts opened—the dear dark souls getting something more than stray crumbs."[16]

So brightly does she paint these word pictures of "things seen from afar" that her readers can almost forget the reality of her physical debility and limited ministry. She writes out lessons from weakness, redefining reality in the light of faith:

> *The same lesson re-iterated all round by God—the simple A.B.C. lesson that where inadequacy & inefficiency on the human side are His conditions for working. "He sealeth up the hand of every man, that all men may know His work." (23 February 1905)*

> *The blessedness of being hemmed in . . . Oh we are slow to see that it is only our weakness that He needs! (6 April 1904)*

> *Time is nothing to Him once the conditions are fulfilled. And He has eternity for the expanding of His thoughts that He thinks towards us. (16 April 1905)*

> *It has been much with us of late, that it is only beyond what is humanly reasonable & possible that we see the Glory of God. (5 January 1905)*

The workers saw vision merge a bit with actuality just before they departed for summer break. For some time, Blanche had been looking for a little cottage outside of town where workers could go for rest when Algiers days were too hot and heavy. Then came an opportunity, quite unsought, requiring a sum only a little greater than a cottage would have cost—a rambling old native house, in a shady garden, crowning a hillside of vineyard and firwood and wild olive. After legal complexities typical of such transactions, the house came into their hands. In Lilias's words,

> *It seemed like a fairy tale of dreams suddenly dropped down to earth—yet with a curious sense that it was no dream but a wonderful bit of God's unfoldings. . . . Such visions come of what God might make of it—& the only answer I get when I ask Him what it means is "He Himself knew what He would do." (26 May 1905)*

Faith not withstanding, it was a very frail Lilias who left Algeria for a rest in Wales in August 1905. Once again, God gave her just what she needed when she needed it most:

> *These last days have been such a weariness bodily and flatness of soul that Llaudrindad seemed very difficult to reach—but as the Welsh hills began to skirt round the railway line there was such a coming to a Holy Land . . . & with it came a reviving that made one feel one could not miss the evening praymeeting—The thing that stands out of it is the hymn "Jesus Lover of My Soul"—beginning like a breath in a far off corner of the tent, & swelling and surging & dropping again all around like the waves of the sea in wonderful minors—& the triumph of the last line*
>
> > *"Thou of life the Fountain art*
> > *Freely let me take of Thee*
> > *Spring thou up within my heart*
> > *Rise to all Eternity"*
>
> *carried one's spirit out in faith that He would do it, for body & soul—& the consciousness of His answer came there & then. (7 August 1905)*

The "reviving" of that first evening was just a foretaste of what was to come. Several weeks previous, while in Paris, she had acknowledged a certain weakness in her temperament—"an overmuch sympathy."

> *Like a flash comes too . . . the connection between spiritual liberty & spiritual authority. Personally I see how both are cramped by a*

giving oneself away in overmuch sympathy with those around—i.e., sympathy with "the natural man" in them.

It makes "crosslights" innumerable in the human soul that break up the absoluteness of God's light & God's will—& it weakens their fibre as well as one's own. It becomes an "other consciousness" as to what they are feeling or wishing, as subtle & strong as self consciousness & the measure of the loss of God consciousness & the fearless freedom that springs from it. (19 July 1905)

As harmless, or even noble, as such sympathy might appear on the surface, Lilias had come to recognize in herself a kind of bondage in relation to it—"the susceptibleness on the human side which has hindered the simplicity of obedience to the Holy Ghost." In her own "Good Friday" of the soul, at Llaudrindad, she brought her natural temperament to the Cross:

It has opened up to me a whole new area that has to be "subdued unto Himself"—the whole region of natural temperament that lies at the back of the self-life in man & needs to be transformed by the renewing of our mind—translated that does not mean annihilated but transformed by a new mind and body. He can take that very susceptibleness that has been a snare & make it into a means of contact with Himself. (11 August 1905)

Lilias was totally unprepared for the "Easter" which would follow—the special gift of Christ's near Presence: "He *did* come, in such a glorious manifestation of His grace & power & tenderness that one felt one had hardly known Him before! And with it came such a light on the *positive* side of Friday's lesson—that all needing delivering unto death on the human side is just what He can make 'alive unto God.'"[17]

The days that followed were full of blessedness for Lilias as she drank in the messages and conversations with others gathered at Llaudrindad. Two additional months with family and friends in England further prepared her, body and soul, for her late October return to Algeria. And her encounter with Christ that late summer day in Wales went down in her diary as an anniversary of the heart never to be forgotten.

At the end of the darkest year in which their work virtually came to a halt, Lilias had written "I am full of hope that when God delays in fulfilling our little thoughts, it is to have Himself room to work out His great ones."[18] Faith alone sustained that hope through years of weakness and limitation. Yet even as windows were being shut all round, doors were opening—in Algeria, in the Arab world—and stand ajar almost a century later: in a written legacy, hammered out of the very atmosphere of impossibility. For Lilias, at last, after the darkest and longest siege, faith would begin to be rewarded with sight. Heavenly surprises were just around the bend.

16
WANDERING BEES
1906—1907

A bee comforted me very much this morning concerning the desultoriness that troubles me in our work. He was hovering among some blackberry sprays, just touching the flowers here & there in a very tentative way, yet all unconsciously, life—life—life was left behind at every touch, as the miracle-working pollengrains were transferred to the place where they could set the unseen spring working.

—Diary[1]

The home in El Biar was all the women had ever dreamed of—and much, much more. On 9 March 1906 they spent their first night in the rambling old house, "picnicing after Blida fashion," only to realize the next morning that it was the eighteenth anniversary to the day of their arrival in Algiers! They named the house *Dar Naama,* Arabic for "The House of Grace." Grace was the name of Blanche's mother, and Lilias said, "beyond that it has to us the deeper meaning of thanksgiving to 'the God of all grace' who gave it—and hope 'that through that grace' it will 'minister grace' in its turn."[2]

Blanche was in her element. From the beginning of their friendship, at a spiritual life conference in Switzerland, Blanche had responded to Lilias's faith and vision. They were one in purpose when they first set off to North Africa and continued to be so with each advance in ministry. Though Blanche did not share Lilias's passion for travel, she did share her passion for the evangelization of Algeria. She accompanied her on many daring itinerations, taking charge of the housekeeping aspects of the journey as she did at the headquarters (Rue du Croissant) in Algiers. Although in no way limited by the supportive role she played in implementing Lilias's countless ventures, here at *Dar Naama* she would develop her own unique ministry of hospitality—and find the home her domestic heart craved.

Much energy was expended during the next several weeks getting the place ready for a mission workers' conference, to be held at the end of the month. Lilias writes:

> *It is marvellous how this old house lends itself to the purpose from roof to court. . . . There is no doing of any ground plan—you might as well do a ground plan of an anthill or a rabbit warren. All except the "House" which is foursquare round a court like the Alger one, is a labyrinth of rooms on different levels joined by passages & staircases so interlocked that even now there are two or three places where I generally take a wrong turning. (23 March 1906)*

Lilias reveled in the possibilities for the future, as workmen restored the rooms and courtyards: the large central court with its spacious glass dome and white Moorish arches and pillars; the "Orange Court" named for its citrus trees; the smaller court with its rows of little rooms on each side, so suitable for a "native conference" someday, replete with well and bakehouse. Visions of a training center, a half-way house for fledgling believers, and rallies for Christian workers filled her mind as she made one lovely discovery after another.

About fifty workers gathered for that first convention. After the first meeting, their speaker, Charles Inwood, dedicated the whole place to God. At the end of the conference, Lilias wrote, "every room has been hallowed by prayer & praise & love. . . .'Jesus' was the very first word of the first meeting. . . . 'Jesus the Very Thought of Thee'—that was the first hymn—& the other hymn that always *rang* with a strong spirit cadence was the Llanthony Abbey one, 'Let me come closer to Thee, Lord Jesus / Yes, closer day by day.' "[3]

Dar Naama was kept open, at the beginning, only through stop-gap help. Even with limited staffing, however, it immediately became the convalescence place for weary bodies, and for Lily, the summer resting place of choice. She describes the house's unexpected gifts, revealed as the months progressed:

> *It is such a "House of Grace"—things without number that we knew nothing of when the purchase was in the balance—five wells—cherries—nettles—pears—figs—walnuts—pomegranates besides the oranges which were the only visible fruit tree—each as they ripened & were discovered has come as a new surprise from God's Hand. . . . Surely God has unknown purposes for His Kingdom wrapped up in the place! (12 August 1906)*

The diaries come alive with some of the loveliest watercolors to date: the orange court with its dark green august oranges; the well in the orchard; the first cyclamen—"with their little angel wings all flying with joy"; the firwood where "there is always a breeze" even on "the hottest days"; a bit of *brousaille* (the native fennel plant) on the hillside in its autumn "clothe of gold."

Photographs pasted into the diary likewise enliven the pages, bringing into whimsical juxtaposition Algerian and European scenes: men and women in native drapery, and English women wearing long skirts, fitted waistcoats, and large picture-frame hats, seated around a table in the orange court taking tea. Much below the surface of appearances is the strong impression that they have indeed been touched by grace; the long drought is ending; there are other surprises awaiting them.

The first surprise was the closing of the house of opposition across the street from Rue du Croissant, "so sudden as to be manifestly divine," after three and a half years of antagonism. With such concrete changes locally as well as in the overall political scene, there was freedom again in Algiers. Algerian residents began to test the waters, and slowly old programs were revived—embroidery and Bible classes for girls and women; Arabic and carpentry classes for boys; evening cafés for men; Sunday meetings in the old mosque room with a screen dividing men from women; house-to-house visitation. New programs came into existence such as a class for small boys, similar to the girls' embroidery lessons but in the decorative brushwork for which many had the old native genius.

Another surprise presented itself early in 1907 when Lilias received a letter from a North African Mission friend, letting her know that two ships would be touching in Algiers for a few hours with six hundred delegates on their way to Rome for an international Sunday School convention. The U.S. leaders of the convention (one being Bishop Hartzell of the Methodist Episcopal Church) desired to bring the challenge of foreign missions to the convention, and they wished to meet with missionaries in Algiers and learn the conditions under which the work was maintained. Lilias wrote:

> *Our first feeling was somewhat of dismay—six hundred of them in for an hour or so—What could we show them or tell them in that time! & moreover what could we shew or tell that would seem . . . worth looking at or hearing about—no schools—no hospitals—no organizations—no results to speak of or to shew for our close on twenty years' fight in Algiers—Should we be able to help discouraging them! (7 May 1907)*

A plan evolved to distribute a printed circular to every delegate on each ship, inviting one or two bands of fifty or sixty representatives to come to the Rue du Croissant for an informal meeting. The printed circular is nothing short of astonishing in both its elegant presentation (a nine-page booklet bound in ribbon) and comprehensive summary of the history and current mission work in all of Algeria—complete with a map and photographs of Algerian nationals and sites of ministry in Algiers, Kabylia, and the Southlands—and that for only a couple hours of potential exposure! With directness and simplicity Lilias presents their realities, appealing to the visitors' hearts as well as their minds:

Dear Friends,

As you pass along our North African shore we send you a call for sympathy and prayer. If, all the days that the coast-line is in view, you hold the land and its missionaries before God, you will leave a track of light and blessing behind you.

And as this is the one port of a Moslem Country at which you will touch, we want to give you a special welcome, through such delegates as may be chosen to represent you.

We have not much for you to see, for of all the coast Algeria is the part most curtailed as regards such aids to the work as Mission Hospitals or Schools, these being disallowed under French law. We are therefore shut up to the simplest and most direct forms of evangelization. Colportage and itineration, book depots, classes, meetings, visiting cafes where the men congregate, and the prison-like houses where the women are shut up. These are the means that lie open to us, and even for these we have had, in some instances, a hard fight.

We are not sorry for our limitations; they help us to keep the one aim of soul-winning clear-cut before us; but they prevent our having the ordinary outworks of a Mission Station to show you.

And even as regards what we have in hand, all is as yet in the initial stage. You have the chance of seeing things at their first beginning.[4]

Lilias and her co-workers made the court into an exhibition with maps, photographs, camp outfit, objects from the desert, and products of the industrial work of the Kabyle mountains in its various stages. They gathered in the Arab room some of the women occupied in their native arts of girdle weaving and couscous making, and in the inner room, girls at their embroidery, sites to which only women visitors could be admitted. Down in the mosque, they had a short meeting to which the native brotherhood were invited, and another few minutes' rally in the court above before the American friends left.

Lilias commented:

> *We cast the whole thing on God, & settled with one consent that we would believe in Him to use the very weakness of it & keep us all intent on shewing, not what we had done, but what we had not done.— We gave into His Hands too, the matter of the time-limit. If one day were with Him as a thousand years, He could make much of an hour. (May 1907)*

One can only imagine the assault on the senses of these American delegates as they first disembarked from their ships in the balmy Mediterranean harbor, boarded carriages which delivered them to the top of the Arab town, and began their descent through the crowded, stench-filled streets winding down to the large dented door of Rue du Croissant. One delegate, Mrs. Walker, writes her impressions of that memorable day—being greeted by Belaid, "a huge negro" with a "smile of joy that brightened our hearts"; the "wee class of tiny children in an inner class room, a few benches, a small organ, a Bible picture-roll, a very few helps for teaching."[5] What gripped her heart, and made her and others realize the extent of the need for missionaries, was a scroll stretching around the inside walls of the court, marking into squares indications of the millions of native peoples in Algeria who had never heard of Jesus and of the slim proportion of Arabic-speaking missionaries, and above, the words: "Lord, what will Thou have me to do?"

The two ships came and went, leaving behind a strong and loving sympathy with their parting prayer: "Thou who dost not fail and art never discouraged, bless our friends."[6] While on their way to Rome, the delegation of each ship, completely unaware of the other, raised three years' support for two and three workers respectively (the exact number of workers for which Lilias had been praying!) to join the work in Algiers. The delegations also appealed to Bishop Hartzell to begin an organized church in Algeria, with the promise of financial backing for the first four years. They telegrammed for Lilias and Blanche to be their guests at the convention in Rome, a suggestion the women met with strong agreement.

Lilias planned their return trip to Rome around visits to the mission stations between Tunis and Algiers—Bizerta, Bone, Constantine—to tell the workers there the story of the past weeks. She concluded that *only those who realize what it has been to be stopped up short at every turn from taking the chances of expansion that open, can imagine what it is to see the horizons that widen now with America behind us on the human side, & God arisen in the strange swift way on the Divine. (25 May 1907)*

With five new workers—Annie Whisler, Sasha Perkins, Alexandrine Gayral, Mabel Grautoff, and May Ridly—1907 was a year of expansion. Work could now be maintained in Algiers while pairs in varying combinations took turns manning the Blida work and visiting mountain villages. Villon and Olives followed up the previous year's campaign to the oases of Figuig (on the southwest border of Algeria near Morocco) with a winter campaign to unvisited villages around Laghouat, an oasis almost three hundred miles south of Algiers, aided this time with bicycles, while camels carried their supplies.

Lilias's detailing of one typical day of village visitation gives insight into both the methods and difficulties of that type of work. Striking off a main road to a footpath which wandered toward the clusters of *ghorbis* (Arab huts) set in prickly pear hedges, she was delighted to chance upon some elusive tent people, who after the heavy rains had come out of their secluded dwellings in isolated pockets in the mountains to gather torrent stones for road mending:

The only chance for a hearing with such like is to work from the seen to the unseen: so I began with the stones—how one was not very big, but that as two, three, twenty, fifty, went into the basket the weight grew heavy—& so with the burden of sin—the lying & the thieving & the quarrelling. They were a bit puzzled at first at having to get hold of an abstract idea, & stones & sins got a bit mixed—were stones sins? Or sins stones? But soon their Oriental minds got hold of the simile & when Blanche went on to tell them how alone they could not carry the shouarre full of stones but had to call a man to help them, so God had sent Jesus to carry their sins away—some faint glimmer crossed their faces—then "fast—fast—it is fasting that will take you to heaven" came in a chorus of voices. (11 February 1907)

Their joy in making contact with the child-like people was tempered by the questions raised by the tent people's automatic response: *"fasting* will take you to heaven." How much could the good news of Jesus penetrate in such a short encounter? Lilias longed to spend an entire week living in a tent by them to bring the light within their reach.

In September Annie Whisler and Lilias, along with the Villons, returned to some villages outside of Rovigo, to pick up where they had left off in June—this time with a tent to enable them to stay in the area for a longer stretch of time. Lilias recorded her feelings about the experience: "It is like an Elixir to get together again the camp outfit that has lain by so long."[7] After several weeks, Lilias and Annie separated from the Villons and struck off in a new direction: southeast to Bou Saada, half-way between Algiers and Tolga. The two journeys, physically into the south by way of a horse-drawn diligence and spiritually into the hearts of people by means of Christ's love, are beautifully recorded in Lilias's travel journal, "A Week in a Strong City," in text and watercolors—a presentation clearly intended for publication.

Back in Algiers, a romance was quietly brewing within the missionary community, enhanced perhaps by mutual involvement in the work with the Arab boys. Lilias records "the linking as we believe for God's service & kingdom of the lives of May Eustace & Michel Olives" and adds, "Her mother has seen him & given her full & restful consent."[8] The new union provided the solution for the long-held dream of a permanent station in Blida; with the betrothed couple's glad consent, a house was purchased and prepared in anticipation of the newlywed's first home.

With three permanent stations to maintain and a workforce of eleven men and women, the missionaries realized they needed a more formal system of organization. They took on the official name, Algiers Mission Band, and reorganized their mission finances along "simple more efficient" lines, with Lilias and Blanche bearing the ultimate financial responsibility for salaries and programs, underwriting them from their own resources and the unsolicited gifts of others.

Though it was something she neither sought nor resisted, the mantle of leadership inevitably fell upon Lilias's shoulders, she having both the vision for the ministry and the ability to inspire and mobilize others in the work. Matters as apparently trivial as the buying of bicycles for colportage or significant as Blanche's purchase of Dar Naama, awaited Lilias's approval. "Leadership with its inevitable discipline of loneliness was thus accepted, yet she would say, 'One of my first thoughts when I get to heaven will be *'How* good to be relieved of responsibility.'"[9] Looking back, those who worked with Lilias praised her approach and well-tempered leadership: a guidance that focused on respect and not control.

Early records list all workers, including Lilias, simply as "Staff," yet every decision or forward advance was cleared by a prayerful go-ahead from her. An earlier diary notation she made after interviewing Paul Villon for the work gives evidence of a mutual understanding of authority and accountability: "All is settled with the Villons. . . . And it is so good that, with his natural independence of character, he is perfectly ready to work under orders, & give in his report every week, & to have his days planned out for study, Arabic, visiting etc."[10]

Lilias, no doubt, was sensitive to the potential difficulty of a man working under the authority of a woman—particularly in that era—and was reassured that this would not be a problem to him. Later, as the mission staff expanded to include more men, she would refine the organizational system to capitalize on their leadership.

The year 1907 also saw the initiation of a bimonthly *Journal* to be circulated amongst their prayer supporters through a round-robin system of receiving, signing, and sending it on to the next on the list, until its return, like a homing pigeon, to Rue du Croissant. These labor intensive works of love were edited by Lilias from her diaries, then copied by hand, hers and co-workers', into ingenious native-style booklets—hand-bound covers with folded end flaps, cutaway windows revealing a picture and quotation representing the theme around which the booklet revolved, all richly illustrated by photographs, sketches, and paintings from the hand of Lilias. The purpose of the *Journal* is revealed years later in a diary entry listing the criteria for selecting extracts for publication:

1) that as far as possible some links should be given with each station, that all should be linked by prayer; 2) that the points where God's Hand is specially sensed at work should be emphasized that prayer

> *may focus on them; 3) that individual touches should be included to keep all bright & living. (1 January 1921)*

A wonderful image of the little band is provided in a July diary entry accompanied by an exquisite watercolor on a background of jade green—a bee hovering over a spray of pink blackberry blossoms:

> *A bee comforted me very much this morning concerning the desultoriness that troubles me in our work. There seems so infinitely much to be done that nothing gets done thoroughly. If work were more concentrated as it must be in educational or medical missions there would be less of this—but we seem only to touch souls & leave them. And that was what the bee was doing, figuratively speaking. He was hovering among some blackberry sprays, just touching the flowers here & there in a very tentative way, yet all unconsciously, life—life—life—was left behind at every touch, as the miracle-working pollen grains were transferred to the place where they could set the unseen spring working. We have only to see to it that we are surcharged, like the bees, with potential life. It is God and His eternity that will do the work—Yet He needs His wandering, desultory bees! (9 July 1907)*

St. Francis had his larks, Mother Teresa her white-robed Sisters of Charity. Lilias had her little band of wandering, desultory bees drawing life-giving pollen from God, then lighting here and there over the face of Algeria—slums, villages, oases—touching a street urchin, a mountain woman, a Sufi mystic with life—life—life.

17
SPRINGTIME OF LIBERTY
1908

The needs-be is that we should yield to His touch, in heart-sensitiveness and quick, full co-operation, whether the inward call is to action, or utterance, or prayer, letting Him work His way, as the hidden spring frees the silted channel—our aim, as Faber puts it, "Only not to impede the sweet grace from above!"

—*A Thirsty Land and God's Channels*[1]

The new year opened with a concentrated effort to ready the Blida house for Michael Olives and his bride, May. Under Blanche's domestic supervision the "dismal little cottage" was transformed with much cleaning and whitewashing into a "dear little home." The pride of the place was an "Arab Room" constructed at the back of the house in a lean-to "where natives can be made at home as they never can be in European surroundings."[2]

Michael and May settled the house with their furniture, carried up by person or beast, as no cart could get up the lane to the cottage set in the middle of a field. They named it *Oulad es Sultane,* translated "Children of the King," a reference to an old tradition of it being part of royal property ages ago. "It is Royal property again," writes Lilias, "this bit of it, now that it is dedicated to the service of the King of Heaven. . . . May its dwellers be all worthy of the title, & live in the power of it in the fighting days to come!"[3]

The next objective for 1908 was to attend to the translating of the Gospel of Luke from Dr. Nystrom's formal version into the colloquial language, a project begun some three years previously. When the revision committee met in the previous fall to go over the revised text, they found, to their great sorrow, that it was too much in the eastern dialect of Constantine to pass in the Western province. With pain and reluctance, they set aside the translation until they could find an Algerian Arab to help them with native phraseology. As Lilias says, they felt bound to do the "very utmost to give the people a wording over which there could be no mistake or misunderstanding."[4]

In February, Lilias and Helen Freeman went to Cherchelle, a coastal town seventy-five miles west of Algiers, for ten days to compare the various translations of Luke to have all in readiness for the revision committee meetings at Dar Naama in March. During the month-long session, Hadj Brahim, a young Arab man with a keen mind, "wide awake all round & yet a native of the natives,"[5] came up daily to help them with the enormous perplexities of translating spiritual concepts into a language in which often there were no suitable words for the task. Lilias reflected on the process:

St. Luke is slowly growing into its final setting—there are words and phrases which will always be linked with prayer victories, when no cues come to the involved passage, untranslatable expression & suddenly solution would come, dropped down from heaven upon one another, on Hadj Brahim himself & in that case all the more evidently of God that, as often as not, he did not realize where the point of difficulty lay.

There are other side touches too that bring Him near—yesterday "Fear not little flock" came in the chapter that we were working on—& we were getting at the right word for "little flock"—"Would that expression—jelieb—I think it was—mean such a little flock that it would not be worth the shepherd's care?" asked M. Summers. "No, if it were a very little flock the shepherd cares for it all the more," answered Hadj Brahim—and up shot the echo in thanksgiving to the great Shepherd who has such a very little flock in these Moslem Lands—He "cares for it all the more." (29 March 1908)

A conference was called in May for all the workers along the coast of North West Africa to meet at Dar Naama to talk over problems that seemed to face the young native Christians—"the strange slackness that comes over the converts so often when the first little flame dies down."[6] Mr. Summers, Bible Society secretary for Spain and North Africa, agreed to preside over the three-day meeting in which the focus was on two main questions: (1) "Are the converts growing towards the standard that we should hold for the church of the future?" and (2) "Is the aim of our ministry to them measured by the pattern laid down in St. Paul's Epistles—in caring; in sacrifice; in intercession?"[7]

The main meetings were held in the central court; noonday "conversational meetings" took place in the open-air orange tree court, fragrant with blossoms. Photographs capture the fifty-some workers gathered in the gracious setting, but the pictures cannot convey the encouragement and edification rendered by this ministry of hospitality. Unified by common goals, workers from one end of the coast to the other—from Cherchelle west in Algeria to Bizerta east in Tunesia—could see their individual ministries in the context of the whole. Lilias, with her unique ability to see the "bigger picture," envisioned how the various organizations could complement each other in their common purpose of bringing the light and love of Jesus to the Arab world.

In this fresh "springtime of liberty" Lilias began again to think strategically, this time for all of North Africa. An invitation from Miss Ericcson, a missionary to Egypt, to attend a conference along similar lines in Bizerta, resonated in Lilias's mind with Helen Freeman's thoughts of opening a station in Relizane, an Algerian town in the center of the western province of Oran. Lilias accepted the invitation with a strong sense that more was at issue than the conference alone, that there was significance in the very timing of Helen's exploration of the western province with this fresh step forward in the opposite coastline of Tunisia thus providing links east to west, along the coast of North Africa.

Lilias made plans to follow up the Bizerta conference with a "reconnoitering" with Miss Ericcson in Kef, an inland city in Tunisia which for years had held a curious attraction for both Lilias and Blanche, an attraction strengthened by their friendship with a young man, Habib, who lived in Kef and was brought up by a set of men purported to be devil worshipers.

Lily writes in her diary:

> *One day we were talking over with Miss Ericcson whether they should not with their growing band, take up work in another town, it came forcibly to me that Kef was the place, and Habib the link—And now, pressing beyond the thought of the conference came the vision "It will mean going on to Kef & that will mean the first step toward planting Christ's banner there—& probably go on to Tebessa for some fresh linking there too. . . . It is a strategic point of the future, for the railway will link it in time with the lines that are pushing strong into Tunesia & down into the desert—round the Djered—All it wants out in these lands is to get a band in training for the openings that will be upon us in the next few years. (27 May 1908)*

The Bizerta conference brought to light common understandings in native work: (1) the conferees' discovery that brain poisons and sorcery were being used against new converts, explaining some behavior that earlier had confounded the mission workers; and (2) their realization that a national worker was a necessity on each station to help them better understand the character and thought of indigenous peoples. The trip to Kef and Tebessa with Miss Ericcson and Blanche, was recorded in detail in Lilias's diary, along with charming sketches and paintings of the people and views that delighted her eye and heart—and with visions that crowded her soul for the future. Over Tebessa, she mused, "It would be a beautiful centre from which to go down to Tozer some day & the villages to its west—for the road is unfrequented and would attract no unfriendly attention—& soon the mining railways are likely to bring it all within easier reach than the four day march of the present."[8]

Lilias looked at Algeria and all of North Africa with eyes of faith that challenged the visible world with the verities of the unseen. Continually reinforcing this faith was God's created order:

The martens have been reading me a faith lesson. They come in flights at this time of year—lovely things with blue throats & feathered claws—one slept in my room last night & another darted in at the open window before I was up, swept round & out again.

Their faith-lesson is this—that their wings need the sense of "an empty void" below to give them a start—their leg muscles have no spring in them & when they perch by accident on a level place they are stuck fast—poor things we did not know that natural history fact in the past & when we have found them on our flat Alger roof with its parapet protection, we have thought they had got hurt somehow, & more than once we have tried to feed them till they died, instead of doing the one thing that they needed—tossing them off into emptiness.

So we need not wonder if we are not allowed to stay long in level sheltered places—our faith wings are like the martens' & mostly need the gulf of some emergency to give them their start on a new flight. We will not fear when we feel empty air under them. (30 April 1908)

Even as the vision widened to embrace lands beyond Algeria, doors were opening for Lilias to present the cause of the Muslim world before the international Christian church. Her summer break being in England this year, she attended Keswick, where two encounters had a profound impact on her. The first was a long talk with Evans Roberts—"the spiritual 'happening' of the summer personally speaking"—which brought to Lilias a fresh outlook on prayer:

He gave great light on the way God will focus our prayer, if we wait on Him & that then we call quietly: "I want this done" with the assurance "He shall have whatsoever he saith" & he said if we could get two or three who understood these laws of prayer, and would pray through, the atmosphere would clear & blessing would come down. The whole talk has brought floods of light on the entire question. (28 August 1908)

The other encounter was with Dr. Samuel Zwemer—"Apostle to Islam"—with whom Lilias would have many future dealings. Dr. Zwemer, missionary to Arabia, was on temporary loan to serve the dual roles of field secretary for The Reformed Church Board of Foreign Missions and the traveling secretary for recruiting for the Student Volunteer Movement. Like Lilias, he saw beyond denominational boundaries, challenging the church universal to support the work in Muslim countries through prayer and personnel, influencing countless young men and women to go into overseas missionary service. Lilias thrilled to his Keswick address on Islam that "was like a trumpet-call to the church to awake from her apathy."[9]

Through yet another strange twist of God's leading, Lilias, as a result of her friendship with Miss Ericcson, accepted an invitation from the Swedish YWCA to speak at meetings in Sweden and Denmark. Arriving early in September, with Blanche Haworth, in time for the last meeting of the Swedish Keswick, Lilias launched an intensive speaking schedule in churches, schools, and training centers, covering almost two months. In her typical fashion, Lilias prepared the way by writing a paper, which later evolved into the booklet *A Thirsty Land and God's Channels*. It is a lucid and comprehensive presentation of Islam, comparing it to the Sahara—"Dry as the dunes, hard as the gravel"—and a compelling challenge to Christians to be channels "in union with Him from whose riven Heart the streams were set flowing."[10] Her diary pages of this trip are filled with photographs and accounts of stimulating sights, new opportunities, and blessed fellowship. Lilias departed Scandinavia "with fresh heart-knittings that have the sense of a future about them, rather than a past, as we leave them for Germany."[11]

The trip to East Germany was an unexpected alteration. Baroness Kurcks of Sweden encouraged the trip, arranging for Lilias to meet a certain Sister Eva of Friedenshort and to see the Sister's work in Miechovitz. Of this final stage of the journey Lilias wrote, "And God, as is His want, has kept to the last His 'best wine.' "[12] She described the experience in her journal:

Outwardly, the place we have landed in is the ugliest & bleakest & barrenest one has ever seen—a great mining district on the spur of the Carpathians, with the winds of all the Russias blown bitterly across it and the thermostat at 27 degrees of frost.

Inwardly it is all aglow, as I never knew a place to be in all my life—on fire with a spirit of sacrifice that does not even know itself to be sacrifice, it is so the natural expression of love.

It was a small work, with deep roots, till the time of the Welsh Revival when Sister Eva's lifelong search after God & His holiness was met by a full draught from His fountain. That summer His power took hold at Miechovitz, & it has grown at a rate that is amazing. Before then there were 24 sisters—now there are 150, & the household numbers 300 souls, including orphans, students, infirm villagers, creche, training home for girl's night refuge—to say nothing of out-posts, prison work & I know not what besides.

We are lodged in rooms off the Central Hall, where God's Spirit came upon them that memorable autumn day—& before it is daylight the chorales begin there softly, like birds singing in the dawn—& all day long there is a ripple of gladness everywhere, with the very minimum of the needful, made elastic to cover the fresh needs that come incessantly. (14-17 November 1908)

It is no surprise that their "hearts were knit instantly." The week was spent "hard at work with meetings—two & three & four a day—though we feel it is we who want to learn of them,"[13] and with the parting came the certainty that they were joined in yet one more link on their ever-lengthening chain of love.

The continental tour concluded in Berne, Switzerland. Lilias's talks now totaled over sixty, individually prepared for each new situation. She summed up that experience:

How faithful God was in His supply of the need, for He gave some fresh outline from His Word for every one. For that last one came the "benediction" in its missionary light—an echo of Miechovitz.

"The grace of our Lord Jesus Christ,
And the love of God
And the fellowship of the Holy Ghost
be with you."

We have so often listened to it as the soothing ending of a quiet sermon. In its full meaning it is a battle cry. (30 November 1908)

The return to Algiers, after almost four months' absence, was greeted by shadows and lights. Before Lilias's departure for the summer, Chrira, one of the older girls for whom they held much hope, had succumbed to family pressure to marry a Muslim man. Now, in their absence, their beloved Sherifa was married to a Muslim man as well, after having withstood years of inconceivable pressures—native sorcery, curses, and charms—and having outwitted countless schemes to trick her into compromises that would obligate her financially into an undesirable union. Lilias had seen great potential for girls like Chrira and Sherifa, who, having been either divorced or widowed, had by Arab law the right of refusal to remarry, a freedom otherwise not granted. Now she wrote:

We are coming to see that this right is but a nominal matter, and that the will of her masculine relations overrides it. And an Arab woman always belongs to a man of some sort—to her father first, then her husband & if he fails, back to her father—failing him her brother—failing him her uncle & so on: & no appeal seems really to release her: it is part of the iron yoke of Islam that will not snap but by the touch of God's Hand. (29 July 1908)

Still, light shone through the shadows. On 12 December 1908, twins were born to May and Michel Olives—the boy was named Eustace and the girl named Lilias. Lily wrote, "We are all so glad & proud as if they belonged to us personally!"[14] On Christmas Eve "God's Christmas present" came to the land in the first package of finished copies of St. Luke's Gospel, and her response was, "So the first Gospel, that will be understood from cover to cover by the Arabs of Algeria, goes out on a floodtide of hope in the same Lord over all, rich to all that call upon Him."[15]

There were, as well, growing lights on the horizon that even Lilias with her "floodtide of hope" could not foresee. Relationships with other workers had been strengthened and unified within the country; friendships had been formed outside. Hearts had been touched by Lilias's personal appeal on behalf of the Muslim world—adding people in Sweden, Denmark, Germany, and Switzerland to North Americans in their growing list of friends. During this lovely "springtime of liberty" a base of support was being built in interest, prayer, and workers, preparing the way for unprecedented advance.

18

EARLY BUDS AND NORTH WINDS

1909—1910

"Awake O North Wind" has been the word in my heart these days. . . . The north wind puts back the buds that are coming out prematurely—they are getting ready by the repression for a stronger life when the South wind blows.

—Diary[1]

The new year was heralded by the opening of a mission station in the western province of Oran—Relizane was the place, and Helen Freeman the person. Lilias and Helen boarded the train with a clear sense of destiny:

It is not often that one consciously turns a corner in life like this—at least not out here.

We looked up at Miliana as we passed it lying along its mountain side with a silver fillet of snow crowning the crest above. Will that be the next to catch the sunrise? Then hours of travel among low tawny

> *hills splashed with dark lentisk bushes like a panther's skin—then they widened into a plain, the hills falling back from it into pink fretted distance, full of touches of blueish cucald, which means prickly pear plantations—& they mean villages—all untouched—no point of light anywhere nearer than Morocco, once Blida was left behind. (5 January 1909)*

Two images sealed this venture with symbolic promises of God's blessing. The first was a well, alongside the first railroad station in Oran, with branches heavy with fruit hanging over its wall. Lilias painted it in her diary as a sign of the "promise of life & fruitfulness."[2] The second promise, Lilias wrote, "lies in today, our first morning here, being the Epiphany, the day star of the sunrise that is to come."[3]

Through contacts with a local French pastor, they secured a temporary cottage until the half-built native style house was completed, and they began "ransacking the meagre Relizane shops for the necessaries of life" and setting up the new dwelling with the ingenious arrangement of Helen's fashioning of furniture from packing cases and petroleum boxes. Lilias wrote, "we feel in these outstations, more than we know depends on living among the people in absolute simplicity."[4]

Leaving Helen in her new surroundings, with only a few local contacts and Philomene Villon as a temporary house guest, Lilias joined Blanche in Miliana—their next point of advance for the following autumn. Once again, with the blessing and aid of a local French pastor, Mons. Capelle, Lilias scouted the area for a strategic site and found a tiny cottage "to let" at the verge of the native quarter—an open valley sprinkled thickly with white houses, single and clustered, trending down to the riverbed two thousand feet below. "The cottage was so *exactly* right in position and size, that far as it had been from our thoughts to move so quickly, we felt we must put it to the test & ask Mons. Capelle to enquire about conditions."[5] With a sense of opening horizons, Lilias took the evening train to Blida.

Blida was the most ambitious undertaking in their plans and one which occupied much attention throughout the winter and spring. With Michel and May Olives firmly based in the Arab cottage, plans were drawn to develop a compound to accommodate their growing ministry. A new mission house was built completely along native lines: "It is all native . . . without a trace of the 'banal' European element anywhere. . . . Five arches are now being built on a scaffolding of wooden segments. Michel raised a doubt this morning as to whether these same segments were all of one size. 'Yes, O my master, they are quite of one size,' was the reply—'but you must not mix them!' "[6]

A parable of faith emerged in the digging of the well which had originally determined the situation of the Blida mission house. Having dug to a depth of fifty meters without striking water, the "water diviner" changed his determination, suggesting the water course had been diverted by earthquake activity. The local people, naturally curious, began to challenge: "Why does not God give you water, if He is pleased with you?" Lilias was convinced that this was a test of faith and that they should proceed as planned. "We sent a stone on its silent drop into the empty well, and heard its thud on the dry bottom, & sang over it together 'Praise God from whom all blessings flow!' "[7]

Her diary reveals the drama of faith as the weeks pass without their reaching water, nearby water supplies likewise having dried up, and the diggers at last abandoning the site. Then on 16 April, while at Dar Naama, Lilias received a telegram: *Eau dans puit. Alleluia*—"Water in the well!" causing her to write:

> *It is so beautiful that it was on Good Friday that the first trickle began—the very day after the workmen had gone away—& the very day that "the full, perfect & sufficient sacrifice" was being remembered before God with His "how much more" for every lesser gift. (18 April 1909)*

One lovely touch preceded the long-delayed answer: "All the house-material is there, already dug up, instead of having to be brought & carted at much expense from below—stones for foundations, sand & gravel for the 'Tabbes'—as they call the beaten wall—everything except the lime. The house has been dug out of this well!"[8]

Later, Michel Olives uncovered the mouth of the well for Lilias to behold, prompting her to write this response:

> *Instead of the still circle of water I expected to see, it was all heaving & rippling in swelling circles! Then it stopped & grew quiet & while*

> *I was wondering if my eyes could have deceived me, the trembling began & all was repeated. Some periodic up-burst from the hidden spring below—then all grew glass again. I never knew before what the "well of water springing up" meant. I thought of it vaguely as a springing all the time—but this is so much more like His way with our souls. A sudden rising & flooding of the underlying life, & then a sinking back with stillness. (15 June 1909)*

As doors were literally opening beyond Algiers, "a window of fresh possibilities" was raised back in the Arab town as well. One day Blanche and Lilias noticed a pink bill of sale pasted to a house, advertising another native house for a curiously low sum in the thick of the Arab quarter. Once again, visions began to take the shape of reality, as they saw in this the possibility of a half-way house, a place to initiate young workers before thrusting them into independence: "It would make *such* a 'slum-post' both in position & character. A step . . . towards living among the people such as never seemed possible here in Algers."[9] The little slumpost was purchased by Blanche and named *El Naama,* "Room of Grace."

The mission band's forward advance into new territory was matched by needed workers—nine new people joined them in 1909 alone, bringing their total to twenty. The Scandinavian trip of 1908 yielded its harvest of two Danish girls—Alma Krebs and Ellen Dagenskolw—and British contacts resulted in Miriam Madson, Fannie Currie, Millicient Roche, Alice McIlroy, and Mary Watling, cousin of Mabel Grautoff. Perhaps the most unexpected recruit was Michel Olives's brother Laurent, who came to Blida for the dedication of the baby twins and stayed on to supervise the Blida building, joining the permanent staff soon thereafter.

It was not long before the growing band was scattered into a "very thin fighting line." The young women, "Missions Helpers," were assigned to various stations—Rue du Croissant, Dar Naama, Blida, Relizane, Miliana—where half their time was given to household cares, the other half to direct service among the people. Laurent Olives took over the native café adjoining Rue du Croissant, drawing around himself young boys for carpentry and Bible classes.

Even as Lilias lamented "things undone that seem infinite,"[10] the reinforcements permitted unprecedented advances in ministry. The summer of 1909 witnessed the first children's camp at Dar Naama—gathering twenty little "girgaff girls" (members of the embroidery class at Rue du Croissant) from Algiers with native women as housemothers. Lilias described and made illustrations of the girls at camp:

The Arab court is full of sunny gladness—the shrill tremolos of youyuyuyyou's which marks all Arab rejoicing from a wedding feast downward, resounds when they are let out to play or called in to eat. They come from the orchard in a procession, with heads wreathed like so many Bacchuses. This [illustration] was Fata' bent Fateema's head dress of violet & white wild flowers today—& Hawawaches in generally a mass of winding tendrils around her fragile face. (28 July 1909)

Dar Naama likewise was the site of spring conferences for the entire band and the meeting place for the revision committee, this time translating the Gospel of John. Lilias wrote about that process:

It is even more full of interest than the revision of St. Luke, & from the very nature of the truths taught in it, needs still more careful weighing. It is not the question of just giving a gospel of words that the people can understand, but to give them the germ of a spiritual language in which the things that the Holy Ghost teaches can be expressed—the dearth of it seems in the inverse ratio to the richness of the tongue for all secular purposes. (27 June 1909)

They made advances in their work through new technology. Using a printing press given to them by their friends at Sister Eva's Training Home in Friedenshort, they printed their own tracts and mass quantities of the round-robin journals, hence speeding the distribution of the still hand-illustrated, hand-bound booklets.

Another concession to modern technology was the purchase of a van, which Lilias describes as the "only possible solution for those *douars* (groups of Arab families) on the tablelands & plains, trending away & far beyond reach from any European center," adding that "a couple of men, or a man & wife, could use it for weeks together without any of the exertion of pitching and re-pitching a tent."[11] A bright red van especially fitted for its previous owner—a lion tamer!—was purchased and dedicated for God's service. Lilias writes, "We just look at it and *wonder.* If we had the planning of it we could not have invented anything better for its purpose."[12]

Patterns evolved in the work—classes and programs at each station visited regularly by Lilias; fall and winter trips to mountain villages and southland oases; spring conferences and summers breaks—and always, for Lilias, ongoing relationships with her native Algier "family": "lazy," but well-intentioned Ali, Mohammed the silk-weaver, gentle Belaid, the young Hawawach and Fata bent Fatima whose presences she valued all the more for her knowledge of their unalterable imminent marriages, and two-year-old Melha, "preternatually intelligent" with the most knowing ways: "This morning she nearly convulsed the women's side of the curtain in the morning meeting, by suddenly remarking, while holding out a picture cube of a gorilla, 'That is my father.'—it *had* a grisly likeness to the old gnome with his shaggy hair & beard."[13]

On another occasion, Lilias wrote about the same child:

> *Today's story is a very pretty one. The little pickle Melha . . . went right up to her nearly blind father & pointed to one of the pictures on the wall—one of the Lord calling a little child to Him—& said "Look at Jesus." "I have no eyes O my daughter—I cannot see," was the answer. The baby thing lifted head & eyes to the picture & said, "O Jesus, look at father!" . . . was not that a bit of heavenly wisdom? (28 July 1909)*

The keynote of this year of great advance was the verse "Awake O north wind and come, thou south." Strangely, without consultation, it was the text for Sister Eva's last message at the April conference. She was with them in Algeria at the time for a period of rest and recuperation from her work at Friedenshort. Lilias responded to her message: "We could almost hear the crackle of the dead wood breaking off as she described it, with the keen winter blasts that bring all into readiness for the spring."[14] Little could they imagine the prophetic aspect of her utterances, the northerly winds that would certainly assail them!

First to come were unprecedented blows on the little band of native believers and enquirers who had begun to meet again. Subjected to brain drugs, which, given in food or drink, produce a paralysis of mind and will, they were vulnerable to hypnotism and "spells"—phenomena the mission workers had come to recognize as Muslim means to coerce converts back into the old paths. One after another the native Christians withdrew from them—and their newly avowed faith—as they fell under this subtle but powerful attack of darkness. Great though her hopes were for the native Christians as the nucleus for a future church visible in Algeria, Lilias reluctantly came to regard the many premature deaths as a delivery for sincere but fragile converts attempting to live a Christian lifestyle in a Muslim household. "Safe with Him," she wrote after the death of a beloved Arab friend. "I think we need to have the Moslem sheep to shepherd to know what that means."

Lilias, in a letter to Dr. Samuel Zwemer, addressed the special challenges which faced the converts from Islam to Christianity. Acknowledging the "look of dumb agony" over the severance of family ties, the occasional relinquishment of property rights, she maintained that more than direct persecution, they experience moral suffering. Her exposition on the use and effect of drugs, merits quotation, for its unique and comprehensive insight into this extraordinary phenomena:

> *We feel that the danger that they run here is of a worse order. All around them is risk of brain-drugs and spells and hypnotism, and we have come to the conclusion that a large proportion of seeming backsliding of converts may be traced to these combined influences, for I cannot but think that spells (i.e. definite Satanic influences invoked and brought to bear) have their part in the havoc wrought. As regards the physical side of the attempt, we think, from comparing notes on symptoms with a missionary from India, that Datura is largely used for drugging; but whatever the drug may be, it is well known in their*

domestic intrigues, and can be administered unnoticed in food or drink. It seems to excite the emotions and paralyse the will-power. According to the description that we have had from one poor soul after another, a great darkness comes over their spirits and lasts for several months before it wears away; they feel, meanwhile, that they cannot come near us or have anything to do with us. . . .

[A] story comes to my mind that may seem incredible, but was told me by the missionary concerned, who fought and died in the ranks of N.A.M. (North African Mission), with a passion for souls that few have shared. One of the converts in her solitary station was a young fellow of good family. All went well with him for a time, then, suddenly, he left off coming to the Mission House, and all touch was lost except round by Heaven. The winter came, and the workers were clearing out the fireplace when they caught sight of this man's name on a bit of paper. They smoothed it out and deciphered it. It proved to be a charm written to prevent his setting foot in the house, or having anything to do with the missionaries. They prayed, in the name of Jesus, that the evil spell might be broken, and burnt the paper. Within an hour the convert was back in the room, bowed and broken-hearted, confessing to God his backsliding. Later on he told the missionary that he knew he had been drugged, and that he had shrunk, with a shrinking that amounts to hatred, from the thought of coming near the mission.

I cannot but feel this is a matter that we should study from all its aspects, and that we should learn to put a definite prayer-guard round the converts in this direction, and to learn the delivering power of the cross of Jesus and His Almighty name, when they are entrapped. So far as we have seen, when they are walking in the light up to their measure, the attempts have failed to take effect, or soon worked off; but when the soul is already weakened by some compromise it falls an easy prey. I send this for what it is worth for publication, but I am glad of the chance of unburdening my heart to you about it.[15]

Then a typhus epidemic began to rage in Algeria, this time affecting their own band. Alma Krebs was the first to be afflicted, her life hanging in the balance in the hospital, while Rue du Croissant was placed on two-week quarantine. The crisis passed; two others were taken ill, and young mission workers were called off assignment to care for them, forcing the closing down of the work at Rue du Croissant for the interim.

The greatest blow of all occurred at the end of May with the death of their beloved Laurent Olives, who succumbed after almost a month-long battle against the dreaded disease. Lilias wrote,

> *Today brought a sorrowful summons to the farewelling of Laurent Olives. A sudden change for the worse came in the night, & he was lying prone by the time I got there, hardly conscious except when the sound of the blessed name of Jesus brought back a rally in the ebbing powers. He only lived an hour after I left—"Jesus—Vive Jesus!" were the last words the watches caught.*
>
> *It is the first death-break in our band, & it leaves a sense of personal loss: there was a gentle thoughtfulness in all his ways, rare in a great stalwart fellow such as he. There is a hush of sorrow over the band of his carpenter lads & Badash with a sober look has taken a bunch of flowers to the chamber where he lay, & he's seen his face once more.*[16]

In the days to follow there were further losses in the band; Sasha Perkins and Mabel Grautaff were recalled to England for family illnesses, and Annie Whisler was given doctor's orders for "six month entire rest." Soon thereafter, Edel Jensen left Algiers permanently for another post. Lilias turned to Scripture with somber reflectiveness:

> *I have been reading today, with the sound of God's warning voice in it the story of David's numbering the people [in II Samuel 24]—& have been seeing the danger of that same looking to numbers instead of to God alone, with the enforcements that this last year has brought. Gideon's lesson [in Judges 7] again only intensified. (19 May 1910)*

Lilias was unprepared, nonetheless, for a further possible breech in their dwindling ranks:

> *Both the Olives and the Villons are speaking of leaving us in these coming months—leaving us only, not the native work, thank God—& if they can, as they think, to more settled work than ours, with a more solid outcome. Now that the initial steps of breaking up the ground have been passed through, we cannot try to hold them. To us however, & in its personal aspect as regards our own bit of the field, it is another north wind blast. (17 October 1910)*

The next month, her fears were confirmed, with the Olives announcing their intention of joining the new Baptist Society being started among the French-speaking lands, and the Villons announcing their intention to work with the American Episcopal Church in Algeria—ironically, the very work inspired by Lilias during the landmark International Sunday School Convention 1907 visit. The Olives' desire was to continue in Blida on the same lines, but under new direction. The Villons' work would be to the principal towns in Algeria and, in the country, to Kabylia.

Regardless of personal impact, Lilias invariably took the "high road" when it came to reporting each new development, but her pain sounds through those measured words, "It is another north wind blast." It was a loss of dreams almost close enough to touch—they had planned to open a station in the oases of the Oued Souf as base for deeper penetration into the Southlands, but this hope was dashed even as the Villons prepared for one last winter in the city of El Oued. Perhaps closest to the heart, however, was the loss of Michel and May Olives. May had been with them since 1898, a "daughter" to Lilias, and the twins definitely were considered "family," as indicated by photographs, sketches, and progress reports sprinkled throughout her diary.

On the face of it, the reasons were clear and understandable: "more settled work than ours, with a more solid outcome." One wonders about specific factors that may have contributed to this decision at this particular time. Did the "trained faith" of the remarkable senior leaders offer adequate consideration of the needs of a young family? Were the two men, the only ones in the band, adversely affected by the rash of female recruits? Did they chafe under female leadership that was, however gracious, nonetheless firm and insistent upon total accountability? Did the death of Laurent Olives—brother and brother-in-law of the two men—have any bearing on their decision?

The questions remain unanswered. The indicators, however, point to sustained positive relationships between these families and the band. The Villons send warm and detailed reports from the Souf during their final Southland sojourn. The Olives continue on location at Blida, and through the years their lives intermingle with the band—the family enjoying summer breaks at Dar Naama, the children familiar presences in Lilias's life.

But for now, during this season of fresh loss, Lilias's questions cut to the soul: "When will the north wind have done its work? *When* will the south wind rise from its land of eternal summers?"[17]

19
SOUTH WINDS BLOWING

1911—1912

"Houses and lands" they were falling to us one after another, & we gave God thanks; but a great longing awoke with the remembrance of the rest of the promise that was being so abundantly fulfilled. Could not He who was giving us such lavish "hundredfold" over its first clause and its last, grant us the same over the promised "brethren & sisters and mothers" that lay between!

—*Back-ground and Fore-ground*[1]

The new year began with bright hopes for the "houses and lands" recently added to their work as Lilias began her station rounds:

Train to Relizane, Jan. 6.

Via Blida for last night. The sense of Epiphany came before the dawn, in the tremulous clanging of its church bell on the plain below—so gentle at first that it might, almost, have been the tinkling bells of the wise men's camels—and growing into a "crescendo" of joy—as will that "manifestation" come to be, at a better daybreak. . . .

It is good to see here in Relizane how the Feet of the Good Shepherd are going after His sheep one by one. . . .

The new little house is perfect . . . the same sense of having been built for us long ago, room by room, as we have had over all our dwellings. The nightly barking of innumerable dogs and the muezzin's cry from the mosque, a stone's throw off, make one realize that we are at the very door of the natives, and they are in and out all the time, as often as not with some tiny offering. (6 January 1911)

A more surprising twist came in the taking of yet another house, an old Moorish dwelling, in the Arab town. The first intention was to rent the ground floor for a reading room, a quiet place for language study away from the noise and activity of Rue du Croissant. As negotiations proceeded, so did the availability of the upstairs court, opening up possibilities for a second idea that Lilias had been pondering for some time:

The longing has sprung up again afresh these last weeks, in the subject of getting girls of leisure out, as "Short Service" helpers. It has come with the sense of kindling and burning that so often marks the opening of a new turn in God's road. (14 February 1911)

Lilias placed an offer on the rooms, which was accepted, and while they awaited moving day, they celebrated the opening of the other new Algiers house: the little slumpost, El Naama, or "Room of Grace," for its small beginning work:

> *So sweet & pure the little place looks now that all is ready—& we all met there this afternoon to give it into the Hands of the Prince of Life & Love to be a fresh dwelling place for Him in the heart of the native town. For one feels so delightfully in the thick of them there—with the muezzin call sounding at the little latticed window and the edging of bright headgear & inquisitive faces round the neighboring parapets when we appear on the roof. It is a big gift from God. (15 March 1911)*

Even as they were inaugurating this new venture, Alma Krebs was on her way to Tozeur, where they had taken possession of a native *fondak* or inn—a joint venture with Albina Cox from North African Mission—"the first house for God's Kingdom in that great desert." Lilias reflects in her diary:

> *Tonight's last act was to go up to the roof room & plant Christ's standard in Tozer on the fresh map there, by the red dot that means a settled post. Alas the dot had in so doing, to be taken from El Oued, for this afternoon brought our farewell to the Villons who will have left for Constantine before we get back—& there is no saying when dear El Oued will be named again.*
>
> *It was a sorrowful bit, that good bye, though without the bitterness in it of any sense of a wrong step on their parts. Time is so short that it behooves us each to lay out our days to what it seems to us will give the widest & surest return in God's Kingdom & this is what he is doing. (24 March 1911)*

During a brief interlude from real estate ventures, Lilias and Blanche spent ten days in Genoa working on papers following up the Lucknow Continuation Committee proposals, which were developed the previous month with other mission organizations, particularly as they concerned

Muslim women: calling for literature developed specifically with their needs and interests in mind; suggesting a hostel for women-students in Cairo. Lilias's recommendations for literature were especially far-sighted, given the lack of women readers, but she countered possible objections with these words:

> *New literature for Christian women. Do fellow-missionaries sigh over the words and think it is a far day to the need for that? It may not be. We have a God who lives in eternity, and knows no time limits. We can be getting ready for the showers, like the autumn crocus of these southern lands, that rears its head in faith, while, as yet, there is hardly a cloud in the sky.*[2]

Back in Algeria, Lilias continued to explore further possibilities for expansion. New "promise buds" were opening around Helen's work in Relizane, first in a "farm class" of native children, maintained by Christian colonists; and then, in an opportunity to open another station a bit further south, in Mascara, the nearest town with a large native quarter. They scouted a tract of land in Bou Hanifia—lignum vitae forest, cornfields, and river bed of oleanders with wonderful facilities, given the needful irrigation for orange growing. Helen purchased the land the following year with the aim of its becoming an industrial farm where inquirers and converts could find a living. "'Houses and lands' again," writes Lilias, "it is as if the pressed-back current of last year were breaking out in new ways all round."[3]

Keeping pace with the addition of houses and lands was the expanding, once again, of the staff, with ten new members joining the band during 1911 and 1912. This included eight women and two men—a young national, Joachim Pons, to carry on the boys' work in the café, and Mr. Smeeton, a "white haired" Englishman who had been a great supporter of their work for years and who would continue to build an ever-broadening base of prayer support for the work as well as develop practical ministries, particularly to blind men in Algiers.

A most serendipitous new element to their workforce was the addition of the short servicers—educated girls who could "come on a self-supporting basis for a time of service in all the countless ways in which such can be rendered with a small knowledge of the language, if hands and hearts are ready."[4] The recruitment for this work was uppermost on Lilias's mind during her summer break in England, and she had this to say about the results, "All opened up like a flower with never a need for a pull at the petals. Contact with girls of leisure has sprung up unsought and plenishings, unsought also, have come in for the Hostel."[5] With Blanche Bannister from The Olives Training Home and Kathleen Butler to guide them in the ways of service, plus Elsie Thorpe on location at the Hostel (Dar el Fedjr) to head the work, a steady stream of young women would come to Algiers for short-term service on a self-supporting basis, until World War I brought this to a halt.

Lilias, a keen appreciator of young people, took special delight in the humor and spontaneity of the young additions to the band. The first pair, coming with the new year, added a welcome dimension to Lilias's extended family:

> *We had what the Americans would call a "surprise party" tonight in coming down to supper and finding the whole of the younger generation in native costumes of the bedcovers & curtains of their rooms for the most part, with their tableclothes draped round their heads! The above plenishings being all made of haiks & fautas they lent themselves perfectly to the draping & the long table full of bright swathings looked fascinating. (1 January 1912)*

Growth in the band, people and places, ushered in necessary corporate advances as well, first in a Home Council in London, next in a Field Committee in Algiers, consisting of the three seniors—Lilias, Blanche, and Helen—and the three next in standing. "It fills us with rest and hope," Lilias wrote, "that burdens, questions, aims, unfoldings, are taken up and shared henceforth by younger hearts and brains."[6] Efforts to consolidate the band both geographically and generationally were likewise forwarded by adding an annual two-day rally in late autumn before the launching of the various programs in the stations and outposts. Lilias commented on the changes:

> *Before us all dawned, I think a new horizon—of the glory of the task to which God has called us—a glory in its every hardness & in the sense that we are working for the future & its coming day. "We were dreamers dreaming greatly." (23 October 1911)*

Another "bit of consolidating of a lighter order" evolved at Dar Naama—the first issuing of an Algiers Mission Band quarterly magazine, described by Lilias:

> *It is for "Private Circulation" and B.G.L.H. (Blanche Haworth) is the Editor: it has brought out already a deal of latent writing capacity, and will be a first linking all round. It is called "El Couffa"—a couffa being a native palm-leaf basket: we are said never to go out without carrying one, whence it stands on the title-page as our ensign! (5 January 1912)*

The five or six years of surviving editions of this "in-house" publication provide posterity with perhaps the most intimate view of the band. A scrapbook in format, printed off a multi-copier, it is generously illustrated with hand-colored drawings and pasted inserts—maps and photographs, station reports, samples of native decorative brush-work and *girgaff* (embroidery) designs. It also included excerpts from, among other things, Lilias's past journals and diaries. Providing history of early seminal work as well as current updates of various stations, the magazine concluded with a literary supplement showcasing a wide range of materials—specimens of new story parables, text cards, colloquial hymns replete with text and scores, lectures on Islam, and even systematic grammatical aids!

What impresses the reader decades later is the breadth and scope of the contributions. International events are reported—biographical sketches of English heroes, scientific updates on the uses of radium—as are mission endeavors such as Amy Carmichael's work in India, along with work in China, Korea, and throughout the world. Poems and stories from such diverse writers as George Herbert and Rudyard Kipling, Robert Browning and François Fénelon are interspersed among unsigned writings in the unmistakable style of Lilias. One can only imagine the anticipation of the mission workers, particularly those in isolated posts, for this publication, rich in resources, both sacred and secular.

Nowhere is Lilias's counsel concerning ministry spelled out more clearly, with characteristic wit and humor, than in the "Letter M," an open letter to missionaries, carried for eight consecutive issues. Here Lilias explores a range of relevant topics—friendships, careless words, treatment of local help, disciplined minds, attitude problems, God's loving providence—drawing on a wealth of practical wisdom gleaned from more than two decades on the field. Only a taste can be given here, but a compilation of these letters would provide a concise handbook for the profit of any Christian worker:

> *How many of us have said and sung with all our hearts "Anywhere with Jesus," but at the time we did not realize all that it meant for us. Indeed at home, and surrounded by all that home means, we could not know. When the test comes we must not forget that "Anywhere" means for missionaries something different from life in England, and let us take very good care not to make a misery of anything that "anywhere" brings us.*
>
> *To us in Algeria it must mean sometime or other, Arab food. Do we object to it? And mice, do we mind them? And mosquitos, do we think them dreadful? In some parts it means close contact with dirt and repulsive disease. Yet if Jesus is there what have we possibly to complain of? It means living among a stiff-necked and untrue people and struggling with a strange and difficult language. And yet let us evermore write over all our miseries, big, and for the most part very little, these transforming words "With Jesus." And then the very breath of Heaven will breathe upon our whole being and we shall be glad.*[7]

As their longing increased for the native "brothers and sisters" whom they had come to claim for the kingdom, a "bud of hope" came from an unexpected source—Si Mohammed ben Kaddour, a member of their very first Sunday class during their earliest days in Algiers. The women's outstanding memory of Si Mohammed was his attempt to trick the original trio—Lilias, Blanche, and Lucy—who at that time could hardly string together a quarter hour's talk in Arabic, by solemnly giving his name in the register as *Mohammed ben el Kelb*—"The son of a dog"—in the hope of seeing it go down in the book!

By chance, on the tram between Dar Naama and Algiers, Lilias came across Si Mohammed after many years' absence during which he had lived a wild life. Now, in the later stages of consumption, he turned again to the women, asking to hear the hymns of long ago and opening his heart to the "Good Shepherd" with a sincerity and ardor they had rarely seen among the Arab men. Throughout his final weeks on earth, he feasted upon Scripture, reading it aloud to the men who gathered around him. He died a Christian death, refusing to say the last *Sheheda* ("There is no God but Allah, and Mohammed is his prophet")—the Muslim's "passport" to heaven—impressing his sister Chrira with his peacefulness at the end. "I am very happy, very happy," she reported him saying, "I am not vexed at dying—Jesus is at my head."[8]

Boualem, Chrira's husband, who was likewise with Si Mohammed ben Kaddour at the end, was deeply impressed, later becoming a believer through his witness. When Boualem's sister Zehour became ill, Lilias saw an opportunity to bring her into the loving embrace of Dar el Fedjr, the Short Service Hostel in Algiers, where the "DayBreakers" (short servicer girls) could help nurse her to heath. To Lilias's great joy, Boualem and Chrira agreed to accompany Zehour in the little Arab guestrooms—joined soon after by Zehour's husband, mother, and nephew—a breakthrough to a new kind of ministry.

Lilias had long believed that they could minister most effectively to individuals through the family. She viewed this as an opportunity to gain "fresh leverages" with Zehour's family and envisioned a future ministry to entire families where, away from cultural pressures, they could daily receive spiritual nurture. The experience surpassed expectation:

> *It has been a wonderful week—a sudden little shower of the Spirit has fallen on the family at the guest house. Night after night we have felt the earnestness increasing, & tonight, the last night, it came to*

the story of the Crucifixion. A great hush of God's presence was over them, in which we felt that He was, according to His promise, using the power of that Cross as His drawing force—it was wonderful to feel the intentness of each soul of the five. . . . there was a sort of gasp of relief when it came to the resurrection. And as far as we could tell, in the time of prayer that followed every one of them came simply like little children to His Feet.

We are "like them that dream"—it is the first time that we have seen anything like a collective work of the Spirit—and oh if He keeps them true it will mean a new thing in being able to stand by each other instead of hindering one another that has so often happened when the wife only or the husband only, was touched. (18 February 1912)

Closely following this wonderful beginning came a new work among the young Arab men, once again starting with returns from the past—Omar and lame Mustapha—with whom they had been so involved in their earliest years in Algiers. Now, however, they came with fresh understanding and a deeper commitment to a truly Christian lifestyle. With great joy, Lilias watched the growing number of young men meeting together to wrestle with heart-issues and to study Scripture. The revision of Acts could not have been better timed for showing the meaning of the life of discipleship to these young followers of Jesus. Lilias described them in these words:

And now the "brethren". . . have begun to gather, night after night, with Boualem & Omar's eagerness over the study of Acts together. We feel the linking of real brotherhood of spirit. It is like watering thirsty plants to see their eagerness after their long day's work—over the simple bare word of God. (16 July 1912)

There were still difficulties. Aissha, Boualem's eldest brother, resisted the new-found faith of the Birgebaa family, terrorizing them with countless creative schemes, particularly in regards to economic control. He held his brother-in-law Hamidan in his power, charging him with unpaid debts from his wedding five years previous, threatening him with legal summons if not paid immediately. When that was paid, he took Hamidan's son hostage until he paid for the furniture given at that same time. (One brother protested, "He has got me in a cage, & I can only hop backwards & forwards, & now & then he pulls out a feather!") The young men struggled constantly with the pressures of the culture; the young "housemaidens" would advance in understanding and trust only to be bartered into the imprisonment of an early marriage. The little boys could be rowdy and troublesome, lying and thieving being favorite pastimes. But, increasingly, these were "in-house" problems—normal struggles of young Christians—in their ever-growing family of faith. There was every indication, in Algiers and the outposts beyond, that a sweet spring breeze was blowing; the long wintertime of difficulty was behind.

Lilias had found, quite improbably, on this hostile soil, a true "home and family." During a break in Majorca, she referred to the "homelike details" of her room, adding, "Home meaning of course the African shore!"[9] A decade later she would confide in a friend, "How true it is, there is no man that has left house or brethren or sisters or father or mother, wife or child or land for My Sake and the Gospel's but he shall receive now and in this time brothers and sisters and lands."[10] She would also recall the "word" that had come to her many years before when they drove down from the French quarter to take possession of 2 Rue du Croissant, their first native home: "Upon this house there shall be peace forever from the Lord." Now, after these many years, that promise took on a new interpretation: "The peace of a house in those days meant its stability—its element of continuance, the heavenly seal on obedience to its calling."[11]

Against all human odds the "English Lily" had survived the harsh elements and was firmly rooted in North African soil. She was nearing sixty years of age; her "home" was multiplied in stations over the face of Algeria, and her "family" extended from veteran colleagues and young mission workers to beloved native friends throughout the land.

Her diary draws 1912 to a close with a benediction and a prayer:

> *It has been a year of grace—an Anno Domini for which we praise the Giver. May He gather all its fragments of the Spirit's working into His eternal purpose and keep them there.*

"Of broken shells He maketh, so He wills
The everlasting marble of His hills."
Amen.[12]

20
SWEET HOLY CHANGE
1913—1916

The printed message is the one that may reach the furthest and the swiftest with the "witness" that will bring in the Consummation.

—Diary[1]

On 9 March 1913, Lilias observed her silver anniversary, marking twenty-five years of service in Algeria. Looking back over that time from the perspective of her recurring phrase, "Blessed are they who wait upon the Lord," now certain "blessings" were indeed tangible. There were now twenty-five members in the band and nine permanent stations or outposts. Station reports published in the *El Couffa,* giving totals for the first three months of the year, provide a sense of the activity of the mission band: Meetings—1,422; Industrial Training—2,409; Medical Services—614; Other Visitors—1,486; Resident Guests—54; Visits Station Villages—818; Distribution Scriptures—78; Distribution Tracts—381.

The widespread mission family was encouraged to be unified through three annual gatherings at Dar Naama: the spring conference with a main speaker and theme; an autumn rally launching the various programs of the new season; and a New Year's house-party after the Christmas activities at each station. Communication was strengthened in between these times with the publication of monthly prayer lists and the quarterly magazine, *El Couffa.*

With the stations and outposts manned, Lilias was able to settle into routines and patterns based at the mission headquarters at Rue du Croissant, taking an active part in the local program, making station rounds each winter and spring, and continuing village itineration in the early fall and spring. Lilias likewise enjoyed new liberty to pursue her vision for reaching Muslims: refining strategy, developing printed materials, and mobilizing an ever-widening base of support, both prayer and personnel.

In July of 1913, Lilias, along with Blanche, Helen, and the next four in seniority, attended the International Sunday School Convention in Zurich. During quiet hours on the steamer, Lilias set down a general outline of advance in the work, built along native lines socially, in contrast to the European methods commonly followed in the early days of foreign missions. She observes,

> *To begin with, evangelistic meetings are an European idea—they do not really suit the mentality of the Arab man or woman. They are so innately afraid of each other that self-consciousness is never lost—under all they are hearing urges the question "what will my neighbour think of my being here" and "to whom will he—or she—tell it."*[2]

Lilias listed specific ideas evolved over the years through trial and error, some quite revolutionary for the time:

> *If we study the native lines of intercourse there would be:*

1. *For the men, the native cafe on a Christian footing.*
2. *The native story-teller or blind Christian with his tum-tum (i.e., drum) or its equivalent. Mr. Smith is getting passage after passage of the Bible now into a rhythmical recitative in which one can almost hear the native lilt and swing.*
3. *For the women a Christian "Ziara" [retreat] to take the place of the outings to shrines which are their only chance of fresh air.*
4. *The Dar Maalema [House of Crafts] for the little girls to learn embroidery & needlecraft, as they have done from time immemorial in Moslem days.*
5. *The Guest-house for men and women in families.*

These are outline thoughts that have come, as trails on which they would move naturally, with no hampering of an uncongenial setting. (July 1913)

The high point of the Zurich convention for Lilias was the message of Dr. Zwemer, "the prophet of the convention . . . he has spoken as one inspired," she writes. He spurred her to these reflections on the subject of prayer:

How all the tenor of helplessness & failure over it is only meant to make way for the prayer-life of Christ in us, & in fellowship with Him in it which will "make all things new"—no longer a weary wrestling to get access & answers, but catching His thought & swiftly asking alongside in His Name—His the upper tone, ours the undertone so to fill in the harmony.

Praying down rather than praying up—that is the summing up—& that again bears on one of the things D. Zwemer said at Zurich—how that the velocity & power of anything that comes down, gains in a ratio of high proportion with the height from which it drops: Even from an aeroplane, a pencil falling will take on the force of a bullet.

> *What might not our prayer power be if it comes down from the throne of the Priest. "Prayer is the true lasting will of the soul united and fastened into the will of our Lord by the sweet inward work of the Holy Ghost"—so it was defined by Mother Julian of Norwich 400 years ago. (31 July 1913)*

The summer ended for Lilias with a "retreat with God" at Klausenpass in Switzerland. During this month she focused on the issue of literature for boys, an interest gaining impetus through an invitation she had received to come to Cairo for the Literature Continuation Committee, spawned from the earlier Lucknow Conference in India. In the beauty and quiet of the Alps, she wrote a paper for the periodical *Blessed Be Egypt,* later published in booklet form—*Literature for Moslem Boys.* Writing down her vision of the possibilities for boys' literature and for vocations for boy colporteurs in its distribution, she asks, "Are we doing our best for the Kingdom of Christ when we are letting boy-lives drift past us, with their priceless chances, into tough Moslem manhood, unchallenged for Him?"[3]

The booklet includes her comprehensive treatise on the stages of intellectual development from early childhood to manhood and an outline of appropriate material to meet the spiritual needs of each corresponding stage. Demonstrating her grasp of boyhood—"boys are ubiquitous, the one human species that seems the same all the world over"[4]—she also introduces her consuming passion for the next several years: developing a literature appealing to the eastern mind—in subject, in setting, and in presentation.

The month in Cairo with the literature committee at the Nile Mission Press was an exhilarating experience for Lilias. Here, in Dr. Zwemer's study, she met with a dozen people from Egypt and Syria, who were "all full of keen insight & purpose regarding the strategic points of advance all round the Moslem world, from the literature point of view!"[5] She and Blanche also seized the opportunity in Cairo to attend a fortnight's special lectures going on at the time—"Apologetics" by Dr. Zwemer, "Phonetics" by M. Gairnder, "Arab Mystics" by M. Swan. Lilias describes this experience: "We have plunged, grey hairs not withstanding, into the study course taking three of the four series of lectures & writing out into the night hours, notes for the younger generation."[6] They would later publish these notes in full, in the *El Couffa.*

Insight into Arab mysticism, as presented by Mr. Swan, gave Lilias the added understanding of another aspect of Islam and triggered a compelling new mission:

It comes as a strong call to bring them the true mysticism of the life hid with Christ in God—a new possibility of access on a hitherto untried side: it is so different than combating the crude cold legalism of the aspect of Islam that comes uppermost; their mystic belief & longings are not generally spoken of—only now one knows of them one sees why "the way" is always the word used by them for salvation by Christ—it is part of that phraseology transmuted—"the way to God" is what these brotherhoods set themselves to teach, with elaborations of method according to the character of the seeker. (11 November 1913)

The new year, 1914, opened with a glow. Never had the band been on such solid footing; "live new buds" were evident at many points of fresh advance: native families were filling the guest-houses, ripe with possibility of the Spirit's collective working; a new ministry for the blind was evolving under Mr. Smeeton's gentle leadership; M. Cook-Jelabert had agreed to be field superintendent to organize and extend the work among the men and boys; a tiny native church was being formed with four native men as nucleus.

In March Lilias set forth with a glad heart to Tozeur. Having reached her early sixties, she was taking her first trip in twelve years to her beloved Southlands. As always, she thrilled at the moment when, abandoning the main line east across the roof plateau, they once again headed south—this time via a train line running all the way to Tozeur. She described the "glamour" of the south:

Sunrise came with great scarab wings of dusty red behind the purple mountains. On the other side the hills stood in madder against a sky of cloisonee blue. . . . A bit longer and the scarab wings had got glorified into white pinions of all the hosts of heaven all against a sky of tenderest shades of turquoise, melting to indescribable green and mauve as it neared the horizon. (21 March 1914)

The climax for Lilias was entrance through the canyon to that first view of desert and, this time, toward their destiny—their very own native house:

How it brought back that day, twelve years ago when we went up coastwards through that other gorge at El Kantara, literally banished from the desert lands, & all those twelve years we had never seen that sea-line again—only had clung to that word that came to us that day "He openeth & no man shutteth." (21 March 1914)

The weeks sped by as Lilias assisted two of the band with the classes of eager-faced small boys and earnest young men, read with the groups of seekers who came in and out of their native house listening with serious thoughtfulness, and visited nearby Nefta, walking about the streets with what she described as "the loveliest sense of God's leading & weaving links among the various seekers with whom we talked."[7] When at last she left the Southlands, it was with the unspeakable happiness of having witnessed the beginning of "God's sequel" promised on that darkest of days so many years before.

In August 1914, England entered the war of nations, World War I. Lilias was in England at the time, on summer break, as were many of the band. Her immediate concern, in regards to the ministry, was getting back to Algeria, which was accomplished—with much difficulty—in late October. The second concern, which would remain the challenge throughout the war years, was maintaining the program at "half speed." Lilias pondered the implications of these limitations coming at the team's most visibly fruitful time in ministry:

"He Himself"—the Master Husbandman—"knew what He would do" in the repression cutting down, cutting back the new growth, "that it may bring forth more fruit" and His "thou shalt know hereafter" car-

ries us on till the day that is nearing, when His sequel shall be seen. . . . so till then He shall have our trust, unquestioning, illimitable. For He is worthy."[8]

The "fruit" produced from this time of repression was a body of literature for the Arab world, which uniquely appealed in both eye and heart to the eastern sensibility of the Arab people and paved the way for an entirely new approach to Arab literature. The challenge in its development was three-fold: (1) presenting material with story lines appealing to the local mind and eastern settings instead of the "hitherto translated stories of Jacks & Bobs whose surroundings are as foreign to children of the east as their names";[9] (2) finding a means of color printing for these color-loving people at a price feasible for wide distribution; and (3) providing translations of the texts in the various colloquial dialects as diverse as each given geographic location.

Immediately following the Cairo visit, a flurry of story ideas had been spawned within the band and among the Algerian believers, ideas for a series of booklets for boys to be issued monthly in Algiers. Then, in May 1914, Dr. Zwemer had invited Lilias to come back to Cairo to help the Nile Mission Press develop a literature for women and children of Arab-speaking lands. Lilias agreed to come for three-month sessions, two successive years, assisted by Blanche. And, in preparation for the first session, she appointed a contributor from each station to help provide ideas, an action which resulted in a stream of ideas from previously untapped talent.

February 1915 found Lilias and Blanche settled in a flat in Cairo, armed with a sheaf of materials gleaned from the band and from their own creative resources. They established a working schedule: the mornings for steady writing, the afternoons for additional writing and for illustrating and collecting material provided by other missionaries—working two afternoons and one morning a week at the Nile Mission Press. Lilias writes of their strong hope and their sense of accomplishment:

Here in Cairo my beloved Morning Star is shouting for joy every morning, poised above the shafts of the great Mohammed Ali mosque of the Citadel. Its shouts seem to bring hope of that true dawn that is breaking over the world of Islam. . . . we are definitely getting ready for such advance as we could not do elsewhere for the interceptions of Headquarters, & the general inertness of Algiers air, so different from the wine-like crispness here that so eases brainwork. (4 March & 16 February 1915)

Their first undertaking was writing and illustrating a series of nine story tracts—equally divided in subject matter among women, boys, and girls—and finding a means to provide the touch of color so dear to the eastern eye. A Syrian convert in charge of a bookstore related an incident that confirmed their belief in the color requirement:

Two natives were buying a day or two ago, & declared that the book they wanted was too dear at a piastare. He shewed them the same book bound in red for three piastres. "Red—very beautiful indeed!" was the answer & the three piastres were immediately forthcoming. (7 March 1915)

The challenge of developing truly indigenous material is indicated in research that went into Lilias's first color leaflet:

The women's [leaflet] is called "Water Lilies" & great has been the labour expended at N.M.P. [Nile Mission Press] to find the real Arabic name, though the flowers enamel every canal with their green & white—"Grass of the Water." Various other names have been rejected—& finally they have discovered that "Brides of the Nile" is their right title. (7 March 1915)

The ingenious solution to the problem of providing color affordably was a process called two-color printing: the application of a single color—red, green, or blue—to details in the simple picture insets and decorative border designs. The four-page leaflets written in the classical Arabic, interfaced with a French translation for the benefit of the French-speaking population along the coast, had enormous appeal to the eastern sensibility. An additional set of "blanks" was prepared—illustrations without letterpress—to allow for translations to be autotyped in countries where Arabic was not understood.

Back in Algeria in early June after an unanticipated delay, the women found that their writing passion continued—they called it "tractitus." A literature committee was established within the band, with the immediate objective of locally printing six bilingual story tracts in colloquial Algerian and French. They planned to issue these month by month beginning January 1916, and to issue six tracts for women and girls as well, using their own "Plex" machine since the number of female readers was too small to justify printed editions. At the same time they continued to prepare new booklets and story tracts for the Nile Mission Press as well as revisions of the earlier story parables first issued in Algiers.

A request from Egypt for "Scripture portions" triggered yet another new line of material from the Algerian Mission Band: textcards on ivory card stock with decorative borders of their own design, the Arabic script done by a scribe since they were of the opinion that "no one but a native can give the subtle lines & curves of the writing as they should be."[10] Once again, the missionaries' ingenuity seemed to know no bounds, as they developed series of textcards around various themes: the "Koranic Series," for example, with a sentence from the Koran followed by verses from the Old Testament and the Prophets. Yet another series, "Questions from the Darkness, and Answers from the Light," posed questions from the Old Testament and answered them from the New. One example reads:

> *"Where is the way where the light dwelleth?" (Job 38:19)*
>
> ---
>
> *"God who commanded the light to shine out of the darkness, hath shined in our hearts, to give the light of the knowledge of the Glory of God in the Face of Jesus Christ." (2 Corinthians 4:6)*

Programs had to be limited during the war years, freeing the missionaries to place greater emphasis on the literature effort. Lilias saw beyond those years, however, to the enormous long-term potential of literature work. Starting with the fortuitous contact with the Nile Mission Press, Lilias infused others with a zeal to participate in this opportunity, encouraging any aptitude for writing and inspiring others in England and America to underwrite publication costs. The writing continued throughout her lifetime—a total of over 115 publications filed and numbered, and 57 tracts, story parable leaflets, and illustrated folders published in Algiers alone. The Nile Mission Press held responsibility for the majority of the literature's publication and distribution, and some of the pieces are in print to this day.

But back in the early stages of their collaboration with the Nile Mission Press, Lilias rejoiced in the satisfying, eye-pleasing publications. Upon receiving copies of the first color series, she wrote, "So those first beginnings are awaiting the breath of life to be breathed on them, like the little clay sparrows in the Moslem legend which the boy Jesus told to fly."[11] She took pleasure in those new advances, exclaiming, "Sweet holy change turns our old things to new."[12]

21
OLD THINGS TO NEW
1917—1919

One feels increasingly in the last decade of normal life, that to get things to go on just as well without one is much to be desired . . . and each generation must find out its own best ways of doing things unhampered by trying to keep to the conditions of the generation that went before!

—Diary[1]

Since the beginning of the war, the mission workers had made no effort to return to the Southlands. Now, with certain objectives met in the literature arena and all major posts manned by the able band, Lilias determined to attempt a return to Tozeur, located just outside the military zone in Tunisia. After five days in Tunis, with what Lilias described as "many vicissitudes as to whether we should be allowed South,"[2] Blanche and Lilias were granted "safe conducts" and joyfully started their journey.

The two-month sojourn in the ancient native *fondak* (or inn) was, as always, a delight to Lilias's soul. It was primitive beyond imagining; when they arrived at the house they "turned out a bevy of cocks and hens and three gazelles,"[3] and Lilias wrote that it was "lovely to wake morning after morning under a palmwood ceiling" and described "the call of the mueddhin before the dawn, praying like a flute and challenging the cry to God for the power of the Name that is above every name."[4]

Blanche, ever the domestic engineer, began at once on the salvage work for their lodgings, "all deep in dust & sand—full of strange little beasts."[5] She also enlisted native help for repairs necessary to make the place inhabitable and hospitable—"white washing within & without & a layer of cement over the rough brick floors to make them sweepable,"[6] preparing the way for Alma Krebs and Albina Cox to carry on the work for the winter.

The women's greatest joy was to find the same spiritual receptivity they had experienced during the first visit twenty-two years before:

> *It is wonderful to come back after all these years & find Tozeur Tozeur still with these eager souls. Surely God has a great purpose for this place. Even the lads come day after day with an untiring desire to hear, in spite of many rebuffs when they come noisily and clamour at the door—& they & the older lads sit & listen by the hour every day, with no other attraction to hold them—If we were young & interesting—or were Arabic scholars—these might be side reasons for them coming on & on. As it is, one can only see in this the hand of God—And even the troublesome ones if one can get them in by themselves, so often sit & listen with their souls in their faces. Those whom we admit, great & small, come & sit & sit with no other plan than "Read to us!" "Talk to us" or "Give us the book that we may read." (20 February 1917)*

Of special interest to Lilias were several men of the *taleb* class—members of Sufi mystic brotherhoods—who came day after day, sitting in the reading room, reading and discussing Scripture with a true soul-hunger. One, she discovered, had been exposed to Scripture ever so briefly years before through a "chance" encounter with the Bible Depot in Tunis: "How the Good Shepherd follows the trail in all His endless patience—even the torn wool on the briars helps Him in His way!"[7] Another, stricken with conviction while studying Isaiah 53, returned later to announce, "I have no sins—they are all gone away!" "Where are they?" Lily asked, and his face answered before his lips, "They are on our Lord the Christ."[8]

Then, without preliminary, the women received instructions from Tunis to leave the area within five days—no explanation given. Was it a practical difficulty, the shortage of food? Or was it spiritual opposition, a counter movement of the Enemy? They did not know the answer; nevertheless, they stayed up late into the nights packing up the furnishings they had so recently settled into this home, meanwhile spending time with their Tozeur friends who came in one by one for final visits. Lilias wrote of their feelings as they departed:

> *Even on the way to the station a hand was stretched out by the baker for a book & we caught the train by five minutes, the little figure of Ma Negeddshe waving to us from outside the station, the last visible link with all the dear souls left behind—and then a strange peace—almost joy settled down on us—& the certainty of one of God's sequels worth waiting for as they have ever been in times past when our ways have been switched off the lines on which we counted. (29 March 1917)*

The immediate "sequel" was a sojourn in Monastir along the eastern coast of Tunisia, which they scouted with the idea of establishing a "second station in Tunisia" to be worked during the months when it would be impossibly hot to stay in Tozeur. There, Blanche "dared [their] sense of abandonment by sending off to Tozeur a batch of camp furniture—against the autumn!"[9] They wandered about the streets of this town, so untouched by European influences, making the acquaintance of local inhabitants with what Lilias called a growing "attrait" to the place—and "a strange sense of rest—God's peace legislating—so we believe,"[10] the feeling of being on the threshold of new things!

Their return to Algiers was followed by a time of recuperation at Dar Naama, which they described as necessary "partly from a bit of fever on the way back—partly perhaps from having lived at higher pressure than we knew."[11] Then they resumed a somewhat curtailed wartime program: station rounds late spring; summer breaks at Blida (permits to England being stopped); the ongoing administration of the band from headquarters at Rue du Croissant, with a station in Monastir being now added to the ranks.

In late February 1918, Lilias went up to Dar Naama for the purpose of securing some unbroken writing weeks for the Nile Mission Press. While there she received a letter from their landlord in Tozeur indicating the way was clear once again for their return, and she discussed the idea with Blanche, who had just taken ill with a fever. Sickness notwithstanding, Blanche responded, "If you say so, I'll get up & we'll go at once." As they talked it over, however, Lilias reports, "we still felt that witholding 'No,' though our hearts leapt to this one more ray of hope."[12]

Lilias's diary entry for February 24 carries a strange tone of presentiment:

> *Blanche is still ill. The hope continues that it may be influenza, but a curious feeling hangs over it—gathered in a strange way a day or two ago—"You come up to write for the natives"—it came almost like a voice —"but instead of that you have to write a chapter of faith to be read up in heaven"—linked with that comes the fact that we are close on the early days of March that have been almost invariably marked by some contest, as if the powers of darkness remembered that they were the date of our coming out for the first time. Ever since the March 1888 when we first landed here, it has been marked by onset after onset. (24 February 1918)*

The next day, a doctor was called in. He did not consider Blanche's case grave at first, yet the fever did not yield and delirium set in—"always quiet & gentle but hardly ever clearing." On Wednesday, 6 March, Blanche looked up at a shaft of sunlight that fell above her bed and said, "A great light is breaking." "Whether she meant light visible or invisible I could not be sure," writes Lilias, "& beyond that she gave no sign that she knew that the river might be near."[13] While the doctor still spoke with hope, he warned them of the danger of heart failure before the fever had run its course.

Then, on Friday evening, 8 March, Blanche stirred from the quiet in which she had been lying for over a week, speaking a stream of English, French, and Arabic for over two hours, sleeping again, rousing only once to ask Lily if she had looked up the trains for starting to Monastir the next morning! Lilias writes:

> *We thought the worst of the night was over, & Miss Smeeton who was helping had gone for an hour's rest & we were alone together—we and the Lord—when suddenly, with no premonitory changes there was a little sobbing breath, & then silence—she had crossed to the other side all unknowing. It was just before daybreak on the morning of the thirtieth anniversary of our landing here. (12 March 1918)*

A new "chapter of faith" was being written on earth as well as in heaven as this friendship of over four decades was brought to an unexpected close. Blanche, who unflaggingly carried out the "Martha" role in their work, was inextricably involved in every phase of the ministry. Although for over a decade they had lived in separate stations—Blanche in El Biar, Lilias in Algiers—from the first day, Blanche was always on call, ready to drop what she was doing to accommodate, implement, and support Lilias's vision. They were partners in ministry in the truest and best sense of the word—itinerating, entertaining, teaching, writing, witnessing, in short, loving the Arab people. Treasurer of the Algiers Mission Band, it was Blanche who bought Dar Naama, embracing with her gift of hospitality hosts of workers and Algerians through rallies, conferences, and summer breaks. And it was Blanche who underwrote one venture after another in the growing line of stations along the coast and inland.

Characteristically, Lilias threw herself into the work, remaining at Dar Naama for the spring and summer. Never one to indulge her emotions, she invariably found comfort in ministry and now, especially, in carrying out Blanche's role of hospitality with the seasonal influx of guests. She was particularly gladdened by the Arab families who came to spend vacations camping in native fashion. She spoke of this as "A new thing on the lines of their own 'Ziares' [family camps] which we have always wanted to see transferred to a Christian setting."[14]

The unpublished pages of her diary, however, take a more personal turn, with Lilias thinking much about life "on the other side," pondering "conflicting theories as to whether those in Paradise are sleeping or waking," wondering if Blanche would be welcoming "those dear baby souls" from Tozeur taken in a typhus epidemic. She writes:

> *I think the thirty years of fellow labouring down here have only taken on a new form. One of the letters of these weeks that has come with the greatest comforting told of two engineers—great friends—who were sent out together to lay down a desert railway line. But when they got there they found that their orders were to begin from opposite ends. It was a great blow, but when they met at last halfway, they saw how much better & more swiftly the work had been done than if they had gone on side by side. (6 April 1919)*

She explores the ever-diminishing barrier between earth and eternity:

> *There is a wonderful sense of expansion—endless expansion—about our love for those who are gone—as if it had escaped earthly fettering—& the pain of the parting is just the rending of the sheath, as it were, to let the flower have its way. And their love for us will have grown in the same way, only in fuller measure into something pure & fathomless & boundless & inexhaustible, because it is "in God." It makes one understand a little how, suddenly, they are the same & not the same, because we are already just that, as far as they are concerned—It is like a river that has got past the surf of the shore, & out into the ocean. (26 May 1918)*

> *A verse in Cant. 2 has lit up into beauty these last days. "The voice of my Beloved—behold He cometh—He standeth behind our wall, He looketh in at the windows (R.V.) shewing Himself through the lattice." It is "our" wall—His & ours, that barrier of things visible that separates us—He on the radiant side of it, we on the dark side—And the breeches that come through sorrow and loss are windows through which that love and light stream in—windows to look out by—not doors as yet. And through them we catch glimpses of His Face looking*

in. And even the multiplied little rifts—the lattice—shew Him too, though more dimly—all the breaks that give an outlet through the sun to the unseen, are infinitely worth while, for those passing visions of the Son of God on the other side! (18 July 1918)

Lilias testified to "that brooding stillness of God's unfathomable peace," yet the sadness which accompanied this unexpected loss can be sensed if not stated explicitly in her writing. Lilias addresses "darkness & oppression":

I have been finding a great blessedness in these last few months in definitely obeying the command "Let them sing aloud upon their God!"—I remembered Pearsall Smith half a lifetime ago, saying in a meeting—at the first Oxford Conference or thereabouts—that he wondered how many present had ever obeyed it. But the seed thought has never got vitalized till now.

One's first waking then has been heretofore so constantly a time of fighting through to a place where one could pray—but the entrance into His gates with thanksgiving & into His courts with praise means an instant leaving all darkness & oppression outside—praising & praising the Precious Blood & the name of Jesus every drift of mist melts away & prayer can begin straight away under a clear sky. (5 February 1919)

Helen Freeman, who came up to Dar Naama at the end of July, writes to the other Blanche, Blanche Pigott:

Here I am at last settled I hope, for the next three months with our beautiful Lily—At every turn one is reminded of Blanche Haworth who arranged this house so admirably. Lily is fairly well, very busy during the last days of shutting up at Rue du Croissant. She is wonderful. The reaction that many dreaded for her has not come and she says, "Where God gives strength there is no reaction."[15]

The October rally was, according to Lily, "the best & tenderest & deepest time with God that we ever had together as a missionary body here."

She added, "Blanche's hymn—written for the Rally of two years ago, with its refrain, 'With one accord/For Christ our Lord,' chimed in & brought her in with us still."[16]

It was a year of great loss, but Lilias's final diary entry for 1918, ended with the ring of affirmation:

> *It has been a wonderful year—heaven opened & the angels of God ascending & descending in ministries one never knew before & such visions of the land where they belong. In leaving [this year] behind, more than all else is the sense of shadowless, fathomless light & love. The sum of all that love means & will mean in its eternal power & beauty, with the earthly limitations broken away. (30 December 1918)*

With the homegoing of Blanche Haworth, practical issues called for attention. Lilias was sixty-five years old with a serious heart condition for which she refused to curtail her activities, although it did require consideration—albeit invariably *after* the fact. Helen, who was almost a decade older than Lilias, had health problems that year, which were likewise a reminder of her age and vulnerability. After the 1918 rally, the Algiers Mission Band committee stayed on to consider the way of the future. Lily writes to the point:

> *One feels increasingly in the last decade of normal life, that to get things to go on just as well without one is much to be desired—it is what nature aims at when the ripening time comes for seed & fruit. The latter must be ready for independent action! & as long as the tree wants to keep tight hold of them they cannot do their own work—& each generation must find out its own best ways of doing things unhampered by trying to keep to the conditions of the generation that went before! (17 September 1915)*

The committee's decision to put the mission on independent footing had immediate as well as long-range implications. Alice McIlroy was installed temporarily at Rue du Croissant as "second," freeing Lilias to stay on indefinitely at Dar Naama, a situation which in time became permanent, when headquarters eventually were transferred to this location. Closing Shushan (El Dar Fedjr), the Short Service Hostel in Algiers, and moving its furnishings to Dar Naama likewise signaled a new era, and with it came God's words of comfort: "I will do better unto you than at your beginnings."[17]

The ending of the war brought Monsieur Cook and his wife, as previously planned, with all the possibilities of work among Arab men as well as help with the ongoing work with women. The Sunday morning meeting was brought back to Rue du Croissant from Shushan, the old crypt being equipped as a little church, with Monseiur Cook as chaplain. Women were included, albeit within native curtains as custom required.

The Armistice liberation brought regions beyond within reach, and two of the band ventured farther inland into the desert town of Laghouat-- almost three hundred miles south of Algiers. As the workers paired off for spring itinerations, Lilias returned to Tozeur for two months with Alma Krebs—this time without the slightest local resistance—preparing the house for others to continue the work, as she had with Blanche two years earlier. She describes their activities:

> *The greater part of the day goes in hours of close talks with groups of men of the Taleb class who sit in groups of three or ten at a time, cross-legged on the golden matted dais of the reading room in their flowing robes, and argue round in circles, shifting their point whenever beaten, till at last there will come a lull when a straight message from God's Word can be driven in, & the thirsty souls that are almost always among them, lift up their heads and listen earnestly. It is strenuous work for Alma, for any slip would be seized on instantly by the opponents, and doubtless published around: God comes to her help wonderfully, in spirit and mind and body, for the daily strain. And towards evening we lock the door with its huge brass key and go out among the palms, where the pale green new flower sheaths are shooting up*

> *above the copper coloured clusters that remain and around us lies the undergrowth of figs and apricot and pomegranate in its spring tracery: the beauty of it all is full of rest. (4 April 1919)*

This return to Tozeur was not only a follow-up of her final joint venture with Blanche Haworth, but a continuation of Lilias's interest in the Muslim mystics, kindled during her first visit to the Southlands in 1895. As early as 1900 she had felt a special bond with these "brothers of the sun" when visiting Tolga and entertained by the local sheik in a brotherhood zaouria.

She returned to Tolga in the winter of 1902, with the intention of setting up their second outpost, only to be expelled by the French authorities. Political unrest made further visits imprudent for the next decade. It was in Cairo, in 1913, through the lectures of Mr. George Swan (in connection with the School of Oriental Studies) that she came to a deeper understanding of the Muslim Mystics' way of thinking and, with that, the conviction that they, with their hunger for things of the spirit and their missionary zeal, should be a special focus of study and outreach. With a new freedom in the political atmosphere, she returned to the Southlands in 1914 with the intention of setting up a permanent station in Tozeur—a hope once again deferred, this time by cutbacks in staff and resources resulting from World War I. Her 1917 visit to Tozeur with Blanche, setting up a station in a rented *fondak* (or inn), and the continued response of the Sufis to the light and life and love of Christ, sealed her determination to return, a desire realized at last in 1919.

Later, Lilias would write about the Sufis, referring to their inscrutable expression and aloofness of manner that held any questioner at a distance: "Till you show by some word that you understand them and care for them and are 'reaching forth' also to 'the things that are before,' they will remain within their shell."[18] Lilias penetrated that shell with her love, sensitivity, and profound understanding of their way of thinking. "She knows about The Way," they would say of her. Their reception of her—an outsider, a European, moreover a *woman*—was nothing short of remarkable. She was received into their private homes, even into the zaourias that housed generations of Sufi families. Likewise, her hospitality was accepted, their mission homes becoming bases from which she could offer readings and instruction from Scripture.

The artist in her responded to the artist in the Sufis, their great writers of old being as much poets as philosophers. Yet she never lost her spiritual focus. In contrast to the cold formalism of orthodox Islam, she found in certain Sufi mystics—particularly of the lay brotherhoods—a sincere hunger for things of the spirit. Her approach was to establish their common ground: the desire for union with God. Building on the bond of Muslim mysticism, she presented true *Christian* mysticism—the union with God which comes from a personal relationship with Jesus Christ.

Toward this end, she poured her energies into establishing Tozeur as a permanent winter station, manned by pairs of members of the band. She dreamed of a day when people of the brotherhoods, having come to Christ, would be missionaries to peoples of the Southlands. Ever a visionary, she pictured a Christian zaouria, where Europeans and Arabs would live along side, each benefiting from the wisdom of the other.

Lilias's special bond with the Sufi mystics would color the rest of her life. With increased numbers in the band and new political equilibrium, she now experienced an unprecedented freedom to travel. Extended visits to Tozeur—and later Tolga—would constitute a major aspect of her yearly routine. In time, some of these Sufi friends even would become part of her world in Algiers. These relationships would provide for her an extraordinary insight into their unique "southern" character and mentality and become the basis for developing ever more effective ways of communicating to them essentials of the Christian faith. Indeed, her spiritual treatises for the Muslim mystics are virtually without equal to this day.

The end of the war brought additional reinforcements: Pierre Nicoud and Augusta Butticaz (Swiss workers); Mr. and Mrs. Buckenham, and Short Service Secretary Rosy Govan (later Stewart, author of the Lilias Trotter biography *The Love That Was Stronger)*. This increase helped to further expand and strengthen the base of independence for the mission that was so desirable to Lilias. She sincerely wanted to hand over the work to others when the time came.

Now, for the very first time, Lilias spells out in concrete terms the finances of the mission—this with an eye to the future:

Our early days out here were spent, as with most shipping in construction, in dry dock as regards the need of faith, financially speaking—(And this is the "tender mercy" of our God, for we had many another faith test to battle through). We were on the solid ground of having, among us, enough for our requirements & that of the work, with the help of our dearly beloved A. K. [Alice Kemp] who sent year by year a sum that covered the salaries of the few paid helpers. And though stations & workers have increased, many of the latter have brought with them their own support, & more. So that though individually we were out of our depth, some of us, collectively, with stray bits of other help that came from time to time from without, we could still feel our foothold. (16 September 1919)

Lilias writes of a fresh stage of faith, "a gentle swaying off that foothold," enlisting men workers—and trusting God for the requisite income to support them financially. Of particular concern to Lilias was the work among Arabic-speaking men and boys, there being but four male workers along the coast of North West Africa sufficiently qualified to speak in the native tongue. She began to pray specifically for twenty Arabic-speaking men—ten for their own band, and ten for other missions alongside.

The printed journal at this time reflects the missionaries' steps toward a "new era"; as Lilias summed it up, "It is time we should make a new beginning." The new format actually returns to the old hand-written version in Lilias's script, delicately illustrated with line drawings in her unmistakable style, numbers being set in geometric design of Arabic origin. People and places come alive in picture and phrase—the round "baby-face" of Mimoun from Miliana; young Fatima, baby strapped to her back; the courtyard of Blida's Dar el Aine; the outskirts of Tozeur lined in palms trees. And the reader is drawn into Lilias's love for the Arab world.

The closing words in this journal entry for 1919 convey Lilias's attitude of heart:

It is a solemn turn of the year this time, for it finds us committed to a deliberate faith in God for our needs, instead of the old half con-

scious trust. This committal means the needs be for a great nearness of spirit to Him . . . more than that, a one-ness of spirit. "The Spirit of understanding . . . & of fear of the Lord." And herein lies the blessedness as we launch out afresh. (26 December 1919)

22
LAUNCHING OUT AFRESH
1920—1922

We are proving these days that time is nothing to God—nothing in its speeding, nothing in its halting—He is the God that inhabiteth eternity.

—Diary[1]

This fresh stage of faith the band had entered, trusting God for increasing financial requirements, was sealed with the beginnings of needed reinforcements and the greatest freedom they had ever known. According to Lilias,

> *we find, in going forward, that we are allowed to distribute & to sell without hindrance. We seem to have reached the point where doors are opening on everyside, & can be entered as fast as God sends men & means in a way that seems almost like a dream compared to the block of the long years of the past. (1 May 1920)*

The arrival of Mr. and Mrs. Buckenham, in January of 1920, heralded a steady stream of recruits arriving over the next three years, ten of whom were full-time workers. Lilias shifted workers about the thirteen locations, teaming them for greatest effectiveness, both in learning the language and manning the various stations. She writes in March:

Mr. Buckenham has started off on his first initiative, wherein we rejoice—It is the gathering together of the handful of men & lads from the Sunday service, into a diminutive class meeting after & where he spoke by interpretation his brotherly slap on the shoulder & grasp of the hand . . . goes a long way to the overcoming of Babel's limitations. (28 March 1920)

In spring visits to the western stations, Lilias sensed a change in the spiritual climate and observed the creative ways in which the band ministered to their charges:

It is Mascara [a mountain town outpost] now, and one feels again a lift in the atmosphere—a sense that buds are giving. . . . Love as usual is the leverage, & it is a time when love takes a shape they can understand—to come and live among them, away from one's friends, does not seem anything out of the way—but the changes of serving them now that the black smallpox & "the yellow wind" which they call typhus, are raging, is something more tangible in the way of "love manifested." (27 May 1920)

Observing the lumbering motor buses between Relizane and Mostaganem—"the one visibly good thing the war has left in its track"—Lilias marvels over this new means of access to villages previously unpenetrated by European women: "How often from the railway line I have looked longingly at these prickly pear patches lying like faint peacock tinted stems along the mauve & ochre foothills & wondered how they were ever to be reached. Now God's time has come & with it His way."[2]

Summer at Dar Naama once again brought its influx of visitors—shifts of workers for a "fortnight's rest" during the hottest months, Arab families camping a week or so at a time. To Lilias, the greatest joy of all was the arrival of Mohammed Ali—the "Bible Boy" of Tozeur—to begin instruction in the Christian faith:

> *"Ali" he wished to be called now, having left the things of Mohammed away in the past. Meantime it is wonderful—more wonderful than words can say, to have a bit of Tozeur really under our roof and free to learn & follow to his heart's content. I don't know anything that has ever called forth deeper praise to God. (30 June 1920)*

All the activity, though a delight to Lilias, invariably took its physical toll on her, as indicated through correspondence between her friends. Helen Freeman writes to Blanche Pigott from a resting place in Castiglione:

> *Lily and I are spending a few days at this restful little seaside place; she has been so overdone with her own work and other people's. The work has been heavy for her, but so encouraging. She has utilized the summer months by inviting Arab families to come and stay in a set of rooms set apart for them in Dar Naama. More than once Lily had two-and-twenty natives under her roof, including children—and God has greatly blessed.*[3]

Lilias adds her own note to the letter, revealing yet again how such respite and rebuilding bolstered her creative productivity:

> *I must add a scrap while the quiet time lasts. There is no housekeeping to think of, and a wonderful "sea of glass" just outside the windows basking in the hot air, and with every spar and sail of the fishing-boats reflected in it, even the clouds and their tints sometimes. We are in a sheltered bay. Helen reads me stories while I work at pen-and-ink illustrations. I am on a little folder now of our Lord's sevenfold "I ams" of St. John—The Bread, The Light, The Door, The Shepherd, The Resurrection and Life, The Way, The Vine. They are so wonderful*

in their consecutive unfolding of the way He meets the needs of the soul.[4]

The year 1920 closed with one victory after another—"retrievals" as Lily called them. She recorded each with an elation almost childlike in its sheer wonderment. First was the official signing for the Tozeur house after six and a half years of haggling with the vacillating landlord: "The passage in Ezekiel about the priest that ministers to the Lord has come freshly today, lighting up the ever growing sense that all we have to do is just to put things ready to His Hand & see what He will do."[5]

Then there were the baptisms of three of their own Algerian men—Ali, his brother Amar who joined him for training at Dar Naama, and blind Aissha from Algiers—following "examination" by Monsieur Cook.

I think there were not many of us who did not feel something of an inward sob of joy when the three came in, one after the other, erect & stedfast looking in their burnouses & long white gandouras. We wondered how they would get through their testimonies! Aissa began, in his strong mountain gutteral—that his trust was in the blood of Christ for salvation, that he had resisted God's voice about baptism, but that now—true native inconsequence—God had blessed his waiting by bringing two others to join him! Amar came next, in his pure Tunesian Arabic, telling how all the prophets were sinners, & that now he had found the Sinless One to bear his sins. Ali came last, with his face aglow. He told how he wanted to go into the grave with the Lord & come up to walk in the newness of life till His return—& the glow on his face brightened into radiance as he stepped down into the water. (23 November 1920)

The "crowning joy to the dying year"[6] was word that two of the band had arrived in Tolga, ending the silence that had begun that day nineteen years before when Lilias and Blanche had been commanded to leave. Lilias remembered how with heavy hearts they had left the mud dwelling where the bands of brotherhood men on pilgrimage to a neighboring shrine gathered eagerly to listen to Scripture, taking with them a bit of palm "in pledge of victory," which remained over Lilias's map of Algeria—reminder of this hope and promise: "He openeth and no man shutteth."

Lilias's special concern for the next couple of years was establishing Tozeur as a permanent winter station. With the house at last their own, and new recruits coming their way, the long-deferred dream of a mission station in the Southlands was becoming a reality. Now, with the Tozeur brothers, Ali and Amar, in training, Lilias had visions of a year-round ministry. The "Sons of Sunshine," as they called themselves, could hold on through the summer months when the sweltering heat was too much for the mission workers' northern constitutions.

In early spring of 1921, Lilias returned to Tozeur for a six-week sojourn. Her apprehension that the mission workers would be resented for having taken possession "of one of their houses & two of their sons"[7] was rebuked by the warmest welcome yet, as she was received as honored guest into the brothers' family home and was visited, as in the past, by a steady stream of earnest seekers from the Muslim college. Once again Lilias set to work to ready the house for the workers who would remain throughout the winter and to equip it for the future, sketching the floor plan in her diary. She writes: "Of all the houses God has given out here, none goes to the depths of one's heart with joy & thankfulness like this dilapidated collection of rooms—some of them not more than hovels. They are just a pure delight!"[8]

A new role awaited Lilias upon her return to Dar Naama. The Tozeur brothers expressed their desire for Christian wives, and Lilias, only too glad to accommodate, became "matchmaker"—a role she would continue to play throughout the years in her effort to promote Christian families—arranging marriages with young women though the North African Mission in Cherchelle. The brothers "feathered their nests"—a room per couple in the vine-covered Arab court—while members of the band, serving as wedding directors, prepared for the two weddings. Ali's wedding was first; his bride was greeted with the guests' customary 'you-yous' of shrill joy, and they all rejoiced the next morning when Ali purchased sweetmeats and nuts for his little bride, customary if the husband is pleased!

Summer found Dar Naama in full swing and Lilias in her element, saying, "We have beaten our record these last days in having sixty-seven souls under the roof."[9] The Arab court was occupied by native families, the other rooms full with the comings and goings of visitors, Algerian and European.

Lilias writes:

> *It is very wonderful and beautiful to see how, all unsought, this house is lending itself, more each summer, to be a sort of camping place to the better class Arab families who can come on their own & fend for themselves. We used to wonder what God meant in giving us a place that is such a conglomeration of little dwellings—few comparatively suitable for European dwellers. Now it is getting plain. Four or five native families or even more can be lodged with that apartness from each other that is needed all round—& we are having that most of the time. (20 August 1921)*

In diary entries, Lilias records and responds to one "retrieval" after another: station reports of ministries thriving in their "new liberty"; correspondence bringing fresh possibilities of recruits; plans for new points of advance; jottings of the "crop of new thoughts for the future." Mixed throughout are accounts of the individuals who peopled her daily life:

> *It is such a happy summer with the dear bunches of the natives about the place. And there is a spirit of love all about—either I get asked out to supper at one end of the house or the other, or a plate of stew is brought, or a hunk of watermelon in its wonderful crimson & green—or a sugar cake or two—or my bathtowels get carried off for a private washing & come back fragrant with a scented jesammine wreath folded in—all little precious tokens—& with them the glad light of the happy spirit of help & fellowship among each other. (25 August 1921)*

The particular challenge of the summer, one that would be uppermost in her thoughts to the end of her life, was the training of native men—leaders, she hoped, for the future Algerian Church. The Tozeur brothers, Ali and Amar, were staying at Dar Naama for the year, working half days on the land with Pierre Nicoud and spending the rest of the day in systematic Bible study. Two evenings a week throughout the summer Lilias brought together the Tozeur brothers with two of the Algiers "brothers," Boualem and Aissha, for the purpose of studying. Then, to her surprise, yet another "Son of the South" showed up in Dar Naama—Si Amar from El Hamma near Tozeur.

While in Tozeur, Lilias had been much taken by Si Amar, a Muslim mystic—"a tall figure with a thoughtful gentle face & a musical tongue"[10]—and she had spent hours upon hours responding to his deeply spiritual questions concerning Christianity. Finally, one day he said, "I have received. I have accepted. I have believed."[11] His arrival in Dar Naama was a cause of great joy as well as perplexity for the women. He, above all the others, showed the greatest possible powers of leadership. But where could he receive instruction to prepare him adequately for such a vocation? And how to mediate the enormous cultural differences existing between the coast and the desert? Lilias writes,

> *We are doing our best to give Si Amar his first lessons in regularity & punctuality—no easy matter with a man who has been accustomed to do things just as they suited him, with no time piece but the sun. We have to remember on his side it must be extremely irksome to be under such restraints as the hands of the watch—& that life must be full of small prickles to him. (29 September 1921)*

A plan evolved to send him to Tangier for a few months' training, pending permit. In the meantime, Lilias savored the opportunity to nurture in the faith this son of the desert "dropped down into our prosaic Alger."[12] High points were Si Amar's baptism and his first "sermon," described this way by Lilias: "Si Amar stood up in a simple unafraid way & went on for fifteen or twenty minutes. It was on false & true profession. . . . It was all lucid & terse, with an unhesitating flow of language & every verse quoted without a mistake. Oh the powers that are there, if God takes & keeps him!"[13]

There were also concerns. The women of the band believed a balance of giving and receiving to be important to the health of the souls of these young Christians as well as a crucial corrective to any who might be attracted solely to the material benefits of such an association. Si Amar, who gloried in the discussion of spiritual matters, was beginning to balk at the responsibilities that accompanied their living arrangement. Asked to give a goodbye word at the morning meeting before his departure, he stood tall and straight and motionless—like a picture in his white robe against the darkness of the arch:

> *Love was his subject—it is a favorite one with him, but alas more on the line of receiving than of giving it. And today's discourse has trended that way—i.e., on how missionaries should treat the converts—One of his remarks was that when the Shepherd had found the sheep he did not say to it "What a trouble you have been to me!" (30 October 1921)*

The "little daily bothers," observes Lilias, "are more difficult perhaps to an ease-loving nature like his than the one great act of surrender that cut him adrift from all the surroundings of his Moslem life."[14]

The new year, 1922, saw the arrival of fresh recruits—Mr. and Mrs. Theobald joined by Pierre Nicoud's bride, Alice, plus Isabelle Sheaf, Jessie Gray, and Alice Kemp, friend of the band since that first day in Algiers. With them came a "launching forth into a deeper tide of faith,"[15] for the necessary funds. A great step forward was the unprecedented decision of the committee to support the Tozeur brothers in a "lay brother" capacity. "I cannot but think," writes Lilias, "that these Southland souls, immature as they are yet, are part of God's answer to our cry of two years ago, for ten Arabic speaking men for the work."[16]

Early spring, Lilias spent a month in Tozeur, this time with Alma Krebs, a Danish worker having a special interest in the Southlands. While Lilias supervised workmen in the finishing touches of their native *fondak* (inn) in preparation for a permanent winter station, she reveled in the opportunity to teach the eager boys and young men who came daily for

Bible lessons. But these invariably sustained and increasing demands had an effect on her weakened heart. Upon her return to Dar Naama, she collapsed and for two weeks was out of commission.

By the end of May, however, Lilias was back, full-force, for Dr. Zwemer's visit to Dar Naama for a conference. It was a time of great inspiration for Lilias and the Algerian workers. The conference aimed at a three-fold advance: literature development, Sunday school development, and preparation for the visit of John R. Mott (founder of the Student Volunteer Movement and organizer of the International Missionary Council) the coming year. Dr. Zwemer left for a trip to Morocco, accompanied by Monsieur Cook—a trip that was significant, among other things, for his brief stay in Tlemcen, near the border of Morocco, which prepared the way for work among the educated men there, proud conservative spirits, previously resistant to Christianity.

Si Amar was now back with his Christian bride of Lilias's arranging and Lilias was busy mediating the domestic problems of the native families at Dar Naama, while also diagramming the band's autumn journeys on a map: western, central, and eastern routes from the coastline, penetrating south to their desert destinations, Figuig, Chardia, and Touggourt.

The year drew to a close with Lilias rejoicing at the prospect of eight persons in Tozeur for Christmas: four of the band joined temporarily by the Tozeur brothers and their brides. She looked back over the year to a range of new horizons "that would have seemed a dream during the hemmed-in years of the past"—the opening of Relizane's substations, Zemmora and Tiaret; the establishment of the Algiers post in the suburb of Belcourt; the stirring of new work in Colea and Tlemcen--bringing the number of stations to fourteen and workers to twenty-nine. "The main thing that stands out in looking back over the year," writes Lilias, "is the changing spirit amongst the Moslems—indefinable as yet, but as unmistakeable it seems to us as the first faint spring-breath."[17] She adds,

> *We have here at Dar Naama a reproduction of a Danish picture. It is a frozen river, grey in its icy deadness, but that breath of the spring is beginning to conquer, & through the midst of it the first flow of the current has begun to gleam, reflecting the purple firtrees & the daffodil sky of dawn in its curve. . . . it is worth, a thousand times over, to*

spend one's life among the Moslems, to see that hour draw near! (22 December 1922)

The lesson reinforced during these years of retrieval and advance was one learned during the long hard years when hope was sustained by faith alone: "Time is nothing to God—nothing in its speeding, nothing in its halting—He is the God that inhabiteth eternity." And children of eternity "can afford to tarry His leisure no matter how short [their] time is."[18]

To Lilias this meant that even when there were no outward signs of encouragement, she would keep a listening heart tuned to her Father's voice, then faithfully do what he said. As she loved to say, *"He* knew what He would do." It meant complete rejoicing when his purpose was revealed in the proving of his promises. And it meant for the future that same waiting on God, content with simple obedience, understanding that the *results* of one's work on earth may be realized long after one's *time* on earth is finished.

Over and over, throughout the pages of her diary, she writes this faith refrain: "Blessed are all they that wait for Him." She firmly believed that time is *nothing* to God—nor to His children, "Les Enfants de l' Eternitie."

23
THE POETRY OF GOD'S WAYS
1923—1924

And all that outworking of His Grace has come so silently—"not with observation" like His work in all growth around—so that one can hardly tell when or how the expansion has come.

—Diary[1]

Lilias was completing her seventh decade of life, and 9 March 1923 marked the thirty-fifth anniversary of her arrival in Algeria. Characteristically, she responded with written reflections:

Thirty-five years—half a lifetime—out here closed last night—& a tide of thanksgiving goes up to God for the "long patience" that has borne with all their negligences & ignorances & has found a way for His mercy & His power to work in spite of all. And all that outworking of His Grace has come so silently—"not with observation" like His work in all growth around—so that one can hardly tell when or how the expansion has come—all one can tell is that we have had nothing to do with its evolution except a measure of blind obedience & oh that that measure had been fuller! (9 March 1923)

Her anniversary gift was the coming of her brother and sister, Alec Trotter and Margaret Egerton—their first visit in all those years. The crowning joy of their visit was a trip to Tolga, delighting Lilias with the double anticipation of her own return after twenty-one years and of introducing her family to the wonders of the Southlands. Helen Freeman writes to a mutual friend:

Lilias has gone off with Mrs. Egerton and Mr. Alec Trotter to Tolga. She is frail now and the journey is long, but the delightful change and the desert air, and her pleasure in having her brother and sister with her will, we trust, very much more than make up for the fatigue. I heard she was radiantly happy. Her brother and sister, to Lily's great joy, fully appreciate Algeria.[2]

Lilias's return—first through the desert gates of El Kantara, then to the mud-walled town of Tolga—brought a flood of memories and the realization for her of the long-awaited "sequel," faith's reward. She writes:

Today came the wonderful moment of passing back through the "Gate" of El Kantara, where twenty-one years ago we went up with the desert closed finally behind us as far as earthly authority went. Now we have the freedom by God's wonderful working of every mile of it, to go on or settle which we will—By faith we took it then—by faith we hold it now—Praise be to His Name! (29 March 1923)

> *And today saw us within the mud walls of this beloved Tolga—dearer than ever before for the hope deferred of all these years. . . . I used to think that relief was the nearest thing that we can imagine in all the unimaginable joys of the life to come. But there is another & a better thing that age shews—& that is retrieval. The "triumph in Christ" that it brings is a true foretaste of the day that is coming. (31 March 1923)*

The place touched her heart as it had so many years before: "Everywhere in the streets there are hands stretched out in welcome—gaunt hands of old men who were in their prime then, strong brown hands of middle-aged men who were but lads when we saw them last."[3] And once again there was the same listening spirit. Members of the mystic brotherhoods gripped her in a special way, kindling in her a passion for their souls which would consume her to the end of her days.

> *All around in this part of the desert the Brotherhoods hold sway, & there must be jewels for Christ's finding amongst these souls. For through the mazes of their fanciful mysticism there is an instant response when one speaks of seeking Him Who is Light & Life & Love. Oh for men to come & help them from our lands at home—men who are Christian mystics in the true sense, knowing the power of Christ "I in them & them in Me." (4 April 1923)*

Lilias's return to Algiers was greeted by similar stories of retrievals. First were reports from the various spring trips: "Doors, & doors & doors—a whole row of them marks the spring story,"[4] Lilias relates in a sequel to the earlier "Prayer Call," a prayer-letter supplement to the printed journals, which anticipated the three-line penetration into the Southlands. A sketch of doors, "not only opened, but as Dr. Zwemer puts it 'nailed back'"[5] is accompanied by accounts of doors opening into the desert as well as along the seacoast and mountains.

The summer's special focus was the training of the Tozeur three, wonderfully assisted by the establishment of a native Bible school by the Methodist Episcopal Church within a stone's throw from Dar Naama. As

Lilias nurtured these men in the Christian life, she sought to better understand the Sufi mentality and character which they represented:

> *There is another point in this year of advance on which God seems to be concentrating one & another of us—that of the Sufis—the fraternities of Mystics who have held agelong sway in the mountain districts of the land, & above all the south desert—I feel more and more that we ought to make a special study of them, for the line of approach that we use for Moslems of the ordinary taleb class slips off these souls without gripping them, whereas, read them a few words, say from St. John's Gospel, or one of the Epistles, and there is a response at once. Of all the millions of Islam, they are far and away the truest seekers after God, albeit in a weird and dangerous path. (9 July 1923)*

Si Amar (called "the Touil" to distinguish him from the younger Amar) presented a unique challenge to Lilias, with his "dangerously brilliant gifts"[6] and laconic southern character. The diaries detail ups and downs—high moments of lucid witness; low points of resistance—yet nothing prepared her for the stunning crisis which brought his time in Dar Naama to an end. In cryptic language which conveyed the impact of the blow without revealing details, Lilias reports:

> *A terrible nightmare storm has broken at Dar Naama, involving such a story between the Touil & his wife's family—that he must leave us at once till he can clear himself or confess. . . . much is explained of the misgivings that we have felt since he came back from the Djered. . . . One feels stunned all the same—& only able to go on hour by hour with the interviews—backed with such loving help from them all, & a stalwart brotherliness from Mr. Theobald for whose being here just now we thank God. (23 September 1923)*

The Tozeur brothers, though not implicated in Si Amar's misdoing, were required to leave for a time of soul searching, as they had come under his dominant sway, and they could not risk continued contact at present. Clearly, Lilias was crushed, but not defeated, and she determined to understand better his "complex nature," anticipating the time when once again they all could be united in kingdom work.

The year of lights and shadows closed with a poignant return to Tolga—and an unplanned side trip to the Oued Souf—Lilias's final journey south, and her first back to that place in twenty-nine years. She was once again in her element as she settled the primitive Tolga mission house: "the rooms already homelike with their three days work put in—All in a chord of dark-blue draperies with touches of orange & flame-colour & cream as befits a South Land station."[7]

Once in Tolga, a dream began to take shape, spurred by their American friend Mrs. J. A. Walker, who desired to go to the end of the rail line to Touggourt. Just that month, a new invention was on trial, "citrouens"—caterpillar cars on a tank system—which made the run between Touggourt and El Oued in ten hours instead of the three or four days on camel. So, on 4 December the women found themselves climbing the dunes in a citrouen, arriving in the Souf. Lilias writes about the experience: "Oh what these crests were, with the great silence brooding over all! & what it was to see at last the low lying line of the first Souf palms, & then to reach the stretches of beehive houses & their dusky dwellers—no words can tell it!"[8]

The two weeks spent among the Souf people confirmed their readiness to listen and set within Lilias's heart the conviction that here, indeed, was another winter post of the future. As they prepared to leave, listeners gathered around them with outstretched hands, "We want you—we would like you to live here," and Lilias laments, "Oh if the shadow of life's dial would go backward & make it possible!"[9] She consoled herself with the fact that they had again linked up with the present generation "for whatever God has to reveal of His purposes."[10] She saw a lesson in the gypsum crystals which lined the walls of the Souf homes:

> *Each of them sprang out of some atom of a growing point round which clusters crystalize, this endless beauty of form. If we may but be a crystallizing point from which God can work, it matters nothing—how*

> *insignificant that starting point. . . . "He calleth those things that were not as though they were." (8 December 1923)*

Lilias's final days in Tolga were poignant with the realization that in all probability, this would be her last sojourn in the south. Palpable in the pages of her diary is her love and vision for this stretch of the desert between Tolga and Tozeur, a stretch that, in her words, "we have always felt was especially given to us for our corner."[11]

She describes Christmas there:

> *Once more—after twenty-two years, Christmas Day in Tolga—& again Christmas like in its deepest sense with just a touch of the fondouk (native inn) to make it beautiful—common brick walls—earth floor & unglazed windows—such a tiny touch, but fitting in with the wonderful sense of being "weak with Him" which is the key note to the beginnings here—"Wrapped in the swaddling clothes, lying in a manger"—that is how the world's redemption dawned. (25 December 1923)*

Upon return to Algiers, Lilias focused on preparation for the Mott Conference, March 1924, in Constantine, the first of a series of Near East Conferences planned by Dr. Mott for the purpose of addressing the missionary challenge to Islam. Lilias was developing a paper to present at the conference on the need for shelter homes for the Muslim child-wives divorced repeatedly and tossed aside while still in their teens. She also would be involved in the broader concern of discussing questions of ministry with the seventy to eighty delegates from North Africa.

The conference was exhilarating to Lilias, particularly the addresses delivered by Dr. Mott who, like herself, thought strategically not for one given geographic area but for each area's position in the larger world scheme. As an outgrowth of the conference, Lilias received an invitation to join the Algerian delegates at the final April conference in Jerusalem. Lilias, who had fully intended never again to leave the coast of North Africa, recognized in the invitation as the "chance of a lifetime" as well as an opportunity "for the bringing into line of the work here, and drawing it into that great solidarity that is unifying the fight against Islam, & gleaning the hard won wisdom of the other battle fields at its long front."[12]

It is difficult to imagine anyone enjoying the retracing of the steps of Jesus more completely than Lilias. Reflecting on the imprint on "one's heart of hearts, of the utter loveliness & worshipfulness of the human Life that was lived out there," Lilias concluded, "one feels that the vision that came of the Life can never fade."[13] Her first impression of the Holy Land was of the "strangely small scale of everything":

> *But before nightfall one came to realize that this is an intrinsic part—that God wants to shew us that nothing is great or small to Him who inhabited eternity in its dimensions of space as well as of time—& that it is a pivot land—& pivots are apt to be small things in the eyes of those who do not understand their meaning. (26 March 1924)*

The Jerusalem Conference, held in a Russian monastery on the Mount of Olives, was rich in content and in "heartlinks" with the "blessed company of faithful people with whom we are heirs through hope"[14]—the Bevan Joneses of India, the Eric Bishops, and Canon Gairdner of Jerusalem, and the Motts and Zwemers, to name a few. After the long and difficult years mobilizing and upholding the forces in Algeria, Lilias here received the encouragement of kindred spirits, and, in turn, revealed in the committee meetings what Mr. Basil Matthews described as "the unquenchable, mystical, fighting love of Miss Trotter of North Africa."[15]

Lilias writes at the close of the time:

> *This morning brought the last standing "within thy Gates O Jerusalem"—the last most likely till we stand there together with Christ. There seemed something of the wrench & ache of parting with a heart-friend, as we left the land behind. . . . one of the gifts of these two weeks has been a strange new sense of fellowship with God in the love of it . . . in the longing of the consummation of the story that is yet to come. (8 April 1924)*

Several days in Cairo for literature work brought this phase of her journey to an end, and she summed up her experience: "'In everything enriched by Him' are the only words that describe it—it certainly has been the fullest month of one's whole life."[16]

Now, returning to North Africa via the port of Marseilles, Lilias decided to extend her trip to Great Britain in order to take advantage of three opportunities for the "furtherance & solidifying" of the work in Algeria: the Glasgow Sunday School Convention; the Faith Mission conference in St. Andrews; and the Keswick Conference in the Lake District. In truth, she was in no position physically for such an endeavor. She knew what few realized: the assessment of a French specialist that "her heart was so worn out that there was no physical reason for her remaining alive at all."[17] Yet she simply could not pass up one last chance to tell of the needs of the field, especially of the need for men. Convinced that Christ would give her "power till her work on earth was done,"[18] she threw herself into that work with utter abandonment.

While in England, Lilias set about working on an idea she'd developed in her travels. The "work" which gripped her soul—"somewhere between Tolga and Glasgow"[19]—was to write a text, based on Christ's seven "I Am's" for the Sufi mystics. While in Cairo, she had met with Mr. Swan and had gone over her ideas in outline. On board the ship to Marseilles, she became acquainted with Professor Margoliouth, an authority on the Sufi mystics. He recommended a list of resources and helped her with technical phraseology which for the most part had no equivalent in ordinary Arabic.

She writes of her hopes for the work:

> *It comes, this last of God's rich gifts, as a fresh impulse, together with the bit with Mr. Swan, in getting to work with the outline at any rate, of "The secret of secrets"—though it may need many months of getting "introduced into feeling" as the old Quakers have it, to the needful extent of getting it into final shape—Even so, it comes, somehow, with a sense of pressure & of "message," that I never remember having had since the days, half a lifetime ago, of the first Parable*

book. At any rate nothing like to this extent . . . so I hope it may shew Jesus to some of these dear souls, in their misty intricate groping after Life & Light & Love. It would be worth anything if this might be! (20 April 1924)

The weeks before the conferences, Lilias set about her work on the Sufi book. During her stay with family in Oxford, she visited the university's Bodleian Library, mining the resources for decorative borders, filling in her manuscript with designs of exquisite delicacy.

The pace of the three conferences was punishing by anyone's standard, yet still Lilias gloried in the "fresh knitting in" of new acquaintances, the riveting of old links of friendship. Wherever she went, she made an unforgettable mark. One who met her for the first time said, "I can never forget the impression she made on me—those wonderful eyes! I never saw a face before upon which was so plainly engraved a whole life's history—such a beautiful worn face."[20] A former Oxford don, not an adherent to orthodox religion, observed: "I shall never forget the impression I received, when I first met her; the mere look in her face and touch of her hand made me feel that she was spiritually apart from the ordinary run of people one meets."[21]

Those who knew her for an adult lifetime observed a great calm and joyous peace. Blanche Pigott said to her, "Lily, you seem so rested in soul." She answered, "Yes, because I have no strength left and am living entirely by the power of divine inflowing."[22] Throughout all her activities at this time—meetings at various conferences, rereading of the old red leather-bound diaries of the first years in Algeria, ordering of paints and postcards, visiting old friends and family—one senses a settling of her affairs, of final good-byes.

These are the last days of English travelling. It has been beautiful to see through all the stages of its summer glory—from the primroses to the heather—from the spikes of the beechbuds to their first drifting golden leaves. This last week has been a race of goodbyes, a night in each place & now I have come to anchor with Gundred (niece) for final repackings & a sort of "at home" all day today to people new

> *and old to whom I had not got round—the oldest of the old being a pair of grey-haired women who used to be, somewhere between forty and fifty years ago, young business girls who stood by us loyally in Morley Halls YWCA days! (23 August 1924)*

Three weeks after Lilias's return to Algeria, Helen Freeman insisted on summoning a doctor, who ordered "quiet days" for Lilias. From the "captivity" of her bed she continued to pray for the south and to pursue her writing:

> *With more on hand for writing than I ever remember before, here I lie with no power for putting two thoughts together—only a few stupid sentences at a time in the writing up of the fragmentary pages of this journal with a view to condensing into the belated journal. So once more if this is as it seems to be, the vocation for the winter, it starts with an impossibility. For these, and all His mercies—the Lord's Name be praised. (26 September 1924)*

Out of this "weakness" was born one of Lilias's loveliest legacies, *Between the Desert and the Sea,* a sketchbook of Algeria, replete with sixteen color plates of watercolors and a description in poetic prose of the land she loved so dearly. She still continued writing the official reports and the printed journals during this time, chronicling the goings on of the mission band across the face of her beloved North Africa.

This remarkable year ended with two significant answers to prayer: the necessary supply of money to keep the ministry afloat, funds which she called "the most wonderful bit of God's intervention in this direction that we have had yet,"[23] and the return of the Tozeur brothers, "again the simple straightforward pair that they were when they first stepped out into the untried path."[24]

A new path was being pioneered by Lilias, this time within the confines of four walls: the way of weakness. She ponders its implications in her diary:

Two glad Services are ours
Both the Master loves to bless
First we serve with all our powers
Then with all our helplessness.

These lines of Charles Fox have rung in my head this last fortnight—& they link on with the wonderful words "weak with Him"—for the world's salvation was not wrought out by the three years in which He went about doing good, but in the three hours of darkness in which He hung stripped & nailed, in utter exhaustion of spirit—soul & body, till His heart broke. So little wonder for us, if the price of power is weakness. (27 October 1923)

Lilias had served faithfully for more than three and a half decades with all her powers. Now she would explore the path of *helplessness.*

24

WITH ALL OUR HELPLESSNESS

1925—1926

[God] needs that helplessness as truly as the negative pole is needed to complete the electric circuit & set free the power. And so when one can only lie like sort of a log, unable to even frame the prayers one would like to pray, His Spirit will find the way through that lowest point which He so strangely needs, & lift them up to the Throne.

—Diary[1]

Lilias's diaries for the next two years are packed full of reports, plans, and visions—as always—serving almost to conceal that each entry is the result of much effort, often written up after the fact from "penned notes & memory" during those minutes in which she could muster the strength. Her wry account of the farewells of Ali's and Amar's families, who had spent Ramadan month at Dar Naama, provides an outside view of her true situation:

> *Their method when anyone is ill is to crowd into the room & sit & look at them. If they are very ill they vary it by setting up from time to time the death wail. To leave anyone quietly alone when they are too short of breath to enjoy talking is inexplicable from their viewpoint. However the women took it peaceably that they could only stand and look sympathetic not to say tearful, & then give fervent embraces.*
>
> *Then came Ali, who smiles joyfully over everything—then Amar, who stood hesitating at the door, evidently longing to say something grateful that would not get far enough up the long road from his big heart to his gruff tongue—finally he came in & thrust into my hands a leather embroidered pouch that must have cost him infinite toil, & not a few precious francs to fabricate—& he was gone. (27 April 1925)*

Lilias accepted each setback in her health as another step forward on the pathway Home:

> *It is a wonderful thing to wake up day after day to the realization that the unseen world lies so close at hand—there is about it the same sense of mystery & marvel just out of sight that I remember in childhood behind the raised beach of grey pebbles at Weybourne near Cromer—Nothing visible but that upheaved line, shutting off all but the faint murmur & splash of the beyond. All the fascination of it comes back in this deep meaning now. (17 June 1925)*

Confined to bed, she turned her attention once again to the Sufi book which burned in her soul as a means of appealing to the Brotherhood's need for "objective, verifiable & divine revelation" in contrast to their search in the "subjective realm of their own consciousness."[2] She dreamed of a work of God among the mystics in which they—"with all their intimate knowledge of Islam on the one side & their apartness from it in spiritual outlook"[3]—would become Christ's apostles to the Muslim world. She responded to the observation that repeatedly in times of spiritual deadness it was the preaching and teaching of the mystics which brought in revival:

> *It is true—Tauler had much to do with Luther's kindling—& Tersteegan & the other Friends of God kept the flames alight in the dreary years of the Thirty Years War, & so did Fenelon & M. Guyon, in their dead time, also George Fox was given to raise the witness of the Quakers. And it would be very much like our God, who is a rewarder of them who do diligently seek Him, if He bestowed on these Moslem Mystics of today the heritage of all that long line of their spiritual ancestry of seekers, in making them in their last days, the channel of His life to the wilderness of the Moslem world. (16 April 1925)*

She wrote to a friend during her confinement that she could only manage sentences a few at a time and "then had to lie back and pray about it."[4] It was a monumental task—writing in Arabic and with a vocabulary unique to the Sufi mystics—and painstakingly researched. Yet in spite of great weakness compounded by the challenges of language, within one month of her confinement she resumed the work and completed the first draft:

> *The Sufi book's last chapter got finished (in the rough) yesterday, & with it a curious sense of coming to life again after a long trend downhill. I have a feeling as if it were all linked together,—as if the sowing in weakness of every kind were needed if it is to be raised in power—& yet the sense of being "through" in a sense with this first bit of "the works that the Father hath given me to finish" brings the sense of the first sparkle of the lights on the coast line. (26 April 1925)*

The work "sown in weakness" was indeed "raised in power" in *The Sevenfold Secret*—arguably, her magnum opus. Lucid, elegant, and strong, it appealed to the common ground shared by Christian and Sufi alike: the purpose of discovering the secrets of divine truth and divine power.

Addressing the Sufi's means of seeking divine union through a succession of seven spiritual states, which in the end still may not please an arbitrary God, she presents an alternate path "wherein we have found joy and peace from the first step."[5] She takes the sayings of Christ about himself contained in the seven "I Am's" of John's Gospel and explores how each offers the "secret" for which they long: satisfaction (Bread), illumination (Light), access (Door), leadership (Shepherd), life (Resurrection and Life), progress (Way), and the ultimate union (Vine).

The book, in fact, created quite a stir. Within three years of publication, it went into six new editions in four languages—Arabic, English, French, and Persian—creating a spiritual resonance for seekers and believers alike with its mystical nuances grounded in solid biblical truth. Lilias's foremost concern, of course, was the Sufi mystics to whom it was specifically addressed, and she rejoiced to hear of its reception by members of their brotherhoods. Harold Stalley, of the Algiers Mission Band relates bringing *The Sevenfold Secret* to the Sufis throughout the years and their repeated comment, "This is *our* book."

During this time, the long low room with black-beamed ceiling and white-washed walls, what Lilias called "the garden that is my room,"[6] became the epicenter of the Algiers Mission Band, strategically and spiritually. She continued to receive reports from the various stations and itinerations, as well as flowers from the many sites. "If I have not walked out to see the world this year," she writes, "it has walked in to see me in a wonderful fashion."[7] Likewise, she continued to be integrally involved in each advance: the opening of a station in Bou Saada; the development of a hostel in Dellys for shelterless girls; the purchase of a Renault Commercial car to facilitate itineration on the "circuit plan"—(Methodist style!); negotiations with the Nile Mission Press for a literature center at Dar Naama; and the formation of an advisory council in England—Reba Brading, of early days in Algiers, Honorary Secretary.

A special source of great joy to her at this time was Salvador Lull, a young Spanish colporteur, who joined the Algiers Mission Band that spring, having officially received his father's consent at the beginning of the year.

> *Lull is proving himself worthy of the name he bears* [recalling the Raymond Lull, the renowned missionary to North Africa]. *He is a*

great strong fellow—but with a strong element of the mystic, & of the love of souls. Miss Freeman has just told me a story of him out of these last days. An atheist was taunting him, "Have you ever seen God!" "No," was Lull's answer. "I have felt Him."

The most wrenching decision for Lilias during this time was to close the work at Rue du Croissant, forced because the property was put up for sale after their thirty-three-year tenancy. Lilias and Helen Freeman, who had underwritten the costs of leasing the property through the years, chose not to burden their successors by purchasing it. Lilias noted that if they made such a purchase, a third of the value would be lost in death duties when they died.[8] At the same time, her sadness is conveyed as she records each successive stage of closing their first native home. Characteristically, Lilias looked ahead to the opening of their next station at Bou Saada. Upon receiving flowers from the garden of the site selected for this new station, she writes:

Is it not like one of God's visible touches of poetry that the very day on which the die was cast re R. du Croissant brings that first bunch of violets from that garden! It seems a wonderful place, full of lemon & fig trees in full bearing, & vines of every kind. But that is all uncertain & its the future—here is God's earnest in a bunch of violets. (31 January 1925)

The summer of 1925 came and with it, Lilias reports, "another step on the path Home today in Dr. Dana's injunction that even the two steps once a week across to the armchair for bedmaking purposes must come to an end, for that all is working on a thread."[9] Still, with the cutbacks came a great sense of relief and the sense of being able to concentrate afresh on "the things that need doing without any waste of powers."[10]

The special assignment of the summer was the translation of the Sufi book into the Arabic distinctive to the Tozeur district, bringing Lilias into close daily association with the Tozeur brothers. She delighted in the renewed opportunity to encourage them in their struggling walk of faith:

> *It is a very real joy to see them sit there for an hour or more morning & afternoon putting their heads together literally & figuratively over the questions that arise whether this thought is "too deep" or this phrasing "too heavy" . . . anxious to keep it all to its simplest, that "the readers may not have to go to the tolbas* [Muslim teachers] *to have it explained, lest it should be taken away from them." (11 July 1925)*

Her sister's visit in October—"for a sight of me face to face"—was a joy to Lilias and reassuring to Margaret. Lilias writes, "She is intensely delighted at the full & happy life I am living, & all the loving thought & care around. She calls me 'the Guru' for all the votive offerings that come in!"[11] Friends took Margaret on daily outings for "what the Japanese would call 'beholdings'" and she would return with vivid word-pictures of the same for Lilias.

Christmas Day brought groups of people to Lilias's door, from morning to evening, in sweeps of singing and with "little bits of offerings of every sort and kind," yet, she writes, with all that joy:

> *the deepest glow of gladness was in a gift that the Lord & I gave each other—the actual finishing by the filling in of the pencil notes of the last of the six typo copies, of the Sufis book . . . just after the last glow faded off the pine tree's branches, telling the day was done. Praise be to His Name. (25 December 1925)*

"A new year has never opened here with such possibilities at our feet—or such a sense of spring in the whole Band of us to 'go in and possess,'"[12] writes Lilias as she records each possibility and each new advance for the coming year. She enumerates the items of business for the January 1926 Committee Meetings, at which she presided from her bed! The new van was steered up along the back road and under her window for her viewing, and she deemed it "so crowded with hopes for the future—just as good as good can be in its powerfulness & its finish without a shadow of showiness."[13]

Lilias records the comings and goings of the band through the seasons of the year—retrievals and advances beyond all imagining: "It is very wonderful to watch these horizons unfold—Long ago—fifty years or more in the past, it was a joy to think that God needed me: Now it is a far deeper joy to feel & see that He does not need me—that He has it all in hand!"[14]

Although she could no longer travel to the dearly loved places, she could visit them in spirit. A great map of North Africa hung on the wall above her bed and daily she prayed her way along the coast, then down along the long lines of penetration into the desert. She prayed for each station and each outpost; she prayed for each room in each house. She followed the van on its colportage circuits and prayed for each stop along the way.

Prayer had always been for Lilias an essential spiritual discipline. She was convinced the band could not survive the hostile spirit-atmosphere, much less succeed in their mission, without the divine guiding and empowering which comes from intimate fellowship with God. Just as she had found this fellowship during the early years in Algiers in Fortification Woods and, later, in the rooftop room at Rue du Croissant, now, at Dar Naama, her bedroom became her place of prayer.

Listening humbly to the experience of others and searching the Scripture for further insight into the process of prayer, Lilias continued to explore the mysteries of faith. She notes a lesson that was garnered early in ministry and reinforced through the years with each new step of faith:

> *It used to seem as if our intercession must sweep round through His & bring back the answer thus—now it has come back to the lesson of "the negative pole"—that all starts with Him—& first sweeps round us—down here—low in our helplessness as Moses was that day sitting on that stone, unable to even keep his hands uplifted. (7 August 1905)*

The text from one of her favorite hymns, "May the mind of Christ, my Savior, live in me from day to day," was her heart-prayer:

> *It has come these days with a new light and power, that the first thing we have to see to, as we draw near to God day by day, is that "our*

fellowship is with the Father & with His Son Jesus Christ." If we can listen in stillness, till our souls begin to vibrate to the thing He is thinking & feeling about the matter in question, whether it concerns ourselves or others, we can from that moment begin praying downwards from His throne, instead of praying upwards toward Him. (21 March 1926)

Likewise, Lilias was ever encouraging others to pray. At Dar Naama, the drawing room was set apart one day a week for prayer between the hours of nine and three—"when our Lord hung on the Cross that Islam dishonours"—for workers to come and go as household duties allowed. A morning of prayer was designated for the outpost workers on that same day. Lilias pioneered ways to link Christians beyond North Africa to needs on the field and to individual North Africans. The printed journals were supplemented by "Togethers"—prayer bulletins more current and specific in content, and Christians were partnered to Algerians with special concerns.

Confined now to bed, without the distractions of the life of action, Lilias could devote herself even more fully to the vocation of prayer. A special focus of Lilias's prayers continued to be the Tozeur men—the Touil, with whom she maintained contact through letters, and the Tozeur brothers, who were perpetually in and out of the house, and whom she mentored for God's service to their own people in the Southlands. Ali weighed heavily on her heart as he was the object once again of attack—this time through the discreet drugging by his wife's Muslim family. A study could be made, alone, on her methods of "praying through" for the soul of another. She prayed the Lord's Prayer with special intention for Ali, saying, "It is such a wonderful vehicle for intercession if one puts it in the third person instead of the first."[15] And she prayed the promises of Scripture on his behalf: "Into Thy Hands I commit his spirit, for Thou has redeemed him, O Lord of Truth."[16] Although there were times when their situations seemed hopeless and her prayers futile (Lilias observes, "It is the penalty one pays for really caring, that one is apt to get emptily hungry over souls, instead of hopefully hungry."[17]), she was able to know with certainty that the Touil died a Christian death. And she saw the brothers come, at last, into careful shepherding and kingdom service.

There was an unexpected answer to her ongoing prayer for native leadership—"Another of God's beautiful touches of poetry"—in Si Sultane's decision to take a public stand for Christ after the death of their faithful friend, Belaid:

> *It was at our dear old Belaid's funeral that came Si Sultane's call to be "baptized for the dead"—He has told M. Theobald that when he was asked to speak there he felt "I cannot"—he could see nothing but the glaring eyes of the bystanders & the great knotted clubs in their hands—Then it came to him—"I can die but once" & he spoke out, unafraid. From that day all shrinking & fear have vanished & believing in the God who kept the crowd in stillness that day, he has given his witness unflinchingly, & with a heavenly touch of life power in place of the old facile & somewhat glib utterance of the past. (11 February 1926)*

Concurrent with her ongoing ministry of prayer were the specific writing projects Lilias believed to be the work given her by the Father to finish. With the Sufi book completed, she directed her efforts to a project as profound in its simplicity as was *The Sevenfold Secret* in its sophistication. Eight full pages of illustrations colored in yellow, green, and aqua, *The Voice of the Bird among the Flowers,* a book for young Arab girls, explores the loving ways of God manifested in his creation. "We love the birds because God loves them," states Lily in the title page, "And Christ said: 'Even one of them is not forgotten.' He teaches them and we must listen to their story."[18] The text and Japanese-style paintings—designed "to give the babies of the land their first picture-book of their very own"—illuminates the character of the heavenly Father through his caring provision for little babies, bird and human!

Lilias also turned her attention to several small "stuck-fast" projects: the writing of "Thor's Story," a treatise based on the Norse legend, for the *Moslem World* periodical, and an expansion of her leaflet *Focussed,* based on a 1901 diary entry. Like so many of her devotional publications, *Focussed* was inspired by an insight from God's Creation—"The word of the Lord came unto me this morning through a dandelion"—then published later in article or booklet form. This particular meditation took on new life when Mrs. Helen Lemmel, inspired by its challenge to "turn full your soul's vision to Jesus, and look and look at Him," wrote the hymn "Turn Your Eyes upon Jesus," which later became the theme of the 1924 Keswick Convention.

Lilias now combined her original meditation with Lemmel's music into a new publication, designing a delicate cover-sketch of a firwood and a dandelion—"a great golden star . . . full face to the sun." The leaflet, *Focussed: A Story and a Song,* was printed on ivory stock and bound by a slender cord—a tiny devotional classic of rare beauty and depth.

With these smaller projects completed, Lilias began to write the text for the Algerian sketchbook, *Between the Desert and the Sea,* the paintings having been prepared early in her confinement. This volume conveys, in essence, her love affair with the land—beginning in Algiers, moving from one region to another, westward along the mountain trend of the Atlas, then southward by the way of the east. Paintings culled from her forty years of journals and diaries lavishly illustrate the oversize pages. The text reveals her intimate knowledge and love of a people and a land; the watercolors bring the same to life with unforgettable images, exquisite and exotic. Her foreword begins within a brief explanation of this land framed between the gold of the desert and the azure of the sea with the invitation to come and look at it: "The colour pages and the letterpress are with one and the same intent—to make you see. Many things begin with seeing in this world of ours."[19]

On 3 April 1926, Lilias marked the anniversary of her first year in bed, noting, "I think it has been quite the happiest year of life!"[20] She "counted her blessings" in flowers, writing, "I have such a lovely outpost room—verbena & heliotrope from Miliana—copper-coloured roses from Colea—chrysanthemums from Bousaada & now dates from Msila—to say nothing of the spoils that come in day by day from the woods here."[21] From her "lovely outpost" she followed the band, recording each new development—the Nile Mission Press association bringing Arthur Upson and the literature work onto Algerian turf; colportage ventures into untried territories; gifts of support (seals of God's endorsement of the ministry); and correspondence with possible recruits.

A bit of excitement broke the quiet pattern of the summer when a fire broke out at Dar Naama, requiring the evacuation of Lilias and resulting in considerable damage within the house. No one was harmed, and, as Helen reported in a letter to Blanche Pigott, "Lily was absolutely calm, and when the doctor appeared I do not believe he found one beat extra as he felt her pulse."[22]

The year ended with the completion of her written legacy:

> *The last of this year's three bits of writing work has gone afloat at last, to my relief and thankfulness, in the posting of the ten typed chapters to go with the sketch book that has been awaiting its letter-press ever since D. Mott & Mr. Basil Matthews settled two and a half years ago that it might have a vocation in making people see & care—It has stuck fast till these last few weeks, & then tumbled in & tumbled out again I hardly know how, but hope that it was because its time has come; for when once it came it came in a shower, as fast as laggard hands & eyes could keep pace with it. (4 December 1926)*

Lilias's medical condition baffled the experts. Her doctor called in another physician for an outside opinion, and Lilias comments:

> *His verdict was that it was tres bizarre that I should be in this world, but this being so, I might, under the same conditions remain in it. It is a very solemn thing to realize that physical, as well as spiritual, life depends on that channel to the Upper Springs being kept clear for the quickening of the mortal body by the Spirit that dwelleth in us, till our work is done.*[23]

However mysterious to some, it was perfectly clear to Lilias that she would remain on this earth *till her work was done.*

25
HOME
1927—1928

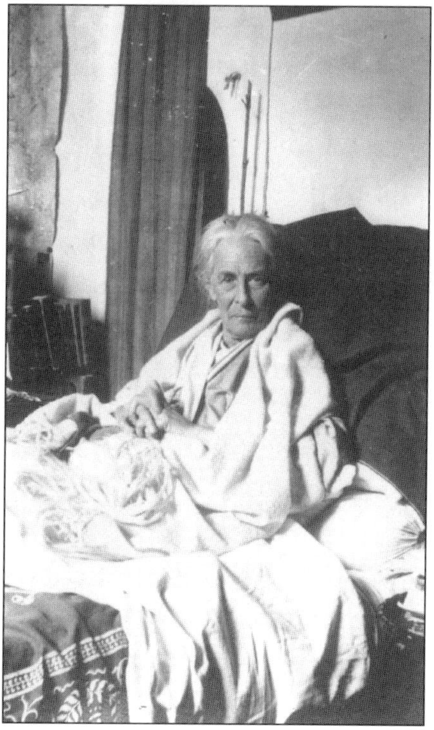

A lesson came this morning over a ripe peach . . . a characteristic of ripeness that I had never noticed before—the ease with which it takes stripping. Up to the last day, before real ripeness sets in, it clings to the outward, & the outward has to be torn from it. The parting with all of it comes now without an effort—the Eternal life at its heart is all that matters.

—Diary[1]

The new year began, as usual, with a written review of the ministry—station work and itinerations, individuals of special concern, growth points for future advance:

> *All these things are so wonderful to watch—all the more wonderful from the watching being from a quiet room full of flowers, instead of from the dust & din of the battle field, good though that was when God gave it. Only now it is easier to trace the working out of these "parts of His ways" & to almost see the still unrevealed thought that links them. (18 January 1927)*

The major writing projects completed, Lilias, now in her early seventies, turned her focus on the consolidation of various matters, personal and organizational. The previous summer, in June 1926, she had written "Directions" clarifying her English and French wills, leaving the purchase deeds of four Algerian properties and her residuary estate to the Algiers Mission Band. Her most personal legacy was her journals and diaries, which she marked for the mission's archives, and her sketchbooks, which she instructed should be cut up and distributed among her family and friends. Now she began the ordering of her "room and contents," undertaken, with her direction, by Belle Patrick (later Collinson) and worked out alphabetically into 125 pigeon hole shelves and drawers. Lilias comments, "It would be lovely, if God so wills, to feel that all is undertaken on that side."[2]

Reba Brading, honorary secretary of the Algiers Mission Band in England, came to Algeria for a three-month visit. Having served with Lilias for four years during the early years in Algiers until health problems forced her own family off the field, Reba brought a unique understanding of the land as well the deep sympathy of friendship. Her husband, Rev. Francis Brading, was on the advisory council in England; their daughter, Lella, was at Dar Naama, caring for Lilias. Lilias's words about Lella were, "Your little girl has crept into the cockles of my heart."[3]

Together they talked over the future workings of the band: the consolidation of the home base and the field base; the appointment of Belle Patrick as assistant secretary to organize prayer groups upon her return to England and act as "liaison officer" between the field needs and prayer partners; the establishment of a guest house at El Biar to serve as a receiving home for men workers and, perhaps, the Christian "Brotherhood" house of the future. Lilias writes, "All these & many other castles in the air get built with wonderful rapidity when Reba Brading & I get together."[4]

Underlying all such plans and dreams was Lilias's fragile health and the band's awareness of a day when she would no longer be the leader of the mission. Lilias referred to the obvious question of who would be her successor in cryptic notes in her agenda book, where she listed the contents of a letter to Mrs. Govan of Faith Mission in Scotland, one item being "specially to pray for General Secretary." She also discussed this concern with Reba:

> *The talk . . . this morning with Reba, opened out other vistas—not as yet ripe for setting down in black & white—but making one feel how swiftly all may work out here when His fulness of time comes, just as He has done on the English side. The very fact of the possibilities of which she spoke, brings a wonderful sense of rest. (26 January 1927)*

Another immediate "consolidation" was particularly difficult for Lilias:

> *A fresh adventure is being mooted in the form of a magazine—quarterly most likely. It has floated in & out of our people's mind for the last year or two—& I've tried for the most part to sink it! & to shew how our scribbles & script, in the form of Journals & Togethers, were much more in keeping with our undeveloped estate, & the more likely to be read for their bit of individual & human make-up. But now knowing that all else has become more than ever irregular & difficult through failure in the eyes & hands to do their bit, I suppose its hour has come—for those who pray must have more news. (3 April 1927)*

The decision taken out of her hands, she got on board with the new quarterly, *A Thirsty Land,* sketching the cover design in her diary. Until the workers could find a permanent editor to take over this venture, she continued to be involved with both content and quality control, noting in her agenda for 31 July 1927 that the "straggled sixteen pages" should be reduced to a "compact twelve pages." Her penchant for excellence also was revealed in her recommendations for the cover:

> *1. photo more emphatic in tone & shewing dune formation & deep footprints*
> *2. the filigree twists in the title suppressed—keeping to the character of the Algiers Mission Band*
> *3. colour of cover ivory & rich coffee brown instead of at present—lemon & purple gray.*[5]

Physical limitations not withstanding, Lilias continued to be involved in virtually every aspect of the band. Her room was the control station of the mission, her agenda book the log in which each maneuver was charted. Daily she listed the contents of letters to be written—often as many as fifteen—and blocked out segments of time for tasks as varied as labeling books for the library or planning the schedule and order of business for committee meetings and rallies.

The business enacted from her bed, with the assistance of her young secretaries, is daunting in sheer scope and output. Lilias kept in touch with the daily operations of each station, strategized the many itinerations on the map spread before her on her bed, and through copious correspondence connected the field with the home base in England. She was intimately involved with lives of individual Algerians, writing detailed letters to them and on their behalf. She investigated new printing equipment and corresponded with publishers over French and English editions of the *Bird Book* as well as new editions of old publications.

Another project that evolved over the months was a collaboration with Miss Woods of Nile Mission Press to develop the pictures from the Band's Magic Lantern presentations, beginning with "Creation" and "Passover Night," into permanent wall posters. She attended to organizational details of the mission—from the development of a more explicit statement of belief to a comprehensive furlough policy. Throughout this immense output emerges a sense that Lilias is ordering the affairs of the mission for the future—a future without herself.

Her agenda book likewise provides an intimate glimpse into her continuing role of training and nurturing fledgling workers. In a response to the application of Dorothy Graham (later Watson) to the Algiers Mission

Band, Lilias expresses their willingness to accept her one year before the required age (twenty-five), based on her previous experience and pending a one-year internship in the French home of Pastor and Mme. Cook, who had served many years in Algeria. Lilias says, "They would be able to tell you much of the ins and outs of native life and Moslem thought and customs, and there would be the advantage of being in a French household and hearing nothing but French around you," French being the language from which Arabic was taught as well as the speech increasingly being used in the coastal regions of North Africa. As well, Lilias directs Dorothy to assist Mme. Cook (a partial invalid) in "practical matters, which would also be part of the essential training for the life out here, where we have to be able to turn our hand to everything, cooking, sewing, etc., leaving plenty of time for study."

What is not explicitly stated to Dorothy, but revealed through the older woman's daily log, is Lilias's sustained support and nurture during that year of preparation. To begin with, though Dorothy may have been unaware of it, Lilias sent a monthly check to the Cooks for Dorothy's room and board. Lilias also writes to her in France asking if she "is studying any book on Moslem questions" and sends her Hugo's first French course to use on her summer break—advising her to "get away for an hour a day at it as well as reading a bit of the Bible in French daily so as not to lose ground." A touching note to Dorothy's mother reveals Lilias's empathy as well as her own motherly heart, as she writes, "we are thinking of her these days in her daughter's start, & how we believe the worst of the lonely time is over & how we will take all care of her."

One can only speculate upon the countless ways in which Lilias nurtured her workers, as well as others outside the band, throughout the many years in her unofficial role of "mother superior." The agenda records promises of prayer and gifts of edifying literature; the entry for 3 April alone lists fifty-two people to whom she sent a calendar of "Creative Prayer" based on the Student Christian Movement's publication of the same name. Evidences of her caring touch fill the agenda: sympathy cards, baby gifts—"a kimona sent with the knitted jacket," congratulations upon success in a violin competition, "violets and new year's greetings" for Blanche Haworth's mother in England, invitations for tea at Dar Naama, and an offer for a vacation at El Biar as a "Guest of God."

Lilias's input also extended to the firmer side of nurture as she instructed and corrected where she felt it necessary. She records the "shock and sorrow" of one worker's sudden leaving, writing to that person about "all its sense of loss." She counsels the eager M'barek, who would in time develop into a strong native leader, "to have patience till the right way opens for continuing his studies," and challenges him at a later date to "remember the two former steps in which God has given him victory & that now comes to third—in burying in Christ's grave the old ambition for earthly learning." Gone is the earlier Lilias bound "too much to human sympathy." Present is the seasoned leader in full stride of ministry.

Even during her confinement, Lilias extended her attention beyond mission concerns to the world at large. Six decades after the fact, Margaret Ross, who worked in the foreign exchange department of the Bank of Algiers, recalls Miss Trotter's keen interest in "the comings and goings of people through the bank. She was not only interested in the titled people who contacted me in the Bank but also the poor Kabyle & Arab street sellers who came in with their foreign currency." Ross sensed that Miss Trotter appreciated topics of conversation that she, a young woman without the problems common to mission workers, was able to provide her. Lilias always showed interest in people that her young friend met from the U.K.—"No doubt some of them were known to her in her younger days."[6]—and through this unexpected connection, friends from earlier years in England were able to make contact with her, to their mutual delight. On one occasion, when trying to visit the ailing Lilias at Dar Naama, Ross was turned away by a vigilant worker. Upon learning of this, Lilias wrote to her, instructing her on her next visit to go to another door where access would not be barred!

When one of the "castles in the air" discussed with Reba Brading became a project in earnest—the building of a men's hostel or guest house at Dar Naama—Lilias was enthusiastically absorbed in it. Enhanced by Blanche Haworth's last bequest being liquidated for the purpose of financial support, the project was a final earthly collaboration of these two great friends. Lilias had envisioned it first as a home for Mr. Tetley upon his arrival as field director, but it evolved along other lines when eye problems forced his resignation. Lilias writes, "One learns as one goes on, not to fear the detours by which God leads on."[7] Evidence of each new development was brought to Lilias: the first piece of turf from the site; a primrose (pressed in her diary) to mark the occasion of the "driving in of the stakes"; architectural drawings for her revising; and snapshots of the house in progress.

Even as she followed each successive stage of the building, Lilias was looking "into the beyond," envisioning a day when a *zaouria* (fraternity house) would be built on the hill opposite, a complement of the guest house. She writes, "if it evolved into a Hostel where colporteurs, European & native, could be trained side by side—that might be in its turn the forerunner of the real zaoura of our dreams, down south where it would be a home!"[8] The plan for that southland zaouria was already drawn up and lodged in a mantlepiece drawer, and three hundred francs for its first sundried bricks were waiting in the mission cashbox.

As 1927 came to a close, Lilias received a letter from Mlle. Page (on loan to them from North African Mission) who accompanied their own Maud Walton on a special venture to the Souf in the Southlands. Lilias pasted the postmark from the envelope in her diary calling it "worthy to be enshrined for it told in a moment that the star of hope that had always shone over Kouinine was a true lodestar." She went on:

> *It is beautiful that once more the star should stand to halt over a fondouk—& that with Christmas Eve a week off—the first keeping of Christmas that Kouinine has ever known. We have one fondouk down in Tozeur—but this new one is of the roughest—little unplastered rooms & probably floored with the sand—flooring & nothing more—I wonder if they have a manger in one of them! (18 December 1927)*

Amidst all her joy at the ever-expanding work of the mission, a cloud was gathering of deepest concern to Lilias as it affected both the future of the band and, potentially, its unity. The problem was first indicated in her diary in the most cryptic terms as a personal test of faith:

> *"I am come into deep waters" took on a new meaning this morning. It started with perplexing matters concerning the future with which the journal does not deal—then it dawned that the shallow waters were a place where you can neither sink nor swim, but in deep waters it is one or the other—"waters to swim in"—not to float in—swimming is the intense, most strenuous form of motion—all of you is involved*

in it—& that every inch of you is in abandonment of rest upon the water that bears you up. "We rest in Thee, & in Thy Name we go." (20 December 1927)

The issue, as it unfolds in the pages of her diary was two-fold. The first was related to a difference of opinion as to whether the men's work fell under the Home Committee or the Field Committee. The second concerned the mission of the band to the outlying and unreached places. Were the stations a means to an end (a base from which they would continue to itinerate to unreached territories) or ends in themselves (developing and maintaining the existing programs)? At the heart of the concern, Lilias believed, were issues of faith: the physical risk of penetrating deeper into territories beyond the reach of outposts; the financial risk of funding these new ventures.

As the time for the spring committee meetings drew near, the pressure on everyone grew more intense. Lilias regarded March, always a "fighting time" for the mission, as the decisive month—"for it looks as if it must hold our united decision whether as a Band we will hug the shore, or whether we will launch out into the deep, out of reach of any landing place if the way should prove stormy."[9]

This particular March held special significance as it closed the band's forty years in Algeria. Like Israel before them, they were at a point of looking back at the forty years in the "wilderness" so that they might fearlessly look forward to "Canaan." In a letter to her "Dearly Beloved A.M.B.," dated 7 March 1928, Lilias anticipates a new step forward in faith, financially as well as geographically. She reviews their position as a faith mission, noting how in the past, financial need had been met in part by their own "independent means" and in part by the help of an "inner circle of friends." She goes on:

Now to come to present facts of the case as they concern us most closely: Miss Freeman and I have both reached the point, not only where supplementing ceases to be possible, but where we ourselves are becoming dependent on God's supply in matters for which we are individually responsible. So it is the time for a united "act of faith."

Referring first to the analogy of the props of a ship being knocked away so that it can be "launched by the weight of its own helplessness," she concludes with yet another analogy she used many years ago in England when, as now, she was presenting the challenge for new "ventures in faith":

> *He Himself has given us a better picture still—that of the eagle's nest of the Spring days, kept secure and restful till the young birds become old enough to fly. Then the mother bird stirs it till they can settle down no more; then comes the plunge into the abyss below, and then the new resting place on her wings. "As an eagle stirreth up her nest, fluttereth over her young, spreadeth abroad her wings, taketh them, beareth them on her wings, so the Lord alone did lead him."*
>
> *Shall we, with the old days closing behind us, stedfastly and unitedly refuse to look to the right hand or to the left for means of present supply or of future advance, but rest with full weight of helplessness upon "THE LORD ALONE."*

The forty years' celebration began in "proper Arab fashion" with its vigil on the eve of the anniversary, 9 March 1928, of Lilias's arrival in Algeria. She describes the anniversary as "a beautiful day in its showers of love all around from morning till night":

> *It began between eight & nine by the door opening for the entrance of little George & Bobbie, in their apricot coloured jerseys—bearing great bundles of carnations—pale creamy pink & white—& behind them a whole string of the dear houseparty with "birthday" gifts of every kind of preciousness, first & foremost a bed table that stands fair & square with its brown feet on the floor, so that papers & files & blotting books will no longer slide as aforetime over each other's heads to the bedspread. . . . Then came a moment pause & then our prayermeeting with its praises first & foremost—& the last surprise was the trooping in, in the late afternoon, of all the native part of the establishment, bringing the babies to be kissed,—the procession ended*

with the two Miss Mays & Miss Newton bearing two little mimosa, one to be planted in the garden here, the other at the Hostel in ceremony of the day. (March 1928)

Two weeks later, the anticipated day of decision came and went in victorious resolve, described by Lilias, "Last Wednesday's committee was, as we expected, a crisis day, for several debatable points were before us, as well as the whole policy of going forward into new ventures of faith."[10] She offers no details as to the scene, as she presided from her bed while the future of the band hung in the balance. Yet the key to the solution is revealed: "Again & again we held on for the heavenly solution & again & again the moot questions vanished into clear agreement and we hardly knew how except that God was in it."[11] Not only did they come to full agreement to reaffirm the special vocation of the Algiers Mission Band to evangelize the great unreached stretches of the interior, but in the months to follow, their unified step of faith was sealed by the stepping up of men who felt called to that particular mission and by several substantial (and unsolicited) gifts to underwrite their expenses.

The crowning event of this historical month was the dedication of the new hostel which was faithfully reported to Lilias along with photographs of the finished home! She records it this way:

Each room had its own special share of prayer, led by one & another from M. Collinson to Si Amar. Edmund, when his father took him at last up the little staircase that mounts to the roof of the roofroom was a bit concerned that this had not been included—& well it might be, for it is a glorious place, they say, for any who desire to go up upon the housetop to pray! & this may be its vocation. (26 March 1928)

With the final consolidations of viewpoint, one senses in Lilias a confident abandonment as she becomes increasingly an observer, still following each development with the greatest of interest. Alongside the advances were changes signifying the end of an era, the most personal being the resignation of Mr. Smeeton, following an illness, ending his twelve-year ministry to the blind. The diary pages record one responsibility after another being delegated to the able care of a new generation. The lesson of the ripe peach—"the ease with which it takes its stripping"—is lived out in Lilias as she releases the past for the future—"the parting with all of it comes now without an effort—the eternal life at its heart is all that matters."[12]

The end of May 1928, Lilias began Sunday afternoon Bible readings in her room, "the other chaplains having vanished" for their summer breaks. She records that the study began where Mr. Theobald had left off, studying the life "over the Jordan" as prefigured in the carvings of Solomon's temple, which she describes as "beautiful vision of 'things that are before' whose foretaste may be ours here & now."[13]

One can imagine those quiet Sunday afternoons as Lilias, propped up against pillows, the map of Algeria above her head, native art and Arabic texts around the walls, adds the wisdom of a lifetime of experience to her scriptural insight. Those who were present spoke of the joy and light in that flower-filled room. Her diary records her notes for those talks about Solomon's temple, beginning with the oxen—"the lowest in the scale of service"—and working through the portals of the porch, to the cherubims around the mercy seat in the Holy of Holies. Perhaps as she expounded on the significance of each carving and the lessons to be derived therein, her listeners noted how fully her own life and character had become the embodiment of those very qualities: the service of the ox, the fearlessness of the lion, the purity of the lily, the fruitfulness of the pomegranate, the victory of the palm tree, the joyfulness of the open flowers, and the pure worship of the cherubim.

Week by week, the diary writing becomes fainter and less legible. It is increasingly apparent that she is moving closer to the "beautiful vision" of the Jordan. The last trailing scribbles from her feeble hand are clarified by the notes of one who listened: "We find the cherubim echoing the song which the seraphims had been singing so long, bringing God's glory out from earth to heaven! 'Thy will be done on earth,' 'Holy, holy, holy,' which is made by all the tiny bits of victory in which each of us has our share."[14] Then, on 27 June 1928, the beginning of her last summer, Lilias wrote in her diary for the last time.

The summer months were marked by increasing weakness and suffering. Lella Brading stood on call as "nurse" with Lilias's two young secretaries—Jessie Johnson (later Stalley) and Edith Armitage—aiding in her care. The band likewise awaited her smallest request. Her mind remained clear, her spirit stedfast as the last vestiges of strength slowly ebbed from her body. In moments between pain and sleep she responded to the loved ones gathered around her bed, laughing at attempts of humor, listening to reports and letters, even asking for prayer for the strength to dictate two final letters, one being to Amy Carmichael of India, with whom she kept an active correspondence.

On 27 August 1928, members of the band gathered around her bed and sang her favorite hymn, "Jesus Lover of My Soul." She looked out the window that framed her garden view and exclaimed, "A chariot and six horses!" "You are seeing beautiful things?" asked Helen Freeman. Lilias looked up and spoke her last words: "Yes, many, many beautiful things."[15] She stretched out her arms as though she would hold them all in her embrace, then slowly lifted her hands in prayer. Almost immediately she became unconscious, and in perfect calm she drew her last breath and went Home.

The fortieth anniversary celebration of the founding of the work in North Africa, planned for 20 September at Eccleston Hall in London, now took the form of a memorial service for Lilias. In two separate services, people from all walks of life and faith gathered to remember her. Their sense of loss was tempered by the realization of her gain, summed up in their singing of another of her favorite hymns: "We Shall See Him Face to Face."

Back at Dar Naama, the Algerians had their own service for their beloved "Lalla Lili" in the court of the house. Si Amar, over whom Lily had labored in prayer so long and so hard, preached the sermon. Si Sultane prayed. Nationals and mission workers sang together without accompaniment, voices blending, men and women, and her body was laid to rest in the soil of her beloved North Africa.

26
LILY'S LEGACY

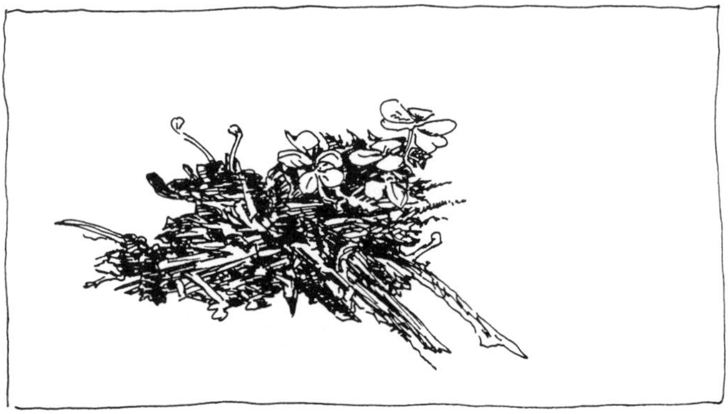

The results need not end with our earthly days. Should Jesus tarry our works will follow us. . . . God may use, by reason of the wonderful solidarity of His Church, the things He has wrought in us, for the blessing of souls unknown to us: as these twigs and leaves of bygone years, whose individuality is forgotten, pass on vitality still to the new-born wood-sorrel. God only knows the endless possibilities that lie folded in each one of us!

—*Parables of the Cross*[1]

A host of witnesses testify to Lily's legacy, through written tributes at the time of her memorial service and in the biographies and articles that followed. Her coworkers spoke of personal qualities: "She never lost her enthusiasm or her capacity for wonder, or her sense of humour, and she loved people to be thrilled with a thought or a place."[2] The younger members of the band marvelled over her openness to their thoughts: "Always interested in new points of view, or new methods, even though she might not agree with them, Miss Trotter was never 'damping,' even to the newest fledged."[3]

Fellow workers marvelled in her capacity for work and the pace which she maintained, insisting that while "her standard was exceedingly high, she was very merciful and encouraging to shortcomers."[4] Her ability as a leader to identify the capabilities and possibilities in individuals permitted her to appoint members of the band to tasks particularly suiting them. "Through her encouragement gifts were discovered and talents developed which their owners at times hardly knew they possessed."[5] Pleasant Hurst, a short-servicer with a special interest in the Sufis, quotes, "I am that sweet-smiling Jesus. And the World is alive through Me." She goes on to write:

> *It was not a Christian, but a Moslem mystic of long ago, who put into the mouth of our Lord these two lines of pure poetry. How "Lalla Lili" would have loved them! . . . When one thinks of the beauty of her utterances, oral and written, it is wonderful to be able to say, that she herself was like that. To read the lives of some of those whose art has charmed us to the uttermost, is to experience a deep depression. But it is not so here. Lalla Lili was like her teaching. To see her was to catch a glimpse of "that sweet-smiling Jesus." It is wonderful to think of the many poor souls who saw her smile, and had their first breath of heaven through her words.*[6]

Colleagues beyond the Algiers Mission Band were inspired by her wide outlook and vision, her touch with world mission problems as well as her grasp of detail. "Her methodical files and folios, and her unfailing attention to business and letters, were all the more remarkable in one who had such great artistic and literary gifts."[7] Her unfailing encouragement to the many Christian workers whose lives she touched is best summed up in the appreciation written by the great apostle to Islam, Dr. Samuel Zwemer:

> *My best impression of her life could best be expressed in two words—it was a life of Vision and a life of Prayer. Her eyes seemed ever looking*

upward, and also gazed below the surface of things. She was indiscourageable in happiness and steadfast in faith, and was an embodiment of her own expression, "The Glory of the Impossible." Personally, I owe very much to her missionary messages, which were my inspiration and comfort in the early days of my pioneering work in Arabia.[8]

She left a vigorous legacy of her work—the Algiers Mission Band was on solid footing when she died, thirty members strong in fifteen stations and outposts, unified in mission and purpose. She pioneered missionary methods and approaches to evangelism for which noted missiologist Dr. Christy Wilson called her "one hundred years ahead of her time."

Her contribution to the literature for Muslims was likewise a pioneering work. Miss Padwick of the Nile Mission Press writes,

First, at a time when most literature for Moslems was dealing (and naturally) with the great points of difficulty and difference between the two religions, Miss Trotter wrote stories that, with all their intimate knowledge of Moslem ways and thoughts appealed first to the fundamental likenesses, the great human needs of all souls. And secondly, at a time when missionary literature, if illustrated at all, was adorned with old-fashioned blocs obtained cheaply from London or America, Miss Trotter gave to all her leaflets a touch of colour and of Oriental beauty, with two-colour designs or little pictures that looked artistically right with the Arabic script instead of foreign or strange.[9]

Lilias's devotional literature—books, leaflets, articles—was circulated through the Keswick Conferences and more broadly by the Algiers Mission Band supporters in Europe, Great Britain, and the United States; it was also reprinted in many languages. As noted earlier, the well-known hymn "Turn Your Eyes Upon Jesus" was inspired by Lilias's reflections first recorded in her diary and later issued in the little booklet *Focussed.*

Yet, for all her accomplishments in organization, strategy, and literature, perhaps her most palpable legacy was, in fact, intangible: a "wideness and lavishness of love that transformed even trivial gifts till they became akin to a sacrament."[10] From the little street urchin of the slums of Algiers to the most sophisticated statesman of the faith, Lilias loved with a love that showed no partiality. "No wonder that Catholics and Jews and Moslems, as well as Protestants, are mourning her loss, for love, in the end, wins love."[11]

The people of Algeria recognized "Lalla Lili" as their lover. One woman arriving sick in Algiers brought her entire family caravan to Lilias in full confidence that "Lili loves me and will not turn me out."[12] The sheik of one of the Sufi brotherhood zaourias asked, after her death, for a French book he could barely understand because on the frontispiece was her photograph —"really her face, how well I remember her."[13]

Seventy years later, the remaining few people who personally knew Lilias remember, above all, that singular quality of love. Margaret Ross, daughter of missionaries with North Africa Mission in Algeria, recounts,

> *Once when about five and my brother three, we were staying at Dar Naama and were told to go and play in the garden but not to speak to L.T. and worry her. She was sitting painting flowers. She called me and I did not go, but when she called again, my brother went up and said, "We mustn't worry you." "Oh, you're not. Tell your sister to come; I want to show you something." This was a beautiful flower, and she told us all about it—all the parts—then spoke of God's creation and love for the beautiful things He gave to us whom He loved dearly. She went on to speak of Jesus and his love. We knew she prayed for us and felt her love for the two little M.K.'s whose father had died of typhus.*[14]

But what about a *lasting* legacy? Today, what is left from this life—so brilliantly gifted—spent in relative obscurity in a work yielding unspectacular results? The Algiers Mission Band continued to carry out its mission—"the evangelisation of the great unreached stretches that extend back of the coast line"—in the spirit of its founder, Lilias. The Band merged in 1964 with the North Africa Mission, known today as Arab World Ministries. Lilias's art, extensively circulated in her lifetime through Algeria and Arab-speaking lands, now for the most part lies dormant in her unpublished diaries and journals and in her out-of-print books. As for the church visible in Algeria, for which she longed and prayed, there were but few who, taking their stand, maintained it publicly against the pressures of their families and society. Today, Algeria, considered one of the most dangerous countries in the world (because of arbitrary attacks of Muslim fundamentalists), is likewise regarded as a notable stronghold of Islam, cold and resistant to the Christian faith.

So was hers a light that flamed brightly for a little while, flickered for a few years, then was extinguished by time and circumstance? Is there no tangible legacy from this distinguished life? In truth, Lily's legacy is impossible to tally on earth. Her love that embraced the temporal concerns of people extended to a passion for the health and destiny of their souls. The records kept during her forty years in Algeria reveal that her "Homecoming" in heaven was welcomed by a host of believers—scores, even hundreds of national believers, who, having accepted Christ against all human odds, worship freely the true God for all eternity.

As for present-day Algeria, hard as it appears on the surface, there are reports of God's Spirit working throughout the land, through miracles, visions, and dreams directing individuals to the light and life and love of Christ. While the greatest response to Christian faith is among the Kabyles, there are among the Arabs evidences of "ones and twos" coming out of Islam, standing firm, joining together with others, and, unaided by missionaries, beginning to talk about a church of Christ in Algeria—Lily's unwavering dream! Who can say whether the flowering today may be, in part, from seeds scattered broadcast, or placed in the hands of children, or lodged in the libraries of Sufi fraternities by Lily's brave band so many years ago?

"[Christians'] works do follow them," wrote Lilias in her first book of *Parables.* In writing of this truth, she prophetically supplied a perspective of her own legacy—and the legacy of all who invest in the kingdom of God.

APPENDIX A
HISTORICAL SETTING IN ENGLAND, 1851

Eighteen fifty-one was a very good year. England had survived its uneasy transition from eighteenth-century agricultural society to industrial nation, emerging mid-nineteenth century as the leading commercial world power. The country's continued supremacy at sea had laid the foundation of an empire and a strong national financial system was spawning a new, powerful mercantile and professional class.

England had overcome her early skepticism of the monarchy which was at its height when eighteen-year-old Victoria acceded the throne of a country in the throes of problems—health, housing, labor, and the uncontrolled growth of cities—resulting from the new, untested industrial revolution. Her Prince Consort, Albert of Saxe-Coburg, had stepped in not only as husband and confidant, but as her private secretary—an unofficial permanent minister—guiding the impulsive young queen in orderly ways of business and hard work.

During the first dozen years of her reign, Queen Victoria witnessed the establishment of both a penny post and the telegraph, as well as the railway mania of the 1840s, when over 6,000 miles of track were laid in Britain alone. The coming of the railway changed not only the face of her kingdom, but marked a great divide in British history, the shift from stagecoach to train.

And if the Railroad Age defined a new Industrial Era, the Great Exhibition declared England's supremacy in the world. Housed in Paxton's creation for the event, the Crystal Palace, a glass and steel phenomenon four times as long as St. Paul's Cathedral and twice as wide, the glorified world fair symbolized the peace, prosperity, and progress of Britain. It was a personal triumph for Victoria's Albert, the driving force behind this event.

This international feat heralded a Golden Age for England, captured in the name, *Victorian,* and characterized by values and virtues personified in the royal couple. Although the nation could not ignore certain realities—poverty, prostitution, and crises of religious faith—the faithful and the faithless agreed, by and large, if not on the grounds of belief, on an ideal of conduct and attitude associated with their sovereign's name. This ideal meant earnestness, respectable comportment and behavior, "character," duty, hard work, and thrift.

If England took its place as a "world nation" the year of the fair, then London, the host city, surely could be considered, in the words of Ford Madox Ford, a "world town." The foundation of a sound Bank of England and healthy credit system spurred the growth of the City, making it the financial and commercial center of the empire. London, both metropolis and emporium, had the nation's highest concentration of population, and its residents consumed the highest rate of the country's goods.

The River Thames, London's nerve center, connected the financial institutions in the East End—the City—with the royal borough of Westminster, which ruled England through Buckingham Palace and through its Houses of Parliament. While reform bills of the 1830s had broadened the base of representation, the governing bodies were still dominated by the landed aristocracy, who, from their stylish town houses, supported a "dining society" and a cultural life comparable to any in Europe.

In the early 1800s, savvy aristocrats with West End estates began laying out elegant squares and terraces to house newly rich merchants and bankers—a rising and powerful upper middle class. The expansion continued throughout Victoria's early reign, filling in the green spaces between the financial/political centers along the river and the established West End. And provision shops and artisans' services appeared between the squares of well-to-do residences.

At the west end of London, directly south of Regent's Park, lay the medieval village of Marylebone. Developed by Robert Harley, Earl of Oxford, as London shifted west into the eighteenth century, Marylebone had the highest concentration of Georgian dwellings in the city. The Prince Regent, in one of his grandiose schemes, targeted this area for the most ambitious and successful efforts of town planning ever to be undertaken—and completed—in London.

The plan was magnificently developed and executed by John Nash. The royal park was laid out as a setting for classically designed villas and terraces, then linked to the busy world of Westminster by means of a new thoroughfare which became Regent Street. Nash took advantage of Portland Place—"the most magnificent street in London"[1]—making it the first quarter mile before cutting its way through and around developed areas, masking junctions with "circuses" then ending the royal mile with a vista towards Carlton House, the prince's residence.

Completed in 1828, though not all the designer intended and after sixteen years of difficulties, the plan did succeed in essentially reorganizing London's West End, providing a triumphal processional mile, south from the beautifully developed Regent's Park to the capitol. Slum properties were cleared along the way, parks and squares laid out, and Buckingham House converted into London's official royal residence—young Victoria its first royal resident.

By 1851, England was the leading world power on the brink of two decades of unprecedented economic prosperity. The monarchy had regained, if not power, considerable influence. London, the indisputable center of the empire, had received a face lift. "The old city was young again, freshly clad in spruce, elegant apparel." It was a good place to be—and a good time to be there.[2]

APPENDIX B
HISTORICAL AND RELIGIOUS SETTING IN ALGERIA, 1888

Algeria lies between the sparkling waters of the Mediterranean Sea and the scorching sands of the Sahara Desert. Bounded to the east by Tunisia and Libya and to the west by Morocco and Spanish Sahara, Algeria, in 1888, is the second largest country in Africa, the tenth largest in the world, an immense mass of mountains, plains, plateau, and desert covering 896,553 square miles.

The great Atlas mountain range dominates the northern region—the Tell. The mountain range lies east to west across the country parallel to the coast, dividing the region, north to south, into five distinct zones: the coastal zone; the plains; the first chain of mountains, called the Atlas Tell; the High Plateau; and the second mountain chain, called the Sahara Atlas. The southern region—the Algerian Sahara—is composed of two main zones covered by vast sheets of sand dunes or "ergs": the Great Western Erg and the Great Eastern Erg divided from each other by a central north-to-south rise called the M'zab.

Most of the country's population is concentrated on the relatively narrow strip of land in the north running parallel to the coast—100 miles deep; 727 miles long. Here, knitted into the backbone of the Atlas Tell are hills and valleys and plains and uplands where people live and work the land for vegetables, fruit, and grain, or graze their herds, farm the forest, and mine the earth. Beyond, in the great Sahara, survivors of the desert extremes eke out a living in the scattered oases from their main stock-in-trade—the date palm.

Native Algerians—Berbers, Arabs, or a mix of both—exhibit more similarities than differences, sharing the same race, the same traditions, the same religion, and the same customs. With the exception of certain Berber tribes hidden in isolated pockets of the mountains, the indigenous population is distinguished primarily by the traditional garb of their region, and by the territorial adaptation of their homes—the wood and thatch of the *doura* on the plains; the terraced houses of the Aures mountains and M'zab regions; the sun-dried brick dwellings of the El Djerid (oases in Tunesia); and the sand hives of the Oued Souf (oases in Algeria).

The history of the Berbers, the earliest known inhabitants, involves foreigners as much as themselves, with a succession of conquerors finding the coastal position of the Maghrib, or Northwest Africa, advantageous to their purposes. In 1200 B.C., Phoenicia founded colonies along the coast of North Africa and ruled North Algeria from its chief city of Carthage. Rome destroyed Carthage in 143 B.C., gradually gained control of the North African coast during the next 100 years, and brought in a level of peace and prosperity until its decline in the fourth century. The Vandals from Europe then invaded and controlled the northern part of Algeria until, in A.D. 533, Byzantine forces came along and conquered it.

Then, in the seventh century, the "strangers from the east"—warlike nomads from Arabia—swept into the country, conquering Algeria and eventually all of North Africa. Brave Berber princes resisted their invaders, but the majority of Berbers fled into the mountains and, in time, all were forced to accept Arab rule and to adapt to the Muslim faith. Thus began what some historians call *des siecles obscurs,* "centuries of obscurity," the era which, in fact, constituted the height of Islam and of its successive Berber and Arab dynasties. During this millennium of dominance, Islam impressed its stamp upon the very soul of the country, permeating every aspect of the culture—legal, civil, educational, domestic, and of course, religious—with its philosophy and its daily practices.

In 1518, the Turks, at the invitation of the Spanish Muslims, or Moors, who immigrated to the Maghrib, took control of North Africa, setting up the "Algerian Regency." Although the Algerians, by and large, refused Turkish rule, Algiers remained under its authority for the next three hundred years—an era remembered for its piracy, the Algerian Regency and Barbary States (Algeria, Tunisia, Tripoli, and Morocco) uniting in their off-coast attacks of commercial ships.

The French navy, in 1830, seized the port city of Algiers, deposed the Turkish *bey* or governor, then occupied the abandoned houses and buildings. When the native Algerians who had fled the city later returned to their homes, they found them occupied and chose to "sell" the property to their occupants rather than contest their seizure. Then they promptly returned to the mountains and plains or to the Arab quarters in the city.

Thus began the progressive conquering and colonizing of the country—making Algeria French by first taking over the buildings, then the land and forests, and finally the minerals from the ground. When civilian administration replaced military rule in 1870, the coastal area was divided into three main provinces—Algiers, Oran, Constantine—and these were made full-fledged *departements* of mainland France. The Muslim-dominated central highland was formed into *communes mixtes,* each with a French administrator. Each commune elected representatives, in theory to represent their concerns but, in fact, to enforce French measures in the Muslim community—a situation which inevitably provided fertile ground for a patronage system. In the Southlands, the military still held sway.

By 1888, Algeria, almost sixty years after the French invasion, had settled into a colonial society in which there were distinct divides between colonized and colonizer, between native Algerians and Europeans (French and non-French), and between Jews and both of those categories. Within the Muslim community was yet another divide between the Arab and the Berber, the latter, ironically, at the bottom of the social scale. Native Algerians were outnumbered in the cities by Europeans who, in turn, were outnumbered in the rural areas by Algerians.

The French Colonial government having succeeded in subduing the native element in the first decades of its rule, attended next to settling the country. Gradually, in the 1870s and 1880s, it built up its ports, began to develop a road system and railroad line east and west, parallel to the coast, and worked to extend rails inland to areas in which natural resources were being mined. Ever so slowly, Algeria was awakening from its pre-industrial sleep, as its resources were being developed and funneled out of the country to its wealthier northern neighbors in exchange for their commodities.

At this time the native Algerians were for all practical purposes invisible when it came to decision making, with voting rights being limited to landowners and civil servants and then only at the municipal level; yet they were visible for services desired, providing pools of reserve labor for the increasing demands of the developing economy. Road signs and place names in the cities were being "Frenchified;" mosques were being converted to cathedrals.

A force remained, however, in Algeria, one stronger than any conqueror that might subdue them. No matter how the people were spread out geographically or separated socially, the element intrinsic to Islam—solidarity—united the Muslim masses in their common language of Arabic and their innumerable functions, feasts, and fasts. Five times a day, when the *meuzzin* cried out the roll call of the faithful, the Arab world united "In the Name of God the Merciful, the Compassionate." The Muslim Algerians stood as one under a much higher sign than the flag of France; indeed, theirs was a cosmic sign: the day-old crescent of the Ramadan moon which sent its call throughout Algeria, around the Arab world, uniting all Islam in its month-long fast into one firm front.

Along the Bay of Algiers lies the gleaming city of Algiers, facing the Mediterranean Sea and encircled by the emerald slopes of the Sahel Hills. The French Boulevard flanks the crescent of the water's edge, and behind it fans the great white amphitheater of the colonial city and its suburbs, squeezed between hills and bay. The capitol city and chief port, Algiers, throbs with the activity and culture which mark any Mediterranean seaport. French colonial society dominates the major residential area as well as commercial and financial centers while other European and ethnic groups, native and foreign, tend to cluster in their own sectors of the city and suburbs.

Above the colonial city, the old Arab town rises in the sunlight, a creamy mass against the deep blue of the Mediterranean sky. The old Moorish section of Algiers was built around the fortress which crowned the rocky heights overlooking the bay. The old city, or Casbah, stands above and apart, literally, from the rest of the city, separated by barriers far greater than any fortification which surrounds it. Entrance into the old native town is a step into the airless stench and dusk of the winding maze of crooked streets. Up and down one walks, through the crush of humanity—plunging down through the Jewish street then up a bit into the Arab quarter. The narrow paved staircases which serve as streets are deep, irregular, and edged with cobblestones. The walls on either side contain cubby-hole recesses here and there housing tiny shops. Between the shops are the nail-studded doors of windowless houses which nearly meet overhead—"that they may buttress each other in case of earthquake."[1]

Beyond the heavy outer door of each house is a long dim vestibule, at the end of which yet another door opens into an open courtyard. Around the courtyard is built a several-storied dwelling housing many families—sometimes several to a room—Kabyles, the earliest inhabitants of Algiers from Berber tribes, often on the ground floor and Arabs above. On the open gallery halfway up, Arab women and girls garbed in short colorful jackets and loose flowing trousers sit scattered on the floor, endlessly fanning the slow-kindling charcoal in earthen firepots, chattering all the while in Arabic.

The world for many of these women is confined largely to this enclosure, except on Fridays, when they and their children will celebrate the sacred day, not at the mosque with the men, but in the ancient cemeteries outside the Casbah on the hills sloping down to the valley. Younger women are beginning to long for liberty beyond their carefully prescribed existence. Such laxity would be accursed in the eyes of the strong-willed women of the old regime, however. They gloried in their prison bars, believing their caging proved their status and value.

The Casbah, in the late 1800s, is as much prison as fortress for the masses of both men and women within its fortification. Some, having experienced a better world beyond, will find their way out. Most will live out the days of their lives within the twilight, like the countless generations before them, counting out the hours with prayers, the weeks and months with feasts and fasts, and numbly holding to their creed: "No God but God and Mohammed is God's Apostle."

APPENDIX C
SELECTIONS FROM THE WRITINGS OF I. LILIAS TROTTER

The following excerpts from the writings of Lilias Trotter have been selected to provide a more comprehensive sampling of both her writing style and her thoughts on subjects of great concern to her. *Focussed* is representative of her devotional works. It first appeared in Christian periodicals and was then reprinted as a booklet. *Vibrations,* a booklet taken from an unrevised manuscript, presents some of Lilias's fundamental thinking on intercessory prayer. *The Glory of the Impossible* elucidates Lilias's remarkable perspective of the challenge of ministry to the Muslim world. And "Moslem Mystics," excerpted from *Between the Desert and the Sea,* provides an uncommon insight into the heart and mind of the Sufi mystic.

Focussed: A Story and a Song

It was in a little wood in early morning. The sun was climbing behind a steep cliff in the east, and its light was flooding nearer and nearer and then making pools among the trees. Suddenly, from a dark corner of purple brown stems and tawny moss, there shone out a great golden star. It was just a dandelion, and half withered—but it was full face to the sun, and had caught into its heart all the glory it could hold, and was shining so radiantly that the dew that lay on it still made a perfect aureole round its head. And it seemed to talk, standing there—to talk about the possibility of making the very best of these lives of ours.

For if the Sun of Righteousness has risen upon our hearts, there is an ocean of grace and love and power lying all around us, an ocean to which all earthly light is but a drop, and it is ready to transfigure us, as the sunshine transfigured the dandelion, and on the same condition—that we stand full face to God.

Gathered up, *focussed* lives, intent on one aim—Christ—these are the lives on which God can concentrate blessedness. It is "all for all" by a law as unvarying as any law that governs the material universe.

We see the principle shadowed in the trend of science; the telephone and the wireless in the realm of sound, the use of radium and the ultra violet rays in the realm of light. All these work by gathering into focus currents and waves that, dispersed, cannot serve us. In every branch of learning and workmanship the tendency of these days is to specialize—to take up one point and follow it to the uttermost.

And Satan knows well the power of concentration; if a soul is likely to get under the sway of the inspiration, "this one thing I do," he will turn all his energies to bring in side-interests that will shatter the gathering intensity.

And they lie all around, these interests. Never has it been so easy to live in half a dozen good harmless worlds at once—art, music, social science, games, motoring, the following of some profession, and so on. And between them we run the risk of drifting about, the "good" hiding the "best" even more effectually than it could be hidden by downright frivolity with its smothered heart-ache at its own emptiness.

It is easy to find out whether our lives are focussed, and if so, where the focus lies. Where do our thoughts settle when consciousness comes back in the morning? Where do they swing back when the pressure is off during the day? Does this test not give the clue? Then dare to have it out with God—and after all, that is the shortest way. Dare to lay bare your whole life and being before Him, and ask Him to show you whether or not all is focussed on Christ and His glory. Dare to face the fact that unfocussed, good and useful as it may seem, it will prove to have failed of its purpose.

What does this focussing mean? Study the matter and you will see that it means two things—gathering in all that can be gathered, and letting the rest drop. The working of any lens—microscope, telescope, camera—will show you this. The lens of your own eye, in the room where you are sitting, as clearly as any other. Look at the window bars, and the beyond is only a shadow; look through at the distance, and it is the bars that turn into ghosts. You have to choose which you will fix your gaze upon and let the other go.

Are we ready for a cleavage to be wrought through the whole range of our lives, like the division long ago at the taking of Jericho, the division between things that could be passed through the fire of consecration into "the treasury of the Lord," and the things that, unable to "bide the fire," must be destroyed? All aims, all ambitions, all desires, all pursuits—shall we dare to drop them if they cannot be gathered sharply and clearly into the focus of "this one thing I do"?

Will it not make life narrow, this focussing? In a sense, it will—just as the mountain path grows narrower, for it matters more and more, the higher we go, where we set our feet—but there is always, as it narrows, a wider and wider outlook, and purer, clearer air. Narrow as Christ's life was narrow, this is our aim; narrow as regards self-seeking, broad as the love of God to all around. Is there anything to fear in that?

And in the narrowing and focussing, the channel will be prepared for God's power—like the stream hemmed between the rock-beds, that wells up in a spring—like the burning glass that gathers the rays into an intensity that will kindle fire. It is worth while to let God see what He can do with these lives of ours, when "to live is Christ."

How do we bring things to a focus in the world of optics? Not by looking at the things to be dropped, but by looking at the one point that is to be brought out.

Turn full your soul's vision to Jesus, and look and look at Him, and a strange dimness will come over all that is apart from Him, and the Divine "attrait" by which God's saints are made, even in this 20th century, will lay hold of you. For "He is worthy" to have all there is to be had in the heart that He has died to win.

Hath not each heart a passion and a dream,
Each some companionship for ever sweet,
And each in saddest skies some silver gleam,
And each some passing joy, too fair and fleet,
And each a staff and stay, though frail it prove,
And each a face he fain would ever see?

And what have I? an endless stream of love,
A rapture, and a glory, and a calm,
A life that is an everlasting Psalm,
All, O Beloved, in Thee.

—Tersteegen

The Glory of the Impossible

You do not test the resources of God till you try the impossible.—F. B. Meyer

God loves with a great love the man whose heart is bursting with a passion for the impossible.—William Booth

We have a God who delights in impossibilities.—Andrew Murray

Far up in the Alpine hollows, year by year, God works one of His marvels. The snow patches lie there, frozen into ice at their edges from the strife of sunny days and frosty nights; and through that ice-crust come unscathed flowers in full bloom.

Back in the days of the bygone summer, the little soldanella plant spread its leaves wide and flat on the ground to drink in the sun-rays, and it kept them stored in the root through the winter. Then spring came, and stirred its pulses even below the snow-shroud. And as it sprouted, warmth was given out in such a strange measure that it thawed a little dome in the snow above its head. Higher and higher it grew, and always above it rose the bell of air, till the flowerbud formed safely within it: and at last the icy covering of the air-bell gave way, and let the blossom through into the sunshine, the crystalline texture of its mauve petals sparkling like the snow itself, as if it bore the traces of the fight through which it had come.

And the fragile thing rings an echo in our hearts that none of the jewel-like flowers nestled in the warm turf on the slopes below could waken. We love to see the impossible done. And so does God.

Gazing north, south, east and west over His world, with the signs of coming spring in one nation after another, two great tracts catch our eye, still frost-bound, as it were, in snow and ice. Hitherto, in the main, they have held out against the gleams of His sunshine that have come to them, and it looks as if it must be long before we shall see grass and flowers appear. They are the Caste Religions of India, and, yet more unbroken in its resistance, the power of Islam throughout the world.

And the watchers there have a fight sometimes, lest the numbness and chill that reign around should creep into their own souls with the hope deferred: and the longer they stay the more keenly they realize the dead weight, impenetrable, immovable, that shuts down like a tombstone the weak little germs of life that lie buried beneath it.

It may be you have, half unconsciously, avoided looking the situation square in the face, lest faith should be weakened. But faith that has to ignore facts is not real faith.

Think over steadily the position of one of these imprisoned souls as he comes in contact with God's message. Try to understand the intense prejudice and conservatism, the absolute satisfaction with a creed that fits so well the religious instincts, and leaves him so free to sin. And then, if a stir begins in the rigidity of his mind and the torpor of his conscience, and his will wakes out of the paralysis of fatalism, it is only to stumble up against a fresh barrier. His very heartstrings are involved in the matter. Think what it means for him, with his Eastern imagination and his Eastern timidity, to face the havoc that confession of Christ would involve—the dislocation of every social detail, the wrecking of home and prospects, and the breaking of the hearts of those he loves. Everything that has made life to him must go, and possibly life itself, if he moves towards the light.

Behind all this and beyond it, both in this case of Mohammedanism and Caste, is the strange, magnetic *hold* of the system over every fibre of the nature. It is so strong that even tiny children are under its spell—creatures that with us would be still in the nursery take a pride and delight in their stern Caste regulations, and their share in the Ramadan fast. And behind that again, and probably the true explanation of the fascination, lies the purpose of the Devil, that there, his two entrenched positions, shall not be wrested from him. He employs every art of hell to keep the truth from reaching the souls bound there: or, if it reaches, from touching them: or, if it touches, from waking them into life and liberty.

This is a distant sight of these great snowfields: but it can give no sense of the icy coldness and hardness that pervade them. For that you need *contact*.

And then the Adversary goes a step further. Not content with dealing directly with his captives, he rivets their chains by dealing with God's people about them. He works on our unbelief and our faintheartedness, and breathes a half-uttered word—"impossible."

But oh! He overreaches himself when he gets to the word. He means it to sound like a knell, and instead of that it breaks into a ringing chime of hope: for

The things that are impossible with men are possible with God.

Yes: face it out to the end: cast away every shadow of hope on the human side as a positive hindrance to the Divine; heap the difficulties together recklessly, and pile on as many more as you can find: you cannot get beyond that blessed climax of impossibility. Let faith swing out on Him. He is the God of the impossible.

It is no new pathway, this. "The steps of. . . our father Abraham" trod it long ago; and the [introductory quotes] bear witness that the footprints of those who "do know their God," mark it still.

Look in the Revised Version at the description of Abraham's launch forth. He *considered* (there is such a beautiful quietness in the word) the whole extent of the hopelessness, and went straight forward as if it did not exist, "being fully persuaded that what He had promised He was able also to perform."

But have we a promise to go on, for these people? Has God spoken anything upon which we can reckon for them?

Do we need more than the following? I think not.

"O Lord my strength. . . the Gentiles shall come unto Thee from the ends of the earth, and shall say, Surely our fathers have inherited lies, vanity and things wherein is not profit.

"Therefore, behold, I will this once cause them to know, I will cause them to know Mine Hand and My Might, and they shall know that I am the Lord" (Jer. xvi. 19, 21).

From the ends of the earth—the farthest away and the hardest to win—they shall come with the cry of broken hopes that nothing can wring from them yet, sweeping away the idolized prophet and the idols of wood and stone among the "things wherein there is no profit." And oh the triumph of the words, "I will this once cause them to know. I will cause them to know Mine Hand and My Might."

And if these promises are not enough, there is an infinite horizon out beyond them in God Himself. If it were only a matter of asking Him to repeat the miracles of the past, faith would have plenty of room. But He is not bound to reproduce. He is the Creator: have we ever let our hearts and hopes go out to the glory of that Name? Look at the tiny measure of creative power given to man, in music, poetry, art—where there is a spark of it, how it refuses to be fettered by repeating itself. The history of His wonders in the past is a constant succession of new things, and He is not at the end of His resources yet. Years ago, at Keswick, Campbell gave us this rendering of John xv.7: "If ye abide in Me, and My words abide in you, *ye shall demand that for which ye are inclined, and it shall be generated for you.*" "Generated for you"—oh the depth of the "possible with God" that lies in these words!

Will you ask Him to do a new thing among these hard-bound races: to "generate" a glow of Holy Ghost fire that will melt its way up through all the icy barriers, and set a host free?

Hitherto the work done has been more like trying to break through these barriers from above, in the hopes of finding solitary life-germs imprisoned—how few they have been and how stunted and weak for the most part, at any rate in Moslem countries! God has yet to show what can be done if He stirs thus by His Spirit from *within.*

No matter if for the time it is a hidden process: the sunlight will be storing underground as you pray, and life will be set moving. Nothing is seen of the soldanella under its frozen crust, till the moment comes when the top of the air-bell gives way, and the flower is there. We believe that God is beginning already a mighty work below the surface in these seemingly hopeless fields, and that it may be with the same suddenness that it will be manifested; and the miracle of the snow-hollows will be wrought afresh by the crowding up of human souls who have won through in the hardest of fights.

Read once more the [introductory quotes]. Let us give ourselves up to believe for this new thing on the earth. Let us dare to test God's resources on it. Let us ask Him to kindle in us and keep aflame that passion for the impossible that shall make us *delight* in it with Him, till the day when we shall see it transformed into a fact.

Behold, I am the Lord, the God of all flesh: Is there anything too hard for me?

Vibrations

A bang and a crash, and a cloud of dust that when it cleared showed a picture of ruin. One of the pillars that support the gallery of our old Arab house had fallen down into the court and lay shattered on the pavement, carrying with it a block of masonry and a shower of bricks and blue and white tiles from the arch above it.

Down below, alongside of us, a native baker had installed himself six or seven years ago. This means that for hours every night two men had swung on the huge see-saw which in some mysterious way kneads their bread, and every blow backwards and forwards had vibrated through our house, and now at last the result was seen in the shattering of masonry that had looked as if it would last as long as the world.

The town architect came, confirmed this as the probable cause of the collapse, and obliged the baker to do his kneading after another fashion!

But God had meanwhile given an object lesson concerning a truth which had glimmered out before in thinking of the strange power of vibrations—once more "the invisible things being understood by the things that are made."

For there is a vibrating power going on down in the darkness and dust of this world that can make itself visible in starting results in the upper air and sunlight of the invisible world, "mighty through God to the pulling down of strongholds, casting down imaginations and every high thing that exalts itself against the knowledge of God." Each prayer-beat down here vibrates up to the very throne of God, and does its work through that throne on the principalities and powers around us, just as each one of the repeated throbs from below told on the structure of our house, though it was only the last one that produced the visible effect. We can never tell which prayer will liberate the answer, but we *can* tell that each one will do its work: we know that "if we ask anything according to His will He heareth us, and if we know that He hear us we know that we have the petitions that we desired of Him."

There are two parables in St. Luke's Gospel that translate this matter of the power of vibrations in the prayer world out of the region of theory into that of revealed truth: the parable of the three loaves in Chapter 11, and that of the widow and her adversary in Chapter 18. It is not a question in either of them, it seems, of prayer for the personal needs of our souls; for these we do not need to come again and again to wring an unwilling answer out of our Father, but to search in His Word till He gives a promise which meets our case and then to step out on it in the bare faith which believes that it receives.

But the question of prayer becomes more complicated when it concerns others—complicated not only by the independence of their individuality and their personal wills, but by the action of the principalities and powers of the rulers of the world of darkness. We have a glimpse of this in Dan. 10. The answer was sent out from God's presence "from the day that he set his face" but it took three weeks to battle through the opposing hosts, and all that time God *needed,* in some mysterious way, the help of Daniel's fastings and prayers down in the darkness, to help fight through and reach him.

Compare the two parables. They rhyme as it were; there is much that is parallel, and yet we see the shade of difference. Both begin with helplessness—midnight in the first, a shut door, a far-off voice that only answers "not now." Loneliness in the second—a widow with no one to take her part, no brother or son to stand for her. And yet in each case "because of importunity" they will not recognise defeat and they both fight through all odds to victory.

But the aim is different in the two. The first is the cry for supply for the individual souls who come to us in their journey through life, the second is the battle that we learn further on, against the principalities and powers in heavenly places, headed by "our adversary the devil." In both there is the stepping down into the place of helplessness first, the Peniel of the crippled Jacob, where power with God and with man is to be found.

Have you ever watched trollies working on a moorside between the quarries above and the road below? How are the empty trucks sent flying up, against all laws of gravitation? It is by the full trucks going down—*down* . . . "I have nothing to set before him." And not by our own power or holiness can we produce any supply. Our cupboard bare, all resources closed around us like the bread stalls in the deserted street—shut up to hope in God alone, that is the first condition. And the second is the importunity which holds on to the end, until the answer has come. A break of faithlessness gives the enemy time to regain his power and to seize again the ground we have gained, like the Amalekites prevailing when Moses let down his hand, "the hand upon the throne of God" (Ex. 17.16 margin) and *through* that throne upon the powers of the enemy.

With our hands placed there upon the place of power we learn the secret of prevailing. "Men ought always to pray and not to faint."

There is one keynote that, once struck, can move heaven and earth; its mighty vibrations ring up to the throne of God and thunder upon the gates of hell: "That in the Name of Jesus every knee should bow." When once the prayer-beats have struck that note of the Name of Jesus, it is only a matter of going on.

We see the power of "the King's name" in the story of Esther. It is when Haman has been delivered to the gallow, and only the voice of Esther is heard, that the king's ring is given to Mordecai with the words: "Write ye also for the Jews, as it liketh you, in the King's name, and seal it with the King's seal." (Est. viii.8). And having the authority of that Name their prayer is the prayer of faith that *knows* it has the petition, and it was "written according to all that Mordecai commanded."

We cannot have the Spirit's commanding in prayer until we have before been living under His law in secret, as Esther in chapter ii.9. "The minding of the Spirit is life and peace"—what far-reaching life and peace for other souls as well as our own, none can tell.

Esther had had access to the King before on behalf of her people. She had surrendered her life and will, if only she might be an intercessor. But now power was given into her hand against the power of the enemy. She was no longer as the friend asking at midnight for the bread of life, she was armed with the authority that was "above" the might that opposed her; she had hold, no longer of the King's sceptre, but of the King's seal.

Oh! This is what we need! Only dim glimmerings come as yet of what it means to wield the power of the Name of Jesus against the world-rulers who lie *behind* the needs of those around us.

With these overwhelming powers against us, the overwhelming needs around us, our own entire helplessness, only one little life on earth, ebbing so quickly—it is essential that if there is a secret of power to be had we *must* learn it.

How did victory come to Esther? It was not that the power given into the hands of the adversary was withdrawn; it was his for the time by an unchangeable decree, even as it is now. But down against that power was brought the might of the King's authority, brought to bear on the side of the oppressed, so that "in the day that the enemies of the Jews hoped to have power over them . . . it was turned to the contrary, that the Jews had rule over them that hated them." It is so still. God does not as yet withdraw the mysterious powers given to the prince of this world, but He can and will send out on our side a "power above all the power of the enemy," and that comes to the same thing, as we see in Esther's story. In her heart, in the heart of the widow, was the same thought: An answer is to be had, and I must have it; and so on they went in the absolute simplicity of this one idea till the answer came, the "vibrations" took effect at last, the last barrier was broken through, and victory was won.

It is a solemn thing to stand on the threshold of a century that will almost without a doubt, so far as we can discern the signs of the time, set Him on the chariot of His willing people. Can we not begin to see the working of the Spirit in the cry that is going up from the hearts of so many of us to learn the secret of a life of prayer? Is He not preparing us to join in the last cry of the Bride, "Come, Lord Jesus"—the cry that will not only "vibrate" but will rend the heavens and destroy the power of "the last enemy"?

Moslem Mystics

The North African desert is, *per se,* the land of the Moslem mystics, though they have ramifications all over the country, and they form the chief missionary element in the spread of their creed. In Miliana we saw only their far back formative touch in the Marabout system with the life pulse gone from within, and the glimpse of reality lost in a fog of superstition. In the desert the mystics might be studied in something very near their pristine form of faith and of fraternity, if only they would let us get near enough to them to study them. Here is the difficulty. The very expression of these Sufi men is inscrutable, with dark unfathomable eyes, and there is an aloofness of manner that holds the questioner at a distance. Till you show by some word that you understand them and care for them and are "reaching forth" also to "the things that are before," they will remain within their shell: and they will withdraw into it in a moment if they think you may ask some of their state secrets. For each brotherhood has its own initiatory rites and formulas, as jealously guarded as any freemasonry.

Even their speech, when it touches on the inward life, is a thing apart, in sharp contrast to the dearth of spiritual expression in ordinary Arabic. The need for something deeper has created a supply, and that a rich and beautiful one. The mystic has his own terminology but dimly understood by those outside.

Many influences from the past have gone to the moulding of him. The monks of the Thebaid, the Neoplatonists of Greece, the Buddhists of India, the Satians of Persia have been each welded in.

The product has been of a twofold order. The development that comes into public view is that associated with the name of dervish, recognisable as a rule by clothing, tattered and patched to the last degree. This patched garment is bestowed on those who have reached a certain point in the stages of the inward life and is an important feature. So important is it that one of the old Sufi books contains a disquisition as to whether the patches should be sewn on neatly or at random—literally, "wherever the needle lifts her head." One saint is mentioned in the same passage who sewed them so thickly one over the other that scorpions hid between the layers.

But it is when they get together that these dervish brothers show the Sufi system at its worst. They meet regularly for prolonged times of prayer, called the *dhikr,* i.e., the "mentioning" of the names of God in continuous chanting repetition. That forms the long introduction: the ultimate aim is to produce so-called ecstasy, and this is brought about by auto-suggestion, hypnotism and other weird processes, till they reach together a frenzy of mental intoxication where they imagine themselves beyond all landmarks that separate the lawful from the unlawful. The result and the reaction may be imagined.

In the other class of the Sufi devotees we find the souls who seek approach to God, not from the emotional side, but from that of philosophy, mental analysis and intricate metaphysics. The world is a fiction, they say; its forms are an emanation of the Divine essence, which will vanish and leave only the radiancy from which it came. Into that essence they seek to be united—united, not absorbed as in Buddhist mysticism; and this union is to be brought about through a succession of seven spiritual stages of asceticism to be attained by effort, and seven spiritual states to be bestowed by God. All is sought under the guidance of a director and in blind obedience to his bidding. They entrust themselves to him, to use their own metaphor, like the corpse in the hands of the washer.

Between these two extremes of the adepts sways the lay brother element, receiving its religious impulses from one and the other in varying force and kept in the path of sanity by having to work for daily bread.

There are crevices where heavenly dynamite is being lodged, for we hear now and again of little groups of these "brothers" who meet and read together the scriptures, and anything of Christian literature that comes their way. Who can foretell the issues of a spark of God's fire?

If, on the other hand, we ascend the scale in the organizations (and it is a highly developed scale) we shall find that among the upper circles of the fraternities are those whose chief outlook on the brotherhood life is as a vehicle for ambition, power and political intrigue. These cause much uneasiness in the colony, and with reason. Each Brotherhood is self-governed and has unlimited authority and can set wide currents in motion. Each is an elaborate system on the same outline, from the hierarchy of the initiated down to the unlettered fellah who hopes in some way to reach God through the mazes of the dhikr. There are large funds at its disposal and immense hospitality is available in the Zaouias, as the fraternity houses are named.

Two or three of the chief Brotherhoods have Sisterhoods recognized and attached: these organizations are worked by the women themselves. All is carried on, as in the case of the Brotherhoods, without a break in the home life, except for periods of retreat. Celibacy has no place in the system.

It is among the rank and file that lies the strategic point for the new message. They have enough to awake a thirst for the unseen, but never enough to satisfy it, for all is subjective. As has been well said, "Their need is objective, verifiable and divine revelation." It is for us to bring them this in the revelation of Jesus Christ. Then will be fulfilled the word by Isaiah the prophet, "The mirage shall become a pool" (Isa. xxxv.7.RV.).

Our dream is of a future where the Christian mystic shall go after the Moslem mystic, and that thus these Brotherhood men, when their thirst has been quenched by the living water, may be drawn into their own development on Christian lines, and bring into the compacting of the Church an element that no others can offer.

NOTES

Preface

[1] John Ruskin, "The Art of England" (Oxford: Ashmolean Museum, 1883) 24-25.

[2] Ruskin, "Art" 26.

[3] I. R. Govan Stewart, *The Love That Was Stronger* (London: Lutterworth Press, 1958) 30.

[4] Elisabeth Elliot, letter to the author, 19 September 1986.

[5] Patricia St. John, letter to the author, 15 January 1988.

[6] John Ruskin, *The Brantwood Diary of John Ruskin,* ed. and annot. Helen Gill Viljoen (New Haven: Yale UP, 1971) 196.

[7] I. Lilias Trotter, Diary, 1 January 1921, Trotter Archives, Arab World Ministries United Kingdom Headquarters, Loughborough, England.

[8] Isabella Strange Trotter, *First Impressions of The New World* (London: Longman, 1859) vi.

Chapter 1

[1] Patricia St. John, *Until the Day Breaks* (Bronley, Kent: OM, 1990) 7-8, text adapted.

[2] Ann Saunders, *Regent's Park* (Great Britain: Clarke, 1969) 84.

[3] Louisa Mure, *Recollection of Bygone Days* ([England]: n.p., 1883) ix.

[4] Mure ix.

[5] Trotter, *First Impressions* 134-135.

[6] "Robert Strange," *Dictionary of National Biography.*

[7] "Robert Strange," *Dictionary.*

[8] "Robert Strange," *Dictionary.*

Chapter 2

[1] I. Lilias Trotter, *Parables of the Cross* (London: Marshall, n.d.) 22.

[2] *A History of James Capel & Co.* (n.p.: n.p., n.d.) 67.

[3] Trotter, *First Impressions* 111.

[4] Mure n. pag.

[5] Trotter, *First Impressions* 161.

[6] Trotter, *First Impressions* 285.

[7] Trotter, *First Impressions* 51.

[8] Trotter, *First Impressions* 69.

[9] Mure n. pag.

[10] Trotter, *First Impressions* 117.

[11] Trotter, *First Impressions* 52.
[12] Trotter, *First Impressions* 308.
[13] Mure viii.
[14] Trotter, *First Impressions* 96.
[15] Trotter, *First Impressions* 302.
[16] Trotter, *First Impressions* 57.
[17] Trotter, *First Impressions* 266.
[18] Trotter, *First Impressions* vii.
[19] Alexander Trotter, *Observations on the Financial Position and Credit of such of the States of The North American Union as Have Contracted Public Debts* (London: Longman, 1839) 355-356.
[20] Trotter, Diary, 24 September 1924.
[21] Trotter, *First Impressions* 78.
[22] Stewart 13.
[23] Stewart 13.
[24] Blanche A. F. Pigott, *I. Lilias Trotter* (London: Marshall, 1929) 3.

Chapter 3

[1] Trotter, *Parables* 17.
[2] Pigott, *Trotter* 4.
[3] Victoria Glendinning, *Anthony Trollope,* 3rd ed. (New York: Penguin Books, 1994) oppos. 360.
[4] Pigott, *Trotter* 4.
[5] Pigott, *Trotter* 4.
[6] Ruskin, "Art" 26.
[7] Trotter, *Parables* 31-32.

Chapter 4

[1] Trotter, *Parables* 17.
[2] Steven Barabas, *So Great Salvation* (London: Marshall, 1952) 20.
[3] Hannah Whitall Smith, *Philadelphia Quaker: The Letters of Hannah Whitall Smith,* ed. Logan Pearsall Smith (New York: Harcourt, 1950) 27.
[4] Logan Pearsall Smith, *Unforgotten Years* (Boston: Little, 1939) 19.
[5] Smith, *Unforgotten* 52.
[6] Barabas 18.
[7] Catherine Marshall, *Beyond Ourselves* (New York: Avon, 1961) xii.
[8] Hannah Whithall Smith, *The Christian's Secret of a Happy Life* (New York: Revell, 1942) 28.
[9] Smith, *Unforgotten* 51.
[10] Smith, *Unforgotten* 59.
[11] Trotter, *Parables* 18.

Chapter 5

[1] Trotter, *Parables* 17.

[2] *Christian History* 10.25: 1.
[3] Barabas 23-24.
[4] Barabas 24.
[5] Pigott, *Trotter* 5.
[6] Pigott, *Trotter* 6.
[7] Pigott, *Trotter* 6.
[8] Emily Kinnaird, *Reminiscences* (London: Murray) 55-56.
[9] Pigott, *Trotter* 5.
[10] Stan Gundry, "Colorful Sayings from Colorful Moody," *Christian History* 1X.25: 9.
[11] Stan Gundry, "The Three *R*s of Moody's Theology," *Christian History* 1X.25: 16.
[12] Trotter, "A Battle That Was Won," *El Couffa* (1913) 65.
[13] Gundry, "Colorful" 9.
[14] St. John, *Day Breaks* 14.

Chapter 6

[1] Trotter, *Parables* 17-18.
[2] Stewart 4.
[3] Ruskin, "Art" 25.
[4] Christopher Wood, *Victorian Panarama* (London: Faber, 1976) 201.
[5] Robert Hewison, *Ruskin and Oxford* (Oxford: Clarendon, 1996) 33.
[6] Bruce Hanson, *Brantwood* (Coniston: Brantwood Trust) 6.
[7] Pigott, *Trotter* 14.
[8] Harriet Whelchel, ed., *John Ruskin and the Victorian Eye* (New York: Abrams, 1993) 131.
[9] Hanson 18.
[10] Hanson 6.
[11] Stewart 16.
[12] Stewart 16.
[13] Stewart 15.
[14] Whelchel 48.
[15] Hanson 8.
[16] Stewart 16.
[17] I. Lilias Trotter to John Ruskin, 25 July 1899, The Ruskin Galleries, Bembridge School, Isle of Wight.

Chapter 7

[1] Trotter, *Parables* 20.
[2] Pigott, *Trotter* 6.
[3] Ruskin, "Art" 26.
[4] Christopher Newell, *Victorian Watercolours* (London: Phaidon, 1992) 13.
[5] Ruskin, "Art" 26.
[6] Stewart 15.

[7] Constance E. Padwick, *I. Lilias Trotter of Algiers* (Croydon: Watson, n.d.) 9.

[8] Padwick 9.

[9] Padwick 8-9.

[10] Pigott, *Trotter* 13.

[11] Pigott, *Trotter* 11.

[12] Pigott, *Trotter* 10.

[13] Blanche A. F. Pigott, *Memoriam* 1928: 2.

[14] Pigott, *Memoriam* 2.

[15] Pigott, *Trotter* 11.

[16] Trotter, *Parables* 22.

[17] Trotter, *Parables* 20.

[18] Trotter, *Parables* 23.

[19] Pigott, *Trotter* 11.

[20] Ruskin, *Brantwood* 19.

[21] Ruskin, *Brantwood* 113.

[22] Ruskin, *Collected Works of John Ruskin,* ed. E.T. Cook and A. Wedderburn, 39 vol. (London: G. Allen, 1903–12) 37: 553-554.

[23] Ruskin, *Works* 37: 572.

[24] Padwick 12.

[25] Stewart 23.

[26] Trotter, *Parables* 22-23.

[27] Trotter, *Parables* 23-24.

Chapter 8

[1] Trotter, *Parables* 24.

[2] *Christian Herald* Nov. 1990: 6.

[3] Theodora Maclagan, *The Development of the Religious Life of the YWCA*, 17.

[4] I. Lilias Trotter, *Bible History Lessons* (London: Church of England Sunday School Institute, 1884) 1.

[5] Trotter, *Bible History* 1.

[6] Trotter, *Bible History* 1.

[7] Padwick 10.

[8] Padwick 10.

[9] Stewart 22-23.

[10] Padwick 11, 13.

[11] Kinnaird 56.

[12] Kinnaird 56-57.

[13] Alvyn Austin, "Missions Dream Team," *Christian History* XV.52: 19.

[14] I. Lilias Trotter, *Smouldering* (London: Church Missionary Society, n.d.) 8.

[15] Kinnaird 57.

[16] Kinnaird 58.

[17] I. Lilias Trotter, *Young Women's Christian Association Monthly Letter* LXIV (Broadmead: April 1887):1-2.

[18] North Africa Missions Records, #106. (n.p.: n.d.).

[19] Pigott, *Trotter* 19.

[20] Trotter, *Parables* 26-27.

Chapter 9

[1] Trotter, "Journal Letters," 8 March 1888, Trotter Archives, Arab World Ministries United Kingdom Headquarters, Loughborough, England. Lilias's "journal letters" were sent to her sister Margaret (now Mrs. Hugh Egerton), from 1888-1890, to be circulated among friends in England.

[2] Pigott, *Trotter* 19.

[3] Pigott, *Trotter* 19.

[4] Pigott, *Trotter* 20.

[5] Pigott, *Trotter* 20.

[6] Pigott, *Trotter* 20.

[7] *A Thirsty Land* 44. "Jubilee Number" (anniversary ed.) Spring. 1938: 2.

[8] Trotter, "Journal Letters," 15 May 1888.

[9] Trotter, "Journal Letters," 26 April 1888.

[10] Trotter, "Journal Letters," 8 December 1888.

[11] I. Lilias Trotter, "Awakened Interest in Algiers," *North Africa,* October 1888: 218.

[12] Pigott, *Trotter* 22.

[13] Trotter, "Journal Letters," 7 January 1889.

[14] Trotter, "Journal Letters," 26 August 1888.

[15] Trotter, "Journal Letters," 7 May 1889.

[16] Trotter, "Journal Letters," n.d.

[17] I. Lilias Trotter, *Back-ground and Fore-ground* (Algiers: Algiers Mission Band, 1913) 2.

[18] Trotter, "Journal Letters," 5 January 1890.

Chapter 10

[1] Pigott, *Trotter* 32.

[2] Pigott, *Trotter* 31.

[3] Pigott, *Trotter* 31.

[4] Pigott, *Trotter* 34.

[5] Pigott, *Trotter* 33.

[6] Pigott, *Trotter* 36.

[7] I. Lilias Trotter, *Between the Desert and the Sea* (London: Marshall, n.d.) 41.

[8] Trotter, *Smouldering* 2.

[9] Trotter, *Smouldering* 3.

[10] Pigott, *Trotter* 36.

[11] Pigott, *Trotter* 40.

[12] Trotter, "Travel Journal," 1893: 48-49, Trotter Archives, Arab World Ministries United Kingdom Headquarters, Loughborough, England.
[13] Pigott, *Trotter* 43.
[14] Pigott, *Trotter* 1893: 40.
[15] Pigott, *Trotter* 1893: 42.
[16] Pigott, *Trotter* 41.
[17] Pigott, *Trotter* 44.
[18] Pigott, *Trotter* 45.
[19] Pigott, *Trotter* 44-45.
[20] Pigott, *Trotter* 45.
[21] Pigott, *Trotter* 47.

Chapter 11

[1] *A Thirsty Land* 44. "Jubilee Number" (anniversary ed.) Spring. 1938: 2.
[2] Pigott, *Trotter,* 26 October 1894: 46-47.
[3] Pigott, *Trotter,* March 1894: 48.
[4] William Langewiesche, *Sahara Unveiled* (New York: Pantheon, 1996) 142.
[5] Trotter, *Algiers Mission Band Journal,* 1895: 102, Trotter Archives, Arab World Ministries United Kingdom Headquarters, Loughborough, England.
[6] Trotter, Journal, 1894.
[7] Trotter, Journal, 15 March 1895.
[8] Pigott, *Trotter* 1894: 50.
[9] Pigott, *Trotter* 11 December 1894: 50.
[10] Trotter, Journal, 11 December 1894.
[11] Pigott, *Trotter* December 1894.
[12] Pigott, *Trotter* December 1894: 52.
[13] Trotter, Journal, 15 January 1895.
[14] Trotter, Journal, 1895: 134.
[15] I. Lilias Trotter, "They That Dwell in the Wilderness," Letter, 1895: 2.
[16] Trotter, Journal, 1895: 102.
[17] Trotter, Journal, 1895: 127.

Chapter 12

[1] Trotter, Journal, 1895: 167.
[2] Trotter, "They That Dwell," Letter, 1895: 4.
[3] Trotter, Journal, 1895: 153.
[4] Trotter, Journal, 1895: 145.
[5] Trotter, "They That Dwell," Letter, 1895: 4.
[6] Trotter, Journal, 1895: 167.
[7] Trotter, Journal, 1895: 167.
[8] Trotter, Journal, 28 October 1895: 180.
[9] Trotter, Journal, 1895: 182.
[10] Trotter, Journal, 18 November 1895: 182.

[11] Trotter, Journal, 28 October 1895: 181.
[12] I. Lilias Trotter, *A South Land* (London: Marshall, n.d.) 4-5.
[13] I. Lilias Trotter, *A Challenge to Faith* (London: Marshall, n.d.) 12-13.
[14] Trotter, Journal, 29 January 1896: 7.
[15] Trotter, Journal, 30 January 1896: 4a.

Chapter 13

[1] Trotter, Diary, 22 May 1899.
[2] Trotter, Journal, 1896: 18.
[3] Trotter, Journal, 1896: 18.
[4] Trotter, Journal, 1896: 19.
[5] Trotter, Journal, 1896: 16.
[6] Trotter, Journal, 1896: 34.
[7] Trotter, Journal, January 1897: 65.
[8] Trotter, Journal, 1897: 66.
[9] Trotter, Journal, 1897: 112.
[10] Trotter, Journal, 1897: 98.
[11] Trotter, Journal, 9 October 1897.
[12] Trotter, Journal, 1897: 93.
[13] Trotter, Journal, October 1897: 118.
[14] Trotter, Journal, 1897.
[15] Trotter, Journal, 1897.
[16] Trotter, Journal, 1897: 114.
[17] Trotter, Journal, 1897: 117.
[18] Trotter, Journal, 1897: 124.
[19] Trotter, Journal, 1897: 126.
[20] Trotter, Journal, 1897: 126-127.
[21] Trotter, Journal, 1897: 128.
[22] Trotter, Journal, 6 January 1898: 1.
[23] Trotter, Journal, 19 February 1898: 25.
[24] Trotter, Journal, 9 February 1898: 26.
[25] Trotter, Journal, 1898: 10.
[26] Trotter, Journal, 1898: 28.
[27] Trotter, Journal, 1898: 69.
[28] Trotter, Journal, 28 May 1898: 49.
[29] Trotter, Journal, 1898.

Chapter 14

[1] Trotter, Diary, 9 September 1902.
[2] Pigott, *Trotter* 86.
[3] Trotter, Diary, 16 April 1900.
[4] Trotter, Diary, 22 April 1900.
[5] Trotter, Diary, 17 April 1900.
[6] Trotter, Diary, 27 April 1900.

[7] Trotter, Diary, 11 August 1900.
[8] Pigott, *Trotter* 89.
[9] Trotter, Diary, 2 February 1900.
[10] Trotter, Diary, 17 April 1901.
[11] Trotter, Diary, 24 January 1902.
[12] Trotter, Diary, 24 January 1902.
[13] Trotter, Diary, 31 January 1902.
[14] Trotter, Diary, 3 February 1902.
[15] Trotter, Diary, 15 February, 1902.
[16] Trotter, Diary, 27 February 1902.
[17] Trotter, Diary, 16 July 1902.
[18] I. Lilias Trotter, "Missionaries and Their Muddles," *El Couffa,* Chapter 7.
[19] Trotter, Journal, 13 March 1896.

Chapter 15

[1] Trotter, Diary, 29 December 1903.
[2] Trotter, Diary, 27 February 1903.
[3] Trotter, Diary, 6 February 1903.
[4] Trotter, *Back-ground and Fore-ground.*
[5] Trotter, Diary, 13 July 1903.
[6] Trotter, Diary, 23 July 1903.
[7] Trotter, Diary, 10 December, 1903.
[8] Trotter, Diary, 29 December 1903.
[9] Trotter, Diary, 29 December 1903.
[10] Trotter, Diary, 29 December, 1903.
[11] Trotter, Diary, 26 May 1904.
[12] Trotter, Diary, 6 May 1904.
[13] Trotter, Diary, 23 November 1905.
[14] Trotter, Diary, 26 November 1904.
[15] Trotter, Diary, 28 January 1905.
[16] Trotter, Diary, 5 January 1905.
[17] Trotter, Diary, 13 August 1905.
[18] Trotter, Diary, 29 December 1903.

Chapter 16

[1] Trotter, Diary, 9 July 1907.
[2] Trotter, Diary, 10 March 1906.
[3] Trotter, Diary, 31 March 1906.
[4] I. Lilias Trotter, *Message from Algiers to the Members of the World's Fifth Sunday School Convention,* (London: Lund, 1907).
[5] J. A. Walker, "From the Secretary of the 'Algerian Mission Band' America," *A Thirsty Land,* No. 44, Spring, 1938: 10.
[6] Trotter, Diary, 14 May 1907.
[7] Trotter, Diary, 23 August 1907.

[8] Trotter, Diary, 5 July 1907.
[9] Padwick 20.
[10] Trotter, Diary, 27 October 1901.

Chapter 17

[1] Lilias Trotter, *A Thirsty Land and God's Channels* (London: Page, n.d.) 12.
[2] Trotter, Diary, 7 January 1908.
[3] Trotter, Diary, 9 March 1908.
[4] Trotter, Diary, 19 March 1908.
[5] Trotter, Diary, 19 March 1908.
[6] Trotter, Dairy, 16 April 1908.
[7] Trotter, Diary, 5 May 1908.
[8] Trotter, Diary, 14 July 1908.
[9] Trotter, Diary, 28 August 1908.
[10] Trotter, *A Thirsty Land* 4.
[11] Trotter, Diary, 4 November 1908.
[12] Pigott, *Trotter* 51.
[13] Trotter, Diary, 17 November 1908.
[14] Trotter, Diary, 12 December 1908.
[15] Trotter, Diary, 24 December 1908.

Chapter 18

[1] Trotter, Diary, 25 March 1909.
[2] Trotter, Diary, 6 January 1909.
[3] Trotter, Diary, 6 January 1909.
[4] Trotter, Diary, 19 January 1909.
[5] Trotter, Diary, 19 January 1909.
[6] Trotter, Diary, 12 June 1909.
[7] Trotter, Diary, 8 March 1909.
[8] Trotter, Diary, 8 March 1909.
[9] Trotter, Diary, 2 July 1909.
[10] Trotter, Diary, 15 November 1909.
[11] Trotter, Diary, 21 March 1910.
[12] Trotter, Diary, 18 April 1910.
[13] Trotter, Diary, 4 April, 1909.
[14] Trotter, Diary, 18 April 1909.
[15] Pigott, *Trotter* 98, 99.
[16] Trotter, Diary, 25 May 1910.
[17] Trotter, Diary, 29 May 1910.

Chapter 19

[1] Trotter, *Back-ground and Fore-ground,* 11.
[2] Pigott, *Trotter* 136.

[3] Trotter, Printed Journal, 28 April 1911, Trotter Archives, Arab World Ministries United Kingdom Headquarters, Loughborough, England.

[4] Trotter, *Back-ground and Fore-ground,* 13.

[5] Trotter, Diary, 6 August 1911.

[6] Trotter, *Algiers Mission Band Journal,* 20 October 1911, Trotter Archives.

[7] I. Lilias Trotter, "Missionaries and Their Miseries," *El Couffa,* chapter 6.

[8] Trotter, Diary, 29 January 1912.

[9] Trotter, Diary, 14 September 1912.

[10] Pigott, *Memorian* 2.

[11] Trotter, Diary 12 May 1914.

[12] Trotter, Diary, 28 December 1912.

Chapter 20

[1] Trotter, Diary, 29 September 1914.

[2] Trotter, Diary, 1 July 1913.

[3] I. Lilias Trotter, *Literature for Moslem Boys* (London: Patridge, n.d.) 4.

[4] Trotter, *Literature* 6.

[5] Trotter, Diary, 6 November 1913.

[6] Trotter, Diary, 11 November 1913.

[7] Trotter, Diary, 26 March, 1914.

[8] I. Lilias Trotter, *Algiers Mission Band Story of 1914* (Coventry: Curtis & Beamish, n.d.) 15.

[9] Trotter, Diary, 7 March 1915.

[10] Trotter, Diary, 8 May 1916.

[11] Trotter, Diary, 30 April 1915.

[12] Trotter, Diary, 25 May 1916.

Chapter 21

[1] Trotter, Diary, 7 September 1918.

[2] Trotter, Printed Journal, 27 January 1917.

[3] Trotter, Diary, 2 February 1917.

[4] Trotter, Diary, 12 February 1917.

[5] Trotter, Diary, 2 February 1917.

[6] Trotter, Diary, 27 February 1917.

[7] Trotter, Diary, 14 March 1917.

[8] Trotter, Diary, 26 March 1917.

[9] Trotter, Diary, 1 April 1917.

[10] Trotter, Diary, 9 April 1917.

[11] Trotter, Diary, 27 May 1917.

[12] Trotter, Diary, 23 February 1918.

[13] Trotter, Diary, 12 March 1918.

[14] Trotter, Diary, 28 May 1918.

[15] Pigott, *Trotter* 175.

[16] Trotter, Diary, 4 October 1918.
[17] Trotter, Diary, 17 December 1918.
[18] Trotter, *Between* 49, 50.

Chapter 22

[1] Trotter, Diary, 12 December 1920.
[2] Trotter, Diary, 29 May 1920.
[3] Pigott, *Trotter* 184.
[4] Pigott, *Trotter* 184.
[5] Trotter, Diary, 12 December 1920.
[6] Trotter, Diary, 12 December 1920.
[7] Trotter, Diary, 9 March 1921.
[8] Trotter, Diary, 9 March 1921.
[9] Trotter, Diary, 12 July 1921.
[10] Trotter, Diary, 19 March 1921.
[11] Trotter, Diary, 10 April 1921.
[12] Trotter, Diary, 23 September 1921.
[13] Trotter, Diary, 16 October 1921.
[14] Trotter, Diary, 9 December 1921.
[15] Trotter, Diary, 4 January 1922.
[16] Trotter, Diary, 4 January 1922.
[17] Trotter, Diary, 22 December 1922.
[18] Trotter, Diary, 12 December 1920.

Chapter 23

[1] Trotter, Diary, 9 March 1923.
[2] Pigott, *Trotter* 196.
[3] Trotter, Diary, 4 April 1923.
[4] I. Lilias Trotter, "Sequel to the Prayer Call" (circular), February 1923.
[5] Trotter, "Sequel," February 1923.
[6] Trotter, Diary, 23 September 1923.
[7] Trotter, Diary, 23 November 1923.
[8] Trotter, Diary, 4 December 1923.
[9] Trotter, Diary, 15 December 1923.
[10] Trotter, Diary, 16 December 1923.
[11] Trotter, Diary, 22 December 1923.
[12] Trotter, Diary, 13 February 1924.
[13] Trotter, Diary, 26 March 1924.
[14] Trotter, Diary, 1 April 1924.
[15] Pigott, *Trotter* 208.
[16] Trotter, Diary, 17 April 1924.
[17] Pigott, *Trotter* 210.
[18] Pigott, *Trotter* 210.
[19] Trotter, *Algiers Mission Band Journal* 1924: 8.

[20] Pigott, *Trotter* 210.
[21] Pigott, *Trotter* 210.
[22] Pigott, *Trotter* 210.
[23] Trotter, Diary, 30 September 1924.
[24] Trotter, Diary, 28 December 1924.

Chapter 24

[1] Trotter, Diary, 21 May 1925.
[2] Trotter, Diary, 22 January 1925.
[3] Trotter, Diary, 16 April 1925.
[4] Pigott, *Trotter* 218.
[5] I. Lilias Trotter, *The Way of the Seven-fold Secret* (Cairo: Nile Mission Press, n.d.) 12.
[6] Trotter, Diary, 25 May 1925.
[7] Trotter, Diary, 16 March 1926.
[8] Trotter, Diary, 20 February 1925.
[9] Pigott, *Trotter* 220.
[10] Pigott, *Trotter* 220.
[11] Trotter, Diary, 7 October 1925.
[12] Trotter, Diary, 1 January 1926.
[13] Trotter, Diary, 21 January 1926.
[14] Trotter, Diary, 19 February 1926.
[15] Trotter, Diary, 23 December 1925.
[16] Trotter, Diary, 15 February 1926.
[17] Trotter, Diary, 30 April 1926.
[18] I. Lilias Trotter, *The Bird Book* (Cairo: Nile Mission Press, n.d.) n. pag.
[19] Trotter, *Between* 5.
[20] Trotter, Diary, 3 April 1926.
[21] Trotter, Diary, 20 May 1926.
[22] Pigott, *Trotter* 228.
[23] Pigott, *Trotter* 229.

Chapter 25

[1] Trotter, Diary, 11 July 1926.
[2] Trotter, Diary, 3 February 1927.
[3] Pigott, *Trotter* 227.
[4] Trotter, Diary, 4 February 1927.
[5] Trotter, Agenda Book, 31 July 1927, Trotter Archives, Arab World Ministries United Kingdom Headquarters, Loughborough, England.
[6] Margaret Ross, Letter, 4 March 1996.
[7] Trotter, Diary, 18 July 1927.
[8] Trotter, Diary, 26 March 1928.
[9] Trotter, Diary, 1 March 1928.
[10] Trotter, Diary, 24 March, 1928.

[11] Trotter, Diary, 24 March 1928.
[12] Trotter, Diary, 11 July 1926.
[13] Edith Armitage, note from Trotter Bible Readings, 24 June 1928.
[14] Trotter, Diary, 24 June, 1928.
[15] Pigott, *Memoriam* 3.

Chapter 26

[1] Trotter, *Parables* 35, 36.
[2] Pigott, *Trotter* 241.
[3] Pigott, *Trotter* 241.
[4] Pigott, *Trotter* 242.
[5] Pigott, *Trotter* 242.
[6] *A Thirsty Land* 44. "Jubilee Number" (anniversary ed.) Spring 1938.
[7] Pigott, *Trotter* 99.
[8] Pigott, *Trotter* 242.
[9] *Missionary Review of All Nations* 94 (Sept.–Oct. 1928): 290.
[10] *Missionary Review of All Nations* 94 (Sept.–Oct. 1928): 290.
[11] Padwick ?
[12] Padwick 17.
[13] Padwick 17.
[14] Margaret Ross, letter to the author, 4 March 1996.

Appendix A

[1] Saunders 84.
[2] Saunders 106.

Appendix B

[1] Trotter, *Between* 8.

BIBLIOGRAPHY:
THE WRITTEN LEGACY OF I. LILIAS TROTTER

Books by I. Lilias Trotter
*Between the Desert and the Sea**
Parables of the Cross
Parables of the Christ-life
The Master of the Impossible
The Way of the Seven-fold Secret

Booklets by I. Lilias Trotter
Back-ground and Fore-ground
A Challenge to Faith
Cherry Blossom
Focussed: A Story and a Song
The Glory of the Impossible
Heavenly Light on the Daily Path
A Life on Fire
Literature for Moslem Boys
A Ripened Life
Sand Lilies
Smouldering
A South Land
A Thirsty Land and God's Channels
Trained to Rule
Vibrations
Winter Buds

Story Parables by I. Lilias Trotter
The Bag of Wool
The Bedouin and His Camel
The Blood Feud of El Hanouchi
The Debt of Ali Ben Omar
The Field of Sahab en Niya
Landsnakes and Seasnakes
The Letter That Came from a Far Country

The Lost Ones in the Sahara
Neseefa the Slave Girl
The Robe of Er-Rashid
The Story of the Nightingale
Water Lilies: A Paper for Mothers

Books about I. Lilias Trotter

I. Lilias Trotter, Constance Padwick
I. Lilias Trotter, Blanche A. F. Pigott (letters and journals)
The Love That Was Stronger, I. R. Govan Stewart
A Path Through Suffering, Elisabeth Elliot (meditations based on Trotter's *Parables of the Cross* and *Parables of the Christ-life* [1992, Vine Books, in print])
Until The Day Breaks, Patricia St. John (1990, OM Publishing, in print)

*All works, unless otherwise noted, are out of print. Copies of these works are housed at the Trotter Archives at the Arab World Ministries United Kingdom Headquarters in Loughborough, England. (See the next page for further information.)

ACKNOWLEDGMENTS

I am indebted to the many people who have been a part of the journey leading to the publication of this book. At the risk of leaving out friends whose listening ears, prayers, and affirmation have kept me on task, I want to acknowledge the following individuals who have been involved in specific aspects of this project.

I am grateful to Lyle Dorsett and Marjorie Mead, who initiated this venture by their enthusiasm for the works of Lilias Trotter, by their encouragement to me to write the story of her life and by providing the link to Wendall Evans of Arab World Ministries. Without their personal support and the backing of North Wind Books, this book would not have been written.

A heartfelt thank-you to Arab World Ministries, Byran Knell and his staff at the United Kingdom Headquarters at Loughborough. They opened their archives, provided space in which to work, and offered permission as well as equipment to reproduce Lily's diaries, journals, and other papers. Words cannot express my indebtedness to Alasdair McLaren, who personally oversaw the archives, prepared the way by organizing and introducing the material to me, and connected me to people and places associated with Lilias Trotter while I was in England. In the months and years since, he has continually followed up leads and acquired information important to this work. Surely he could not have imagined what he was getting into when he first permitted this stranger from America access to the archives.

I will ever be grateful to Jane and Betty Barbour for first introducing me to Lilias Trotter and giving me over a period of time their entire Trotter library. I owe thanks as well to the others who supplied the "missing volumes": Patricia St. John, Roy Davison, Jesse Stalley, and Phil Bourne of Middle East Christian Outreach (MECO) in Cyprus.

During my research numerous people provided crucial pieces of information to fill in the jigsaw puzzle of Lilias's life. At the top of the list is Darcy Heath Weir, who has been a true partner in this venture from beginning to end, sleuthing out invaluable facts in countless places and sustaining a thoughtful, listening interest at each stage of the work.

A special word of appreciation for Rosemary Davidson and Ruth Brooker—United Kingdom and Oxford Correspondents (respectively and respectfully!)—who have humbly acquiesced to their unsolicited title, and responded to each and every request.

Likewise, there are many others who have supplied important information: Robert Egerton, grandnephew of Lilias Trotter, provided a family tree plus numerous resources to fill out the family background; Pete Pierson discovered the published letters of Lilias's mother; Jamie Weir unearthed the history of James Capel & Co., the stock brokerage firm of Lilias's father; and Donald Doud applied his handwriting analysis skills to the mysterious diary entries.

I am grateful to the Ruskin scholars who responded to my inquiries, thus broadening my understanding of Lilias's friendship with John Ruskin and his influence on her art: John Dawson, Curator and Librarian of the Ruskin Museum, Coniston, who culled the *Collected Works of Ruskin* for references to Lilias Trotter; J. S. Deardon, curator of The Ruskin Galleries, Bembridge School, Isle of Wight; and Michael Wheeler, director of The Ruskin Programme, Lancaster University.

Likewise I owe gratitude to The University of Oxford: the archival assistants in the Print Room of the Ashmolean Museum for tracking down the Trotter paintings that John Ruskin used in his lecture "The Art of England," and the Bodleian Library for access to that lecture.

Eileen Hawkins, Archivist for the YWCA of Great Britian, provided important historical information on the organization, for which I am grateful.

A sincere thank you to Christy Wilson Jr., professor of missions at Gordon-Conwell Seminary, for tracing sources that led to information about Samuel Zwemer; to Harold Stalley for a historical perspective of the Algiers Mission Band; and to Wendell Evans, Bernard Collinson, and Ronald Waine of AWM for insights into Christianity in Algeria today. My deepest appreciation to Edmond and Esther Buckenham for their generosity in lending their Algiers Mission Band materials as well as providing their personal recollections and insights. Margaret Ross and Dorothy Watson were also most generous in sharing with me their personal insights and their correspondence with Lilias Trotter.

I am indebted to Dottie Dawley and Darcy Heath for unlocking mysteries with their English translations of French sources, and to Norm Camp for his translations of Arabic to English.

To Dixon Armstrong for launching me into the strange territory of computers, to Don Tibbets for keeping me going, and to Tony Woods for advancing me into the world of windows and fonts—thank you for your patience and generosity. Marge Tallman likewise provided invaluable assistance with computer complexities beyond my grasp!

Without places of quiet for extended periods of work this book could not have been written. Special thanks to Robin Gibson and the Gibson & Valenti Law Firm and to Suzie Bellamy and the Lake Wales Public Library for providing such space.

A special word of appreciation to Milford Myhre, who introduced me to the wonderful properties of the Canon 700 color copier to resurrect the Trotter paintings from their century-long seclusion; to Peter Cake for introducing me to the Print Shop in Loughborough, England; and to the Harrises and their staff at the Print Shop for enduring weeks of daily interruptions in order to help me achieve the most faithful reproduction of the paintings from the diaries and journals. My deepest appreciation to Carol Haynes and Emily Schoenhofen, who made possible the introduction of the art of Lilias Trotter to the reader by underwriting the cost of the color pages of the book. And to Margaret Andersen, whose generous gift made possible the line drawings adaptations (of the lilies from Trotter's paintings as well as the *Parables of the Cross* color plates for part 1 of the book), I wish to express my heart-felt gratitude.

Many thanks to Lil Copan, my editor at Harold Shaw Publishers, who patiently endured my dreams and schemes, channeling them with her practical editorial skills into workable realities.

My acknowledgments would be incomplete without mentioning the Mountain Lake Bible Study group members, partners with me from the beginning in my enthusiasm for Lilias Trotter. They have survived my many references to her life and work; indeed, they participated in a study of *The Sevenfold Secret,* and they drew upon their collective resources to locate out-of-print books and biographical information and made possible the research trip to England as well as the funds for color-copying the diaries and journals.

Finally, my boundless gratitude to my husband, Dave, who has lived with two women, Lilias and me, for the past three years! He has set up and shut down the computer in numerous locations, listened through each new development and each newly written chapter, and remained unswerving in his belief that the time and energy expended on this project was merited.

Arab World Ministries

If you have been challenged by the life of Lilias Trotter and her love for Muslims of the Arab World, you can receive information about supporting missions to the Christian church in North Africa by contacting Arab World Ministries at one of the addresses below or by leaving your name and address in the guest book on Web site http:\\www.awm.org

UK (site of Trotter archives)
AWM, PO Box 51, Loughborough, Leics, LE11 OZQ
Email: 74754.1321@compuserve.com

USA
AWM, PO Box 96, Upper Darby, PA 19082
Email: awmusa@awm.org

Canada
AWM, PO Box 3398, Cambridge, Ontario, N3H 4T3
Email: awmcan@awm.org

The Netherlands
AWZ, Postbus 9199, 1006 AD, Amsterdam
Email: 76001.47@compuserve.com

France
MENA, BP2, 69520 Grigny
Email: menagp@compuserve.com